Praise for *Space To Exhale*

"Rarely have I encountered a book that truly speaks to the soul—*Space To Exhale* does that and so much more.

In her seminal work, Hurley helps Black women feel seen, valued, and celebrated—positing the revolutionary concept of centering ourselves and our needs by designing a life that nourishes, validates, and energizes us. While the book challenges fundamental paradigms on what a 'successful' life looks like, Hurley masterfully moves beyond ideology to offer practical tips and strategies for navigating workplace landmines and cultivating a life of meaning and serenity in the process.

Beautifully written in Hurley's relatable, witty style, *Space To Exhale* is part love letter, part sermon, part guide—a gift to any Black woman striving to live a life that's centered, purpose-driven, and joyful."

—Dana Brownlee,
Workplace Antiracism Advocate, and Author of
The Unwritten Rules of Managing Up

"The most powerful thing one can do is to intentionally curate a life that feels as good as it looks. In *Space To Exhale*, every reader is invited into a sanctuary of rest, self-love, and radical self-discovery. Written for Black women and anyone tired of navigating the relentless demands of hustle culture, this book is equal parts a balm for the weary soul, a shelter for the wounded heart, and a blueprint for a life rooted in ease, authenticity, purpose, and rest.

With each page, *Space To Exhale* invites you to breathe deeper, move slower, and live more intentionally. It's a guide for curating a life that aligns with your highest self—bit by bit, breath by breath."

—Alechia Reese and Dani Bourdeau,
Hosts of the Triggered AF Podcast

"As a Black woman who has experienced burnout myself, I can say with certainty that this book is much needed, and it has the power to change lives. *Space To Exhale* is more than a handbook; it's a sanctuary. It offers practical tools, heartfelt wisdom, and a gentle reminder that living a life of ease, intention, and authenticity is not only possible, but necessary."

—Zee Clarke,
Author of Black People Breathe

"*Space To Exhale* is not just a book. It's a vibe. It's sitting on the front porch sippin' tea. It's a balm for the soul. It's a joyful guide to 'reclaiming your time.' Most of all, it's a love letter to Black women across the African Diaspora. With her warmth, wit, and unapologetic honesty, Lisa Hurley offers a blueprint for thriving in a world that too often demands that Black women and femmes silence our voices and sacrifice our joy.

Space To Exhale is for every Black woman who has ever whispered, 'There has got to be more to life than this.' Sis, there is—and it starts with putting yourself first. This book is your permission slip to live soft, love hard, and exhale fully. Get ready to laugh, cry, and leave feeling seen, inspired, and ready to step into the fullness of your magic. *Space To Exhale* is a whole mood, and you don't want to miss it."

—Joquina Reed,
Founding Steward and Creator of The AntiBlackness Reader Project

"In a world that demands constant hustling over healing, Lisa Hurley's *Space To Exhale* invites readers—especially Black women—into a sanctuary of self-discovery, self-love, and serenity. Lisa's guide offers more than permission to rest; it provides a road map to reclaiming joy, balance, and authenticity. I cannot imagine anyone that does not need this road map.

Drawing on her own experiences as a Black woman navigating a world not built for her, Hurley creates a heartfelt and empowering narrative that speaks directly to the weary and overwhelmed. Hurley's timely words remind us all that we are deserving of lives filled with ease, love, and intentionality. *Space To Exhale* is both a soothing balm and a clarion call to put ourselves first. It is a lifeline for those tired of pouring from an empty cup and an invitation to reimagine what it means to truly live. *Space To Exhale* is the companion we all need on the journey back to self."

—Amira K.S. Barger, MBA,
Communications, Marketing, DEI Executive, and Author of The Price of Nice

"The soft life: That's where real strength and power lie. Lisa Hurley's début book *Space To Exhale* helped me realize that it's time to acknowledge my soft side.

'Capes off. Kimonos on.' is one of Hurley's rallying cries, and *Space To Exhale* feels just like one of those soft, silky robes. It feels like a hug. It embraces the reader with soothing, spa-like vibes of serenity, stillness, self-care, and sisterhood—and it's time for more of us to embrace that energy. *Space To Exhale* is the book that will help us do just that.

Now that I've read *Space To Exhale* I feel armed with additional tools for my journey to curating my soft life. With every anecdote, affirmation, and meditation, Lisa reminds us all that ease is the new wealth and softness is the new strength."

—Jeri Bingham, EdD,
Founder of Black Introvert Week, *and*
Founder of the award-winning podcast HushLoudly

"Standing ovation. I have NEVER read a book like *Space To Exhale*. It breaks boundaries for how books should be written. Lisa Hurley has given us an incredibly impactful gift in the form of a road map to own your soft life. She shares her practices (affirmations, meditations, and more), and allows us into her stories that carry us gently from word to word and page to page. This book allowed me to exhale in new ways. Get ready for the source of truth for Black women."

—LaTonya Davis,
CEO of L. Davis Consulting, LLC and
Founder of L. Davis Academy for Innovation and Impact

"*Space To Exhale* is a breath of fresh air. Lisa has created not just a book but a sanctuary, a space where Black women can truly, finally exhale. Every page feels like a soft hand on your shoulder, reminding you that rest is your right, not a reward. As a Black woman and first-generation American navigating the complexities of entrepreneurship and life, I feel seen in Hurley's words. Lisa names the exhaustion we carry and lovingly invites us to lay it down. *Space To Exhale* is equal parts validation and permission, as well as a guide for choosing softness in a world that demands hardness. More than a book: It's a lifeline."

—Brianna Doe,
Founder and CEO, Verbatim

"Though the book *Space To Exhale: A Handbook for Curating a Soft, Centered, Serene Life* is written primarily for Black women, Lisa Hurley's insights transcend color boundaries, offering wisdom for anyone navigating identity and ambition.

As a Black man, her call to shed societal expectations and embrace rest deeply resonated with me. Lisa challenges the relentless demands of grind culture, offering transformative tools like breathwork, affirmations, and journaling prompts. Her poetic yet practical guidance invites readers to reclaim authenticity, balance, and joy.

Space To Exhale is more than a handbook—it's a balm for the soul, urging us to pause, realign, and prioritize thriving over mere survival. Lisa's work is a timely revolution, inspiring us all to create space for stillness and self-care, unlocking the freedom to live fully and unapologetically."

—Diamond Michael Scott,
Global Book Ambassador and Taoist Nomad, The Chocolate Taoist

"*Space To Exhale* is a transformative guide for those yearning to escape the exhaustion of hustle culture and find comfort in a life of rest, reflection, and intentional living. As someone who centers Black women unapologetically, Lisa invites us to reimagine what it means to live fully—starting with prioritizing rest and well-being. This book is a must-read for those seeking rest, community, and renewal."

—Janice Gassam Asare,
Author of Decentering Whiteness in the Workplace

"Lisa Hurley's *Space To Exhale* is a powerful invitation to slow down, reconnect, and honor ourselves in a world that constantly demands more. With wisdom and warmth, she reminds us that true rest is about self-awareness, boundaries, and the courage to redefine success on our own terms. This book is a balm for the soul and a permission slip for anyone ready to embrace authenticity, rest, and the transformative power of self-love."

—Amanda Miller Littlejohn,
Author of The Rest Revolution

space to
exhale

space to
exhale
a handbook for curating
a soft, centered, serene life

LISA HURLEY

WILEY

Copyright © 2025 by Lisa Hurley. All rights reserved.

Published by John Wiley & Sons, Inc., Hoboken, New Jersey.
Published simultaneously in Canada.

No part of this publication may be reproduced, stored in a retrieval system, or transmitted in any form or by any means, electronic, mechanical, photocopying, recording, scanning, or otherwise, except as permitted under Section 107 or 108 of the 1976 United States Copyright Act, without either the prior written permission of the Publisher, or authorization through payment of the appropriate per-copy fee to the Copyright Clearance Center, Inc., 222 Rosewood Drive, Danvers, MA 01923, (978) 750-8400, fax (978) 750-4470, or on the web at www.copyright.com. Requests to the Publisher for permission should be addressed to the Permissions Department, John Wiley & Sons, Inc., 111 River Street, Hoboken, NJ 07030, (201) 748-6011, fax (201) 748-6008, or online at http://www.wiley.com/go/permission.

The manufacturer's authorized representative according to the EU General Product Safety Regulation is Wiley-VCH GmbH, Boschstr. 12, 69469 Weinheim, Germany, e-mail: Product_Safety@wiley.com

Trademarks: Wiley and the Wiley logo are trademarks or registered trademarks of John Wiley & Sons, Inc. and/or its affiliates in the United States and other countries and may not be used without written permission. All other trademarks are the property of their respective owners. John Wiley & Sons, Inc. is not associated with any product or vendor mentioned in this book.

Limit of Liability/Disclaimer of Warranty: While the publisher and author have used their best efforts in preparing this book, they make no representations or warranties with respect to the accuracy or completeness of the contents of this book and specifically disclaim any implied warranties of merchantability or fitness for a particular purpose. No warranty may be created or extended by sales representatives or written sales materials. The advice and strategies contained herein may not be suitable for your situation. You should consult with a professional where appropriate. Further, readers should be aware that websites listed in this work may have changed or disappeared between when this work was written and when it is read. Neither the publisher nor author shall be liable for any loss of profit or any other commercial damages, including but not limited to special, incidental, consequential, or other damages.

For general information on our other products and services or for technical support, please contact our Customer Care Department within the United States at (800) 762-2974, outside the United States at (317) 572-3993 or fax (317) 572-4002.

Wiley also publishes its books in a variety of electronic formats. Some content that appears in print may not be available in electronic formats. For more information about Wiley products, visit our website at www.wiley.com.

Library of Congress Cataloging-in-Publication Data is Available:

ISBN 9781394290680 (Cloth)
ISBN 9781394290697 (ePub)
ISBN 9781394290703 (ePDF)

Cover Design: Rose Reynolds
Cover Image: © Lisa Hurley, 2025
Author Photo: © Lisa Hurley, by Fred Sly for Pocstock

SKY10104910_050225

*Dedicated to my Mama Bear, Kathleen Hurley:
You are an angel. You are a light. You are everything.
Love you MORE.*

Table of Contents

Prologue		*xiii*
Author's Note		*xv*
Introduction		*1*
PART I	**Know Yourself**	**11**
Chapter 1	Know Your Self: Remember	13
Chapter 2	Know Your Values: Align	29
Chapter 3	Know Your Strengths: Focus	49
PART II	**Love Yourself**	**75**
Chapter 4	Curate Your Thoughts: Manifest	77
Chapter 5	Curate Your Circle: Connect	107
Chapter 6	Curate Your Capacity: Rest	133
PART III	**Be Yourself**	**167**
Chapter 7	Working While Black: Learn	169

Table of Contents

Chapter 8   Curate Your Career: Strategize   205

Chapter 9   Curate Your Energy: Elevate   225

Chapter 10 Curate Your Soft Life: Exhale   245

Conclusion   *265*
Epilogue   *271*
Resources   *273*
Glossary   *275*
Acknowledgments   *281*
About the Author   *287*
Notes   *289*
Index   *297*

Prologue

The Alchemist

My spirit asked for this
I am an alchemist
I'm the antithesis of low

I am transforming now
I am brainstorming how
High and how far I will go

God is at work within
Balancing yang and yin
Making me ready to go

Farther than ever
Like stars up in heaven
I'm finally one with The Flow

© Lisa Hurley

Author's Note

Let us take a collective breath

Inhaling ease, and joy, and peace

Exhaling the exhaustion and disconnection so many of us feel

Breathe
Breathe
Breathe

It is time for a divine recalibration

I am ready for one, and by opting to respond when this book chose you, you are clearly ready for one too

We are aligned and we are agreed:
There must be a better way
Of living this thing called life

Not hurried, or harried, or constantly hustling, but

Soft
Centered
Serene

This is your invitation to a life gently lived

xvi   Author's Note

To a state of grace
To a return to self
To a slower pace

This is your invitation to practice the pause

To divest and rest
To be much more
To do much less

Beloved, this is your invitation to exhale

We have created a sacred space in which to do our healing work
So let us embark on this heart-centered journey together

Inhale
Exhale

Let us commence

~ ~ ~

There is little that is not made better, easier, and more manageable by pausing to take a breath. That said, *Space To Exhale* is not a book about breathwork—at least not solely. That is its core, but there is so much more.

Neither is it a book about achieving perfection. We don't need the pressure of trying to achieve the unachievable. Healing is not linear; it is not a destination that can be reached like a terminus in a station. The journey is always ongoing, but incremental advancements can be made along the way.

Space To Exhale is a book about making progress, bit by bit, step by step, and yes, breath by breath, toward enjoying a more easeful life.

It is about making room so your mind, heart, spirit, and body can heal. About creating a divine vacuum into which abundance can flow.

This book is my gift to you. Thank you for choosing to receive it. It is a gift to myself as well because I, too, am still on my healing journey. And isn't any road trip better with company? I love that we're traveling together

Let's turn up the music and go.

Author's Note xvii

Why Did I Write *Space To Exhale?*

To answer that I must take you back to the summer of 2023. I was exhausted. So were many of the Black women in my circle. And we had been tired for a long, long time. In addition, most of us in the activism space were being repeatedly bullied, microaggressed, and censored. We felt stressed, unsafe, and burned out from trying to navigate spaces that were actively built to hinder us from thriving.

We were—and are—tired of being strong for everybody else, but having no one to lean on when we need support.

There were many group chats and backchannel conversations about us needing to feel safer and more relaxed; about us needing spaces where we do not have to fear censorship or reprisal simply for stating facts; about us needing a space where we genuinely belong. We wanted to be away from prying eyes and from people who, in mixed-demographic groups, usually ended up harming us. My response was twofold:

First, in order to encourage Black women to take a breath and practice the pause, I started posting more frequently about the need for us all to rest. In the middle of the COVID-19 pandemic, when we were all still trying to figure out up from down, I wrote this post:

TFW you're done with the week, but it's only Tuesday.
It feels like somehow Covid has simultaneously sped up and slowed down time. Whyyyyy are the weeks so long?
It feels as if we're collectively:

• Frozen in the present, but focused on the future.
• Panicked, but productive.
• Blessed, but burned out.
• Needing, yet resisting, rest.

Over the past year and a half everything has changed, but we're expected to keep on keeping on as if everything is the same.

💔 Our bodies are tired.
💔 Our minds are tired.
💔 Our hearts are tired.

Our spirits are tired.
 And we're tired of feeling tired.

We need rest.
More to the point, we need to normalize and prioritize rest, rather than rewarding busyness for its own sake.
Today, give yourself permission to rest. Even if just for a few minutes.

Rest.
Rest.
Rest.

Take a breath.
Companies, if you can, show your employees some grace. Give them permission to take a break (A day? A week, maybe?) without fear of judgment or reprisal.

Let your employees rest.

Second, I'm a believer in verbs, so the other thing I did was take action. I created the soft, safe sanctuary I could tell Black women needed: The Great Exhale (TGE). It's an online community for any Black woman across the diaspora who is ready to remove her superwoman cape, take a deep breath, and rest. It's a community focused not so much on networking and clawing our way to the top,* but more so on sisterhood, soft living, serenity, and support.

Of course, because questioning Black women is a global pastime, I received lots of pushback about making the community exclusively for Black women. (Many people have a belief that being pro-Black means being anti-everything else. That is not the case.) However, I knew then what some of us have always known and what even more of us have now accepted in a post-2024 election world: Black women need to stop carrying everyone else and start lifting ourselves and each other. And that begins by prioritizing our self-care.

---

*Don't get me wrong, networking communities are also necessary. There is need, and room for all of us.

Author's Note

Because we're done. DONE. We're done with caring for others to our own detriment.

We're done with being the voice of reason and humanity to people who don't see us as fully human. We're done with dealing with people who prioritize blue bracelets and pink hats over Black lives.

We're done with being the "Strong Black Woman." The era of the Soft Black Woman has begun.

In the pre-launch phase of TGE I also received pushback about the community being "too quiet." Apart from the fact that I'm an introvert, so there's literally zero chance of me creating anything frenetic, my response was, "It's called The Great Exhale, not The Great Adrenaline. The whole goal is to relax." Constant work and everlasting busyness are what is expected of Black women—and that's what inflicts some of the deepest damage upon us. The Great Exhale is an antidote to those harmful expectations. You don't go into a meditation room only to find disco balls, strobe lights, and loud music. You expect zen, peace, and rest. That is what The Great Exhale provides.

I chose to stay true to my vision. I'm happy to say that my instincts were right. The feedback from my community members has been overwhelmingly positive, and one of the things they mention most often is how beautifully calming the vibe is. Black women have to be "on" everywhere else. Inside TGE, we get to relax and simply … be.

We focus on meditation, affirmations, journaling, soft living and, of course, breathwork. There's a lighter side too: I created channels within the community dedicated to joy, to jokes, to celebrating our hair and our culture. We get to frolic and be free. We get to talk about what we want to talk about without having to parse our words, code switch our language, or spend time explaining what we already know to people who are committed to misunderstanding us. We get to post what we want to post without having to be on the lookout for Uncle Algo (the algorithm) or feel fearful of being censored. And since it's important to circulate the Black dollar, there's also a channel named Minding Our Black Business where community members can promote their products and services or those of any Black-owned company.

Space To Exhale is a continuation of the heart work that I started with The Great Exhale. While it is possible that the virtual community could change in the future—evolution is inevitable—what will remain constant is xx

Author's Note

that it will always be a space for Black women. That is my vow. I owe that to my sistas and to myself.

That said, I want us *all* to heal: It's the Reiki Master in me. *Space To Exhale* therefore extends a warm welcome to *everyone* who is ready to live a softer, more serene life. I have always said that if just one person is positively affected by my words or my work, then I have done my job. However, to have my work make an even broader impact and hopefully help more people is part of the assignment that I have been entrusted with. I am being obedient.

The Framework

My firm belief is that we need to move from the exclamation point energy that the world demands of us, to the exhalation point energy that our souls crave. With that in mind, I created the Exhalation Point Framework to help us dispense with hustle culture and instead embrace ease.

The framework is composed of three elements: **Know Yourself, Love Yourself,** and **Be Yourself.**

Know Yourself

Curating a soft life starts with knowledge of self. When you know who you are, it is easier to build a life that is steeped in the energies of peace and abundance.

Love Yourself

Curating a soft life is built on self-love. When you love yourself, you make better choices that serve your highest good.

Be Yourself

Curating a soft life is based on being true to yourself. When you're true to yourself, your inner and outer worlds are aligned, you stay in the flow, and you are able to exhale.

Who Is *Space To Exhale* For?

As I mentioned before, as a Reiki Master, I want everybody to heal. May all of humanity elevate. However, as a healer (and activist) who navigates the world in Black skin, I will always center Black people, and especially Black women, in my work. I say this without apology because it often feels as though Black women are last on everyone's list. In my world, Black women are moved from the margins to the center, from the bottom to the top, from the back to the front.

In my world, Black women matter.

Therefore, when I first conceived of *Space To Exhale*, my goal was primarily to speak to Black women, and about Black women's lived experiences. My goal was to share stories, reveal insights, and provide resources uniquely suited to us. The experts always advise you to write about what you know. So I have.

That said, the book speaks to everyone who is tense, anxious, and perpetually exhausted. It provides moments of reflection, recalibration, and respite. It is for anyone, regardless of race, orientation, gender, or identity, who has ever asked themselves, "Is this ... it?" It is for anyone who has ever realized that their life isn't working as they would like it to. It is an invitation for us *all* to rethink our priorities and move toward living more meaningful, considered, rested lives. And because I live in the energy of seeking solutions, *Space To Exhale* provides tools and tips for how to do so.

This book is for you if:

- You're tired of feeling tired, and you're ready to get some rest.
- You're through with hustle culture and ready to experience a more serene lifestyle.
- You're done with being the "Strong Black Woman" and are ready to step into your Soft Black Woman era.
- You're one of the 92 percent of Black women voters in the US who voted for Kamala Harris.[1] The energy is "Let somebody else handle it. I'm doing me."
- You're *still* suffering from post-election grief; still reeling from the harmful "your body, my choice" rhetoric.
- You're an "only" who needs tips on how to navigate working while Black.
- You want cheat codes on how to avoid pitfalls in your life, relationships, and career.
- You desire to live a life that truly serves your highest good.
- You're ready to finally relax ... and exhale.

xxii Author's Note

If you feel burned out, disconnected, and tired till it hurts, *Space To Exhale* proposes an alternate path—the path of least resistance—and provides you with advice on how best to travel it. Within these pages you'll get validation for how you're feeling as well as tools and inspiration for living a kinder lifestyle. You'll learn about soft-living principles and how to put them into practice. If you value contemplation and prefer quieter pursuits (Introverts: I see you!), you'll also find breathwork exercises, prayers, and meditations to elevate your energy and nurture your soul.

In addition, *Space To Exhale* is for my niece Taryn, my "adopted niece" Ayanna, my goddaughter Joy, and all the young'uns coming up who every now and then need a reminder of how amazing they are—and how loved. A reminder that they are intelligent, worthy, and capable—and that they are nobody's mammy. That they are seen, understood, and valued. That they matter. That there is beauty in their melanin and power in their personality. It's a loving admonition to trust their gut, know their worth, take up space, and choose the path that works best for them. A reminder that it's okay to change their mind, and to take their time. There is no need to rush. Breathe. All will be well.

It's also for the younger generations who sometimes have so many questions and would just like a little advice on how to navigate life—without actually having to speak to anyone IRL. It's for the ones who are open to receiving cheat codes to make their lives a little easier. For the ones who are uncertain about their path but who are nevertheless already clear that they want a gentler experience for themselves than what some of their elders have endured. It's for the young folks who already feel suffocated by the weight of people's expectations and crave the freedom of their self-directed path. Auntie is here to help.

Honestly, this book is for me too.

It's for multiple versions of myself throughout the years. It is for eight-year-old Little Lisa with the Trini accent (before the Bajan one kicked in), big glasses, big dreams, big smile, and small afro, who was so often afraid of just being herself. It's for the little West Indian girl who always loved to play with words. It's letting her know that she can relax and be confident because, ultimately, as Brother Bob sings, "Everything's gonna be alright." Little Lis', you grow up, and you still get to play with words. Best of all, your words help people.

Author's Note

It's for teenage and young adult me who was always interested in yoga, prayer, energy, crystals, Reiki, and healing; who wanted to exist in that world for a living but couldn't see the way forward. It's for the version of me who always craved sisterhood in addition to my big sis but was never quite sure how to achieve it. Guess what, Lis? You get to do all that and more. And you have a whole community of sisters online.

It is for mid-career me trying again and again to prove myself to people who were unqualified to judge me. A love-rooted nudge to remember Who I Am. I never needed their approval. I was meant to walk my own path. And so I am.

I have Type A tendencies, so this book is also a tap on the shoulder to the me of today who still sometimes needs a reminder that I am enough and that I've done enough. There is nothing for me to prove. It is okay for me to rest, to pause, to take a few moments to breathe. It is me writing myself a permission slip to slow down and embrace progress over perfection. It's a permission slip for you too.

You cannot hustle and heal at the same time.

Happily, the book is also for future me who I already know is rich, relaxed, and reaping the rewards of rest. Life is good.

Why Me?

First off, why *not* me? I have all the degrees, awards, and expertise needed to prove my credibility. But also, as the saying goes: I'm not new to this, I'm true to this. I have always been this person. From a young, young age, even as far back as four or five, one of my favorite phrases was "But that's not fair!" Now I grew up in a certain culture, and there was no way I was going to risk actually saying those words out loud (shout-out to my West Indian fam, I know y'all get it), but I thought them, frequently, for myself and for others. Injustice of any kind has always disturbed my spirit. I have always been inclined to root for the underdog. I can't stand to see anyone be hurt or mistreated. Seeking justice is a part of who I am at my core. It is no wonder that I became an activist, calling out that which is not fair, just, or equitable.

In addition, my parents have always been very pro-Black. When I was between six and eight, I remember occasionally wishing that Mummy's afro wasn't quite so huge or that Daddy did not so often wear the dashikis that Mummy had painstakingly embroidered with intricate designs; however, that phase did not last long. I quickly became very proud of how they presented themselves. I did not know the phrase "Blackity Black Black" back then, but that was definitely their vibe. As an educator and intellectual, Daddy focused on Pan-Africanism and is professor emeritus of Africana Studies at Stony Brook University. My pride in my Blackness and focus on the Black experience was bred into me and modeled for me. That, too, is a part of who I am and how I navigate the world. My current focus on Black women reflects who I have always been.

My mother is a healer, giver, and artist. She is also a builder and a doer. She has a bent toward action. If there is a problem and she has the means and capacity to solve it, she will. I inherited many of those traits from her, and she also taught me that if there is something you want to see in the world, you have the power to create it.

For example, my mom is one of the founders of the Barbados Reiki Association, a community of Reiki practitioners. So I learned about building a healing-focused community like The Great Exhale from her. She is a quiet but strong leader who demonstrated that you don't have to be the loudest person in the room to make a positive impact on the world. That was an important message for her introverted second-born child to absorb. She gave me permission to walk through the world exactly as I am. My mom is also highly empathetic and hates to see anyone suffer. We are similar in that way as well. My innate empathy currently expresses itself by seeing and feeling the pain of my sistas and having a desire to help reduce it.

Writing is in my blood: My father and sister are published authors several times over. In addition, they are both poets, and both have a background in academia as professors. My sister is also a former journalist, and she created the curriculum for the master's in journalism at Coventry University in the UK.

It is little surprise, therefore, that for as long as I can remember, I've been writing in one form or another. I wrote my first song at about age four, and I've been writing ever since—poems, essays, ranty posts, you name it. For a large part of my career I was also a marketing copywriter, so I literally spent all day writing. However, I love writing so much that I also do it during my down time. I have a couple of blogs where I write about, well … all the things. Everything from pop culture, racism, and fashion, to spirituality, careers, and mental health.

Author's Note XXV

There's even a little poetry. Some of the poems are admittedly angsty, but there are others that stand the test of time. Case in point, the poems that open and close *Space To Exhale* are decades old. In fact, I wrote the original version of the closing poem "Why I Breathe" more than 25 years ago. It was a foreshadowing. If that doesn't exemplify being true to this, I don't know what does. I have always been on this vibration. I've always been interested in breathing as a conduit to deeper connection with self.

Spirituality, yoga, affirmations, meditation: I have been intensely interested in all things esoteric since my early teens. I'm a lover of good energy and good vibes, so when I first heard about Reiki, I was instantly fascinated. Like many great things in my life, I was introduced to Reiki by my mom back in the '90s. I've been a Reiki practitioner since then, and have my first and second degree in Usui Reiki. A few years ago, I decided to go deeper into my spirituality journey and was initiated as a Reiki Master, also by my mom, who has been a Reiki Master Teacher for several years.

One of the main themes of the book is burnout: What it is and how to address it. While I mention the syndrome from a theoretical perspective, I also have lived experience with suffering from it and overcoming it. Although I am not a mental health professional, I do believe that my "burnout battle" story will be helpful to readers who might be experiencing the same thing.

All of this is to say: I am the right person to write *Space To Exhale* because I have lived the life and done the work. The book is a tapestry of everything my multipotentialite heart is interested in, as well as an extension of my activism and healing work. It is an expression of my traits, talents, interests, experiences—and purpose. And a part of my purpose is to serve my community and my readers from a place of authenticity. To paraphrase Hillel: If not now, then when? If not me, then who?

What to Expect from *Space To Exhale*

This Is a Book of Self-Healing

Space To Exhale is the book I needed when I had to get up after a breakdown. I felt burned out, exhausted, and constantly anxious because of the effects of existing and working while Black. If the phrase "make your mess

xxvi   Author's Note

into your message and your test into your testimony" were in book form, this would be it. It has given me a way back and a way forward. My hope is that if you are in a similar place it will do the same for you.

This Is a Book of Community Healing

It is a reminder that, although there are aspects to healing work that one must undertake alone, one can never fully heal in isolation. We need each other. We need support from the collective; to be rocked in the cradle of our community. We need the village. Let us create one together right now.

This Is a Book of Encouragement

It is a way finder for those who feel stuck on the treadmill of life: Who feel fatigued, stressed, burned out, and overwhelmed. It is for anyone who has ever felt like adulting is a scam. It is for those who are searching for a deeper meaning; for a more fulfilling life, to let them know that it is possible to create the life you truly want. Hold on. Stay encouraged. Better is coming.

This Is a Book of Curation

It is about choices. It's about the small daily actions we can all take to elevate our existence, to make ourselves feel better, to thrive rather than merely survive, and to get closer to living the life we've always imagined for ourselves—in healthy, balanced ways. It encourages us to be the sculptors of our own lives; to cut away that which is not needed (or not good for us), and reveal the beauty that has always been waiting beneath the surface.

This Is a Book of Expansiveness

It encourages us to make room. For ourselves. For our dreams. For our truth. For our destiny, our health, and our restoration. Room to breathe. It reminds us that it's okay to want better for ourselves—and to ask for it. It is okay to want something different from the norm. We're allowed to have our own definition of success, and to clear a path for it to manifest. Importantly, it reminds us to be open to receive; to make space in our minds, our homes, and our lives for what we most desire. Abundance abounds.

This Is a Book of Relaxation

Meditation, contemplation, a conscious daily exhale. It is also a book about baby steps. Slow and steady wins the race. Better yet, just slow and steady. We can opt out of the race. This is not about competition or sprinting to a finish line. There are no awards and gold stars, apart from the ones you can confer upon yourself for treating yourself more tenderly. It is about moving toward a life more tranquil. This is about us embracing our inner tortoise and going slower; about consciously and consistently choosing the path of least resistance.

This Is a Book of Validation

It's not just you: We are all collectively exhausted. *Space To Exhale* is for all of us who are tired of the daily grind; for those of us who are burned out; for those of us who have gotten used to feeling fatigued as our default. It is for everyone who has felt forced to do what is expected of them, as opposed to what their heart desires. It's for anyone who has ever thought "Is this all there is??" I get it. I've been there. At times I am still there. The good news is it's never too late to reinvent yourself. It's never too late to choose differently. It's never too late to embrace calm, and relax fully into your life. This is not all there is. There is more, and you get to experience it. Just choose.

This Is a Book of Sisterhood

It is most especially for my Black sistas around the world: No matter how they try to divide us, we are one. Solidarity. I see you, sis. I feel you. I love you. I am you. You are not alone. It's not all in your head. I know you're tired, sis, but it is time to rest. We finally get to rest. It is time for us to lay our burdens down and put ourselves first.

Of course, it is also for my sisters within The Great Exhale: We get to continue what we started together. We get to keep building a soft, serene sanctuary within our community—and within these pages.

And finally,

Author's Note

This Is a Book of Alignment

So:

Thank you for showing up.

Thank you for slowing down.

Thank you for choosing you.

Thank you for seeing me.

Thank you for giving yourself time and space to exhale.

Introduction

Trigger Warning

Contains references to abuse, assault, mental health issues, racism, and suicidal ideation. If you are struggling or in crisis, or someone you know is, call 988 or visit the American Foundation for Suicide Prevention at www.asfp.org.

Is it just me?

It's the end of the 2nd week of this new year, and I'm already feeling exhausted. I came very close to major burnout towards the end of last year, and I clearly am not fully restored.

So … time to rest.

Time to re-prioritize.

Time to excise the extraneous and elevate the essential.

× I refuse to work myself to tatters.

× I refuse to be a slave to the capitalist matrix.

× I refuse and rebuke all the false emergencies.

× I refuse to make other people's deadlines matter more than my lifeline.

I refuse. I refuse. I refuse.

My plan for this year includes achieving more while doing less, so I'm going to start right now by taking a nap.

Introduction

My long weekend will be a real long weekend.

I will be blissfully useless.
I will leave my calls unanswered.
I will sip tea, instead of serving it.
I will relax my body and brain.
I will spa, as a verb.
I will be a potato.

I will treat myself like my favorite houseguest.
My time off will be time off. I will unplug.
Disengage. Disappear. Be unavailable.
I will be the architect of my own restoration.
I invite you to do the same.
Rest.

I posted these words on social media a while back. Ya girl was tired. And tired of being tired. Naturally, there are many reasons why. Among them: Life, health, and of course, working while Black.

Mostly the last, to be honest. Every day on the corporate plantation there was some new set of foolishness to deal with. I feel like there should be a warning sign posted on the front door of every office building:

Caution: Caucacity[1][*] Ahead.

Here's a snapshot of a typical office shenanigan:

One day at work, I had just delivered a virtual presentation. It went great, and I was feeling good about it. Did a little internal happy dance and everything. Just before the call wrapped, the person leading the meeting gave the customary thank-yous. Imagine my shock and irritation when they thanked everybody on the call except me—the person who had developed the copy concepts and walked the team through the deck.

Before you ask: Yes, they are.

---

[*] "Caucacity" is a word coined by The Kid Mero in an article for Vice in 2012. It is a portmanteau of the words "caucasian" and "audacity." Though it is sometimes spelled "caucasity," I have used the spelling that he prefers.

Introduction 3

They even thanked my boss (also a white person) who not only was not on the call but was not even at the office. They were on vacation. I would, of course, have been okay with "Thanks to the team." My boss had contributed, and therefore deserved to be recognized. But it was … weird … to not thank or even acknowledge the existence of the person who had just presented to you for almost an hour. I felt erased.

I confess that tears came to my eyes.

Now you might be thinking, "*That* made you cry?" Well, yes and no. The tears were not even really because of that incident, but more so triggered by years upon years of similar slights, microaggressions, and disrespect.

The tears were because of the many times my boss introduced everybody on the team by name—except me. Because of constantly hitting the glass ceiling. Because of repeatedly moving from pet to threat. Because of frequently having to train the people I reported to but never being considered for a more senior role. Because of participating in a group project but being asked to take the group photo rather than be in it. Because of being put on a performance improvement plan—a PIP—because I didn't smile enough. Because of being put on another PIP because they wanted to lower my position in the calibration rankings in order to make a case for promoting a white woman rather than me.

The tears were also because of random people examining and touching my hair. Because of being yelled at in front of my entire department. Because of being judged for being "too quiet" but also being judged if I was ever "loud." Because of being interpreted as being angry when I was just existing with my face at rest.

The tears were cumulative.

After a while, working while Black wears on you. This was just one of the days when it broke my spirit. Straw, meet the camel's back.

In my frustration, I turned to LinkedIn and posted the following:

Being the only Black employee on an all-white team is freaking exhausting and demoralizing.

The response was overwhelming. Black person after Black person—especially Black women—jumped into the comments to share their stories of trying to survive in white-majority corporate spaces and of how the

4 Introduction

daily battle impacts their personal lives and mental health. They shared tales of feeling tense, tired, and traumatized.

So while I wish I could say that my experience that day was unique, unfortunately it is not.

Now that incident took place in an office, but what many non-Black people fail to realize is that racism is everywhere. It is not confined to corporate corridors. It is truly inescapable. Frequently, before I even arrived at the office, I had already had to deal with some racially tinged ignorance.

Like the day I returned from my pre-work walk with my fur baby only to be refused entry to *my own apartment* by a tradesperson of pallor who did not believe I lived there. This was his first time at the building, but he felt he had the right to interrogate me. "Are you sure you live here?" he asked, positioning himself between me and my door. I had walked up with my dog on his leash and my keys out, ready to put them in the lock, so I didn't even understand the question. He was about to make me late because he had delusions of grandeur. I mean, if he was in "policing mode," he could at least have waited to see if my key worked. But anyhoo. Those overseer genes are undefeated. I was finally able to get into my home because my white neighbors, who had moved in a mere two days prior, vouched for me. Meanwhile, I had been living there for more than a decade. Sigh.

There was also the day I walked up to the top of my street to catch my bus to work, and my neighbor's dog started to bark. (As dogs do. Just saying.) She yelled out to me, "Do you know why he's barking?" I looked at her confused because, again, this is what dogs do. Also, her dog was one of the "known barkers" in the neighborhood. He barked at everyone. "It's because of your hair!" she shouted. "I beg your pardon??" I replied. "He's never seen hair like that, so he's scared!" I had left home feeling fabulous, in my huge fro and sunglasses, and this white lady with bad intentions, bad vibes, and a bad perm was trying to dull my shine.

"Bitch!" Yeah … there was that day too. The day that I got on the bus to head to the office and the driver cussed me out because—get this—I paid her. Yup. You read that right. She was mad because I paid her with a $20 bill. I usually had change, but that morning I didn't, so I had made sure to tell her early in the trip so she could prepare. When I was ready to get off, I handed her the $20 that I had already told her about. She looked

Introduction   5

down at it, looked up at me, cut her eyes, and called me out my name. I got called the B-word for paying my bus fare. You can't make this stuff up.

I know I'm not alone; many Black women have similar experiences. We deal with the daily paper cuts of racism outside of the office, then we have to go into work, paste on a smile, and gird our loins for a day of misogynoir and microaggressions.

Those of us with children, spouses, dependents, pets, and side hustles do a second and sometimes even a third unofficial, but no less taxing, shift. Childcare, elder care, household management, emotional labor, the administration of life. All the things.

It's a lot.

And it's expected of us. To paraphrase Zora Neale Hurston, Black women are frequently treated like "the mules of the world." We're expected to just keep going. Just keep giving. Just keep working. We're expected to pour and pour and pour into everyone but ourselves until we're completely depleted.

The good thing is we're not accepting that anymore. We are ready to pour into ourselves.

Space To Exhale: A Handbook for Curating a Soft, Centered, Serene Life is the book Black women need to help them prioritize themselves, get rest, and live a life more gentle.

~ ~ ~

More than any other identity group, Black women are tired, stressed, overlooked, overextended, and underinvested in—especially at work. How do I know? I am one.

But don't just take my word for it: A report by Black Women Thriving states that in their professional lives, fewer than 50 percent of Black women feel happy at their job. Sixty-six percent feel emotionally unsafe at work. More than 88 percent have experienced burnout. Additionally, a study by Boston University revealed that among all women, Black women aged 18–65 have the highest suicide risk. The. Highest.[2]

How does this data translate to the real world? Just look at the experiences of former Vice President Kamala Harris, Supreme Court Justice Ketanji Brown-Jackson, former First Lady of the United States

Introduction

Michelle Obama, former President of Harvard Dr. Maxine Gay, and Lincoln University Vice President of Student Affairs Dr. Bonnie Candia-Bailey, who died by suicide in January of 2024 as a result of workplace mobbing.

These highly visible, highly accomplished Black women were bullied, berated, undermined, publicly flayed, and left unprotected. Unfortunately, Black women who are equally as accomplished but somewhat less visible are also subjected to similar mistreatment.

Across the diaspora, regardless of age, profession, industry, career level, educational attainment, and social class, living while Black—and living in the body of a Black woman—can be a torturous experience.

And we are collectively exhausted.

On a personal level, as an activist, as a Black woman operating in majority-white corporate spaces, I am all too familiar with this exhaustion myself. Alas, I am also familiar with attempted suicide. Sometimes, the world gets to be too much.

Since 2020, I have been advocating around issues, including racism, texturism, anti-Blackness, pay equity, introversion, neurodiversity, and DEI, and it has been a Sisyphean task.

With every seeming advancement, society takes several steps back. And with every retrogression, Black women find themselves at the bottom of the proverbial barrel: The most marginalized of all marginalized communities. We feel as though we keep fighting for seats at tables where we are not welcome—and it wearies our souls.

In true Gaslighting 101 form, we are told that things can't be that bad. We are told that we're imagining it, that we're being melodramatic, that we are angry. We, the victims of ongoing microaggressions and psychological harm, are openly doubted and undermined:

> *Maybe they didn't mean that racist comment. Maybe it wasn't a racist comment at all. Maybe "you're so articulate" is a compliment. Perhaps people touching our hair without permission is a blessing. Perhaps being overlooked for that promotion (again) and having to train the CEO's cousin (again) will build character. Perhaps making 64 cents[3] for every dollar white men earn will make it easier for us to support our families and self-fund our side hustles.*

Makes sense, right?

Um ... no.

It's not all in our heads, and it's not okay.

Although the issues described above are the result of systemic forces and structures, some of them can be mitigated against on an individual level. The goal is to focus on what we **can** control, which is a stress reliever in itself.

I believe that Black women can choose differently. I believe that Black women can have it all—though maybe not all at the same time. They—or should I say **we**—can create life-work balance, in that order. We can choose to divest and rest. We can curate a softer, happier existence for ourselves, where rather than simply surviving, we can fully thrive.

We owe it to ourselves.

Black women are praised for being strong and resilient, but what if we didn't have anything to be resilient from?

What if we could experience lives filled with ease?

What if our existence and energy could be gentle?

What if we could create and inhabit spaces where we feel nurtured, loved, and psychologically safe?

What if we could consciously curate lives where we have room to pause, relax, and simply breathe?

Space To Exhale is the book that will help us do that.

Why is *Space To Exhale* necessary *now*? If it wasn't already evident, Black women are clearly in crisis and in need of healing. As a Reiki Master, as an activist, as a Black woman, it is incumbent upon me to do my part to help make things better. I have written this book with the intention of uplifting and inspiring my sisters.

Space To Exhale is a balm to the spirit. It is the word "woosah" in book form. It is a guide that not only gives Black women permission to curate the kind of life they truly want, but it also provides an actionable roadmap to help them do so.

8 Introduction

The goal of *Space To Exhale* is twofold:

First, it validates Black women, as well as anyone who is ready to relax, take a pause, and exhale. To do so, it guides readers through The Exhalation Point framework I outlined in the Author's Note, inviting them to **Know Yourself, Love Yourself,** and **Be Yourself.** The book is therefore divided into three sections, based on the framework.

In the **Know Yourself** section, I encourage readers to remember who they are, stand firm in their values, and cultivate their innate strengths.

In the **Love Yourself** section, the focus is on loving yourself enough to think positively about yourself, surround yourself with people who are good for you, and most importantly, to prioritize rest.

In the **Be Yourself** section, we focus on life-work balance. I encourage us all to reexamine what we really want from life, redefine what career success[†] means to us, and show up authentically in ways that, instead of draining us, amplify our energy.

The second goal of *Space To Exhale* is to educate organizations about why their Black employees might experience the company as unsafe. The book also provides recommendations to help companies make their cultures safer, more welcoming, and more equitable.

Navigation

Approach *Space To Exhale* as you would a buffet. Everything is served, but you get to choose what you'll consume. Take what resonates and leave the rest. Here's what's on the menu:

Invocation: Let Us Pray

Each chapter starts with an invocation: A prayer to set the tone. Read the entire prayer or a portion thereof. A verse, a line, whatever is most comfortable. Go at a pace that suits you. I have used the words "Most High" to open all the prayers. Feel free to substitute whatever term resonates most with

---

[†]In the table of contents, you will have noticed that Chapter 7, "Working While Black," is titled somewhat differently from the other chapters. It discusses what I have dubbed as the Working While Black Effect. While it is not a part of the framework outlined above, I felt it necessary to include a full accounting of what most Black people, and especially Black women, experience in white-majority workplaces. A huge part of why so many of us are exhausted and frustrated is because of how much effort it takes to navigate corporate cultures that were not designed for us to thrive.

Introduction 9

you and your beliefs. If prayers are not your thing, you can, of course, skip them. There are a lot more inspirational goodies for you to enjoy.

Recollection: A Likkle‡ About Me

After the prayer, I share a story from my life and the lessons I learned as a result. I also sometimes share a couple of stories from my mom's life because she has taught me so much about living fully but gently.

Education: Soft-Life Strategies

After each "what had happened" story, there are tips for how you can integrate my hard-learned lessons into your life.

Elevation: Vibrate Higher

As a Reiki Master and eternal seeker, I'm all about energy. I believe that attending to our inner world helps us improve our outer world. Each chapter ends with exercises to help us all vibrate higher. Again: Focus on what you feel aligned with, and set the rest aside.

- **Exhalation: Breathe Easy**
  Naturally, with a title like *Space To Exhale*, there are breathing exercises to help us all pause and regulate our systems.
- **Affirmations: Speak Life**
  How you talk to and about yourself matters. The affirmations are drawn from my archive (500+ deep) and there are also new ones exclusive to the book.
- **Introspection: Journal & Heal**
  There is so much catharsis to be gained from pouring your feelings out onto the page. The journaling prompts provide inspiration to help you get started.
- **Curation: Do the Work**
  Faith without works is dead. The "Curation" sections provide actionable steps for you to put into practice and tips for making your dream life a reality.

---

‡As an FYI, I'm from the Caribbean, so expect a little—or should I say a likkle—sprinkle of West Indian lingo from time to time.

Introduction

- **Appreciation: Express Gratitude**
  Give thanks for the blessings you already have. Few things improve your life and mindset as much as expressing gratitude can.
- **Celebration: Razzle Dazzle**
  Taking time to big ourselves up and celebrate our wins is so important. When life gets heavy, focusing on the good in our lives and in ourselves can make it feel a little lighter.
- **Meditation: Think Blissfully**
  Each chapter closes with a meditation: A mindset cleanse to elevate the vibes.

And with that, y'all ready? We've laid the groundwork, so let's get into it. It's time to take a collective breath and start curating some space to exhale.

Asé.

PART

I Know Yourself

1 | Know Your Self: Remember

Invocation

Most High,

May I deeply know My Self
May I brightly shine my light
May I fully live my life
May I remember Who I Am

May I completely own my royalty
May I adjust my crown accordingly
May I comport myself with dignity
May I remember Who I Am

May I view myself with clarity
May I treat myself with empathy
May I share Divine prosperity
May I remember Who I Am

May I proudly claim my ancestry
May I wholly know my history
May I now fulfill my destiny
May I remember Who I Am

Amen

Trigger Warning

This chapter briefly mentions domestic violence, molestation, sexual assault, and abuse.

A God-Given Glow Up

"Are you sitting down?"

"Um … yes?" I replied hesitantly.

When someone says this you're never quite sure whether it's going to be good news, or your world is about to be torn to shreds.

Fortunately for me, it was the former. Actually, it was AMAZING news.

It was the evening of August 20, 2020, and Polly Irungu was on the other end of the line. She and I had met the previous summer at Afropunk Brooklyn, and she had very graciously taken a few photos of me. Polly is a super-talented photographer (as of this writing, she is the photo editor for the office of the vice president), and she is also the founder of Black Women Photographers (BWP).[1]

That year, Afropunk's theme was "Take Up Space." So I had. The Universe blessed me, and I was everywhere. It is thanks to Polly that my image was featured on Refinery29.com wearing a Barbados-blue tulle ensemble and a pink crown. Little ole me!! (Outside of the frame there was a pop of yellow, in the form of sunshine-colored Fentys. Gotta rep the Bajan flag whenever possible.) That photo was captioned "At Afropunk, Lady Liberty has microbraids, a floral crown, and—yes—she's Black."[2] And let me tell you, when this happened I truly felt like I had made it.

But sometimes the Universe has bigger plans for you than you have for yourself.

So anyway, there we all were in the middle of the global dumpster fire known as the COVID-19 pandemic, and in my personal, perpetually panicked part of the world, a sliver of light shone through. God sent a blessing to make me smile.

Know Your Self: Remember 15

"Your picture is going to be on the Nasdaq screen in Times Square," Polly continued.

My brain glitched. I must have misheard her. Right?! 'Cause ain't no way!!

"Wait … WHAT?"

I just blurted that out. I was so shocked that my manners deserted me.

Polly laughed; she completely understood. She repeated herself a bit more slowly to give me time to process her words: "Your picture is going to be on the Nasdaq screen in Times Square."

"But how? And when? And which one?" I rapid-fired questions at her because I was genuinely confused and in a state of shock.

"Tomorrow," she replied. "It's the one of you wearing the floofy white cloud and that amazing sunburst crown."

I moved the phone away from my ear, tilted my head to the left like a puzzled puppy and looked sideways at the screen, brow furrowed. This had to be some kind of practical joke. Because again: Ain't. No. Way. Me? In Times Square?? I put the phone on speaker and rested it on the table because I couldn't hold it anymore. My hands were literally shaking.

Polly explained that she had pitched a multimedia exhibition to Nasdaq as part of their inaugural Amplifying Black Voices campaign,[3] and they had said yes. So, thanks to her, this little girl from Barbados was going to have a dream come true that I hadn't even been aware of having. If ever there was a "Look, Mom, I made it!" moment, this was it. I am forever grateful to Polly for that wonderful opportunity. Thanks and praises. I'm also forever grateful to my designer Jen Wilson who conceptualized and created the bespoke lewk that had made waves at my all-time favorite festival.

As soon as I hung up, I called my family. "Are you sitting down?" I asked. (I figured it was now tradition to ask that.) I told them everything, laughing and crying at the same time. It was a very loud, boisterous phone call, lol. Fortunately, my neighbors are cool. There was lots of shouting: "Whaaatttt??! OMG!! Congratulations, Lis!!" There were lots of excited screams.

Polly had given me all the details and asked me to take some photos of the exhibit for her since she wouldn't be able to be there. The day of, I told my boss that I would be starting late—I knew better than to say why—and took one of those rickety little Jersey City buses into Port Authority. They're like the American version of a Bajan ZR van. If you know, you know. Rickety or not, the bus felt like a limo to me. I was floating. I confess

16   Know Yourself

that as I walked toward Times Square my eyes started filling with tears. Happy tears. I truly couldn't believe it.

Since we were mid-pandemic, Times Square was a ghost town, which made the whole experience even more surreal. I'm not sure if there were even as many as 20 people there. I looked up at the screen, holding my breath behind my mask, phone poised to capture the moment, and then, finally, I saw it. It was not a prank. It was real. There I was, larger than life, at the center of the universe. Wow.

In total, there were five images in Polly's segment of the exhibit. The first four (amazing!) photos were titled "Our Magic," "Resist," "Black Joy," and "We Are Here." Polly had captioned my image "Don't Forget Your Crown," and in that moment I felt like the queen of all queens.

In an interview with Nasdaq, Polly explained why she had selected these images:

> Not going to lie, it was really hard. It's not [every day] you get the opportunity to have your work shown on a tower in Times Square by Nasdaq. I chose these photos to showcase Black women in all of their glory. I want members of my Black Women Photographers community to remember their power, their joy, and to never forget who they are. I want people to see these photos and instantly feel the joy within them. I want these photos to serve as a reminder to never dim your light or shrink and change yourself for anything or anyone. These photos are some of my favorite photos that I return to when I need that reminder myself.[4]

My Times Square début was a core experience and a core memory. It was a MOMENT. For that reason, I celebrate the "anniversary" every year even if only with myself. I will never *not* celebrate it for several reasons. I celebrate because it inspires me to continue to:

- **Dream big and expect good things:**
  I'm originally from Barbados, and I predate Rihanna by quite a few years. Like several. (Okay, by a couple of decades, lol.) By which I mean: When I was growing up, being featured in Times Square or anything similar to that was not even a remote possibility. Never crossed my mind to dream of it because I had rarely or never seen it. Rarely by people who looked like me and never by anybody from

Know Your Self: Remember 17

Barbados. Nowadays, in the Age of Rihanna, anything is possible. But back in my day? Not so much.

Look how far I'd come.

So this experience reminds me to think big, dream bigger, and allow the Universe to show up in limitless ways. Cause little ole me from Bimshire—another name for Barbados—made it onto the big screen in the Big Apple. (Cue "Empire State of Mind," the iconic track by Jay-Z and Alicia Keys.) And if big things can happen for me, big things can happen for you too.

- **Do me, be genuinely nice to people, and keep showing up:** When Polly and I met, we vibed and chatted for a good while, beyond the "did you get the shot" conversation. This is important because I saw a lot of people acting salty, impatient, and entitled with the photographers. Not cool. Funny thing is, that conversation—and the resultant photos—almost didn't get a chance to happen because I had nearly talked myself out of attending Afropunk that year. But I put on my big-girl pants, turned on my extroverted side, and headed to Brooklyn despite the protests of my inner introvert. I showed up.

  I was authentically myself. I have always identified as a fairy princess, and in those moments, I was one. I smiled. I posed. I twirled. I frolicked. I vibed for the culture. I embodied joy, light, and #BlackGirlMagic. And blessings ensued. Blessings continue to ensue to this day because Afropunk is still using photos of me in both outfits as promos for the event. Every time I see them, I smile.

  Nothing happens if you don't show up.

- **Remember Who I Am, and show up as *that girl*, always:** I'm a woman of a certain age, and those of you who are at that stage know all too well that we gradually become less and less visible. We are considered to be irrelevant, inconsequential, past our prime, and unworthy of being gazed upon. The world treats us like we're a nuisance. Or a laughingstock. It's as if every wrinkle depletes our worth. Not realizing what a blessing it is to live long, people throw the word "old" at us as though it's an indictment of our character; an assessment of our value—or lack thereof. Our crowns become tarnished, or people perceive them as such, and sometimes that gets into our heads and wreaks havoc with our self-esteem.

But the truth is that no matter how old I get there will always be the little girl inside me who loves the limelight; who lives for a jazz hands, lights-camera-action moment. That little girl loves glitter, costumes, crowns, sequins, and tulle. Allllll the tulle. (This might be my Trini side coming through, lol.) That sparkly little sis loves herself and believes that more is more. She is fun, and happy, and a maximalist. She is part and parcel of who I am, and I choose to honor her whenever I can. I will always be that girl.

And sis, I know you will always be that girl too, in whatever way is true for you.

So my Times Square triumph also reminds me to gaze upon myself with kind eyes; it reminds me of the power of self-love; it reaffirms the power of authenticity. It is a reminder, for us all I hope, to show up in our fullness; to adjust our crowns; to remember who we are.

Why It Is Important to Remember Who You Are

You are worthy of living a soft, centered, serene life and having the best of everything. We all are. But sometimes life beats us down so much that we forget Who We Are.

We forget that we are innately worthy. We forget that we deserve nice things. We forget our north star. We get moved off our square. We twist ourselves into a whole different person just to try and fit in or get ahead. We shrink ourselves to avoid other people's disapproval. We attenuate our ambitions out of fear of being too much. We dim our light so our glow won't upset the haters. We hide from ourselves because we fear our own greatness. Then one day, we wake up and we can no longer recognize ourselves. Who is this sad, shrunken, shadowy soul? We realize that this is not who we want to be or how we want to live.

If our "avatar" is in charge—the public-facing persona so many of us develop when we're in survival mode—we might be living a life that is inauthentic and unfulfilling. A life that makes it hard for us to breathe.

A good life, a soft life, must be grounded in authenticity. The life of our dreams must be based on who we are in reality. Not who someone else thinks we should be. Not who our peers pressure us to be. Not who the system tries to force us to be. Who. We. Are.

Know Your Self: Remember   19

Because how are you going to curate the life you want if you are building on a foundation of lies? As our good sister Lauren Hill sang: "How you gon' win when you ain't right within?"

Look, no judgment here because I've been there. I'm sure you have too.

We lie to ourselves about the kind of relationships we desire.
We lie to ourselves about the career we would prefer.
We lie to ourselves that "The Path" is working for us.

(I mean … it might be, but often it isn't.)

What is "The Path," you ask? It looks a little like this:

Go to school → get good grades → be a good girl / be a good boy → girls: Don't laugh too hard; it's not ladylike → boys: Don't cry at all; it's not manly → go to college → graduate with honors → get a job—a *real* job, a *secure* job, a *respectable* job (doctor, lawyer, engineer, CEO) → go back to school, get your MBA → get married → buy a house (picket fence, of course) → bills, bills, bills → have two kids → get a Golden Retriever → get a better job → work work work work work work → climb the corporate ladder higher → retire → expire.

There are nuances to this across cultures, but still … around the globe, "The Path" is remarkably consistent.

However, for many of us "The Path" does not work. It can leave us miserable, unfulfilled, and internally vacant, just marking time until the ultimate slumber.

It can place us in a mindset of "Is this … **IT**??" And who wants to live like that? I truly believe that we are meant to enjoy life. We deserve better and we deserve more.

That's why it's important to do the work of knowing yourself and remembering Who You Are: It gives you the opportunity to forge a different path; one that you have consciously chosen. A path that not only leads to joy, but also offers nondeferred happiness along the way. Remembering who you are provides stable scaffolding from which to construct the life of your dreams. Nothing gives you space to exhale like having the right foundation in place.

20 Know Yourself

When you remember Who You Are, you:

Respect Your Roots

I'z a Bajan. In Barbados, that's a local way of saying I am a Barbadian. And if you couldn't already tell, I am proud, proud, proud of my island. It's small but mighty: A breathtaking 166 square mile gem in the eastern Caribbean. The sea, sun, and sand are a given: The island is visually stunning. But beyond that, I appreciate and respect my Bajan people, culture, traditions, and mores. Barbados is not perfect—no country is—but it's mine. It's sweet like sugar cane, and I love it.

These days, most people immediately think of Rihanna when the topic of Barbados comes up, as well they should. You don't need me to convince you of her bona fides: Our girl is a global icon.

Another person who comes to mind is Mia Mottley, who is the first woman to have been elected as prime minister of Barbados. In addition to leading the country, she has been active on the international scene. From 2020 to 2021, she served as co-chair of the Development Committee of the World Bank and the International Monetary Fund. In 2022, she was named as co-chair of the UN Secretary-General's Sustainable Development Goal (SDG) Advocates Group[5] along with Canada's then-Prime Minister Justin Trudeau, and as of this writing, she is also co-chair of World Health Organization's Global Leaders Group on Antimicrobial Resistance.[6]

For its tiny size, Barbados is truly a land of luminaries. A non-exhaustive list of eminent Bajans by birth and by descent includes folks like Adisa Andwele, Sir Hilary Beckles, Nicholas Brancker, Ryan Brathwaite, Austin Clarke, Grandmaster Flash, Doug E. Fresh, Ché Greenidge, Lene Hall, Alison Hinds, Eric Holder, DJ Puffy, Rupee, Arturo Tappin, Obadele Thompson, and Sada Williams, as well as ancestors like Errol Barrow, Edward Kamau Brathwaite, Shirley Chisholm, Frank Collymore, George Lamming, Sir Lloyd Erskine Sandiford, Sir Garfield Sobers, and Sir Derek Walcott. Google my people, y'all. We outchea. There's a saying that wherever you go in the world, you'll find a Bajan. I would edit that to add: You'll find a Bajan—*excelling*.

Anytime I feel like I've been moved off my square, this helps bring me back to center: The knowledge that I am descended of a proud people. It informs how I move through the world and how I choose to show up.

It keeps me grounded: It is my foundation. I still have my accent; I still speak Bajan dialect; whenever I can rock Barbados blue I do; and I go home as often as I can. I rep Bim* hard.

I remember being in an ESL class at a school I once attended in the US. Yes: They had me, a native of an anglophone country who had majored in linguistics in undergrad, taking English as a Second Language. But anyhoo. The topic of literacy came up, and one of the American people of pallor started down the line of "The US has the highest literacy rate in the world." The African American teacher and I looked at the person with smug smiles on our faces (yes, it was a li'l petty, lol) and then our eyes met with an energy of "Will you tell him or will I?" I went first, explaining that my island Barbados had (at the time) a literacy rate of 98 percent. Not the highest in the world, but definitely higher than that of the US.

The guy tried to argue me down, but then the teacher stepped in. He told the dismayed student, "There's no need to get upset with her. These are publicly available statistics. I know about Barbados, and she is correct." Chad was big mad. We both gave him the deadpan stare with a slow blink and an internal shrug. We don't create the facts. The facts are the facts. Oh, and as of this writing the Barbadian literacy rate is 99 percent. We might be a small island, but we have big country energy.

When I was in primary school, we started every day by reciting the National Pledge:

> I pledge allegiance to my country Barbados
> And to my flag,
> To uphold and defend their honour,
> And by my living
> To do credit to my nation wherever I go.

Those last two lines especially hold a permanent space in my brain. That is the goal. To remember where I came from and bring honor to my country in whatever ways I can. I respect my roots. I remember who I am. I am a Bajan.

---

*Like "Bimshire," "Bim" is an alternative name for Barbados.

Embrace Your Ancestry

I love being Black. And even more than that I love being a Black woman. There is something so sweet and special about being a member of the sistahood. Our melanin, our magic, our movementations … yassss! I would never want to be anything else. I also love being African American. And, of course, I love being West Indian.[†] I love that I was born in Jamaica (where my parents studied at the University of the West Indies), grew up briefly in Trinidad (my mother's homeland), then mostly in Barbados (my father's homeland). Intersectional identities for the win!

I am also happy that my family is my family. I enjoy seeing our DNA express itself in similar-yet-different ways. It fills me with pride to see our traits and talents passed from one generation to another. As the Soca Queen Alison Hinds sings in her classic calypso "Born Wit' It":

> My great great grandmother pass it down
> My great grandmother pass it down
> My mother get it from my granny
> And Mummy give it to me
> 'Cause we was born wit' it[7]

Once, when I was speaking on a panel, the moderator asked me how I identify. I immediately answered: "I am Blackity Black Black Black," and threw up my fist for good measure. We all laughed at my response, and I was kind of joking but mostly not. I am not a person of color. I am Black. Periodt. And yes, there's a difference.

A few years later I was able to back up my reply with science: I had my DNA tested so I could get a glimpse into my ancestry beyond the Caribbean connection. The results were pretty much what I expected. I'm 90 percent of African origin, mostly from Ghana, Ivory Coast, Benin, Togo, and Nigeria. It brought the biggest smile to my face to see evidence of a connection to the Motherland I had always known existed. Of course, for those of us who study actual history, it will come as no surprise that the remaining 10 percent is of European descent. Because slavery. (I mean, where do you think the surname Hurley came from? It is courtesy of the colonizers.)

[†] For the love of God, can y'all please stop calling us "Caribbeans"? That's not a thing.

Know Your Self: Remember

Knowing and embracing my ancestry fills me with a feeling of pride, a sense of connection and community. It fortifies my sense of identity. I feel like I belong.

Lean Into Your Strength

Life has tried to keep me down—or even take me out—more than once. I'm sure it's the same for most of us. It's not a question of *whether* the storms are coming. It's a matter of *when*. I've dealt with molestation (not by family), sexual assault, domestic violence, health issues, car accidents, chronic pain, extreme burnout, suicidality, mental illness, misogynoir, and multiple forms of abuse: Physical, emotional, financial, racial, systemic.

But this, alas, is the nature of life. It's not that struggle will never happen; it's a matter of how you respond. I'm not saying that I never falter—I definitely do. Big time. Sometimes it truly feels like life is trying to bus' me down to the white meat. But I eventually regain my footing, raise my head high, and keep moving forward.

To recover my strength even in my weakest moments I remember the stock of which I am made, I remember whose child I am, I remember those on whose shoulders I stand, I remember that I am part of a community—and my community loves me. I remember that if I have overcome before, I can do so again.

I am more than my traumas. I am more than my trials. I am more than my tragedies. We all are. As Pastor Donnie McClurkin says, "We fall down, but we get up." Remembering Who You Are makes it easier to get back up.

Shine Your Light

The world will do its best to make you forget who you are. It will try to humble you. The system will try to stifle your strength and snuff out your light. Some people are only happy when you shrink into a diluted facsimile of your true self, imagining that they can only be "more" if you are "less."

But I truly believe that part of the remit that each of us has in this life is to thrive regardless. Shine. Sparkle. Take up space. This is where the magic happens. When we show up in our fullness, we help make the world a better place.

24

Know Yourself

When you remember Who You Are, you see yourself in the best possible light. You want better for yourself. More importantly, you *choose* better for yourself. And that can only be a good thing.

Something I learned from Luvvie Ajayi Jones, four-time *New York Times* bestselling author, and my coach at The Book Academy, is the concept of "No words wasted." So, in the spirit of that advice, enjoy this excerpt from a post I once wrote:

> One last thing, sis: No matter how the system tries to convince you otherwise, you are descended of a proud and noble legacy. No matter how people try to diminish you and dull your shine, you are a star in your own right.
>
> Just by dint of you existing.
> You are regal.
> You are magic.
> You are worthy.
> You are enough.
> You are powerful.
> You are luminescent.
> You. Are. Everything.
> So remember that, sis.
> Remember Who You Are.
> Adjust your crown and move accordingly.

Elevation: Vibrate Higher

Exhalation: Breathe Easy

Tree Breath

Unlike most breathing exercises, tree breathing is done standing up.

Stand tall, feet shoulder width apart and facing straight forward. Your arms are relaxed at your sides, your eyes are gently closed. Imagine that you are a beautiful, deeply rooted, magnificent tree. Your feet are like your roots. Imagine your roots going deep into the earth,

(continued)

(continued)

keeping you safely anchored. Your body represents the trunk of the tree. Imagine your trunk feeling strong, centered, and secure. Your arms and head are the branches and crown of the tree. Imagine them swaying gently in the breeze and reaching toward the sunlight.

Now let's start our tree breathing:

Inhale through your nose for 1, 2, 3, 4, simultaneously raising your arms over your head.

Tilt your head back slightly, and hold your breath for 1, 2, 3, 4.

Exhale through your mouth for 1, 2, 3, 4 while returning your head to a neutral position and bringing your arms back down to your sides.

Repeat this a few more times:

Inhale through your nose for 1, 2, 3, 4 while raising your arms over your head.

Gently tilt your head back, and hold your breath for 1, 2, 3, 4.

Exhale through your mouth for 1, 2, 3, 4, as you bring your head back to neutral, and your arms down to your sides.

Inhale, arms up: 1, 2, 3, 4

Hold, head back: 1, 2, 3, 4

And exhale: 1, 2, 3, 4

Head returns to neutral, and arms return to your sides.

With every inhale, you feel happier, healthier, and more energized.

With every exhale, you feel more rooted and resolute, yet also more relaxed.

Feel the energy move from the crown of your head down to your feet, your roots, connecting you to the earth.

Inhale for 1, 2, 3, 4

Hold for 1, 2, 3, 4

Exhale for 1, 2, 3, 4

(continued)

(*continued*)

Inhale for 1, 2, 3, 4

Hold for 1, 2, 3, 4

Exhale for 1, 2, 3, 4

Inhale for 1, 2, 3, 4

Hold for 1, 2, 3, 4

Exhale for 1, 2, 3, 4

Last time: Inhale, raising your arms for 1, 2, 3, 4

Tilt your head back and hold your breath for 1, 2, 3, 4

Exhale for 1, 2, 3, 4

Bring your head back to neutral and relax your arms at your sides. When you're ready, slowly open your eyes and return your breathing to its usual pace.

Affirmations: Speak Life

- I am innately worthy.
- I am choosing to remember Who I Am.
- I am my ancestors' wildest dreams come true.
- I am giving myself permission to shine bright.
- The entire Universe supports me in being my truest self.

Introspection: Journal & Heal

- Answer the question: "Who Am I?"[‡]
- Explore the following: What is my culture or heritage?
- What does the phrase "Adjust your crown" mean to you?
- Complete this sentence: "When I remember Who I Am, I …"
- What does the word "roots" mean to you, in terms of family?

[‡] De gyal dem suga. (Just kidding, y'all. You know I love a little kiki.)

(*continued*)

(continued)

Curation: Do the Work

If you have not already done so, and you're interested in learning more about your ancestry, get your DNA tested. Once you have received the results of your DNA test, write down your thoughts and feelings.

Appreciation: Express Gratitude

What are you grateful for? Count your blessings:

- I am grateful ...
- I am grateful ...
- I am grateful ...

Celebration: Razzle Dazzle

Flex on 'em, sis! What are you proud of? Celebrate yourself:

- I am proud of myself for ...
- I am proud of myself for ...
- I am proud of myself for ...

Meditation: Think Blissfully

Sit or lie down and get comfortable. Close your eyes and focus on your breath.

Breathe through your nose at your normal pace, and then when you are ready, slow your breathing down.

Inhale through your nose for a count of five and exhale through your nose for a count of five:

Inhale: 1, 2, 3, 4, 5; exhale: 5, 4, 3, 2, 1

Inhale: 1, 2, 3, 4, 5; exhale: 5, 4, 3, 2, 1

And again, inhale: 1, 2, 3, 4, 5; exhale: 5, 4, 3, 2, 1

(continued)

(continued)

Keep breathing at this cadence. With every exhale, you feel more and more relaxed.

Now place your hands on your chest, focus on your heart chakra, and mentally tell yourself:

I remember Who I Am.

I remember Who I Am.

I remember Who I Am.

Keep inhaling and exhaling slowly for a count of five each time.

Release that affirmation and prepare to welcome a new one into your mind. Repeat silently to yourself:

I am happy with Who I Am.

I am happy with Who I Am.

I am happy with Who I Am.

When you're ready, release the mantra and get ready once more to welcome a new one. Smile gently, and mentally tell yourself:

I know and love the real me.

I know and love the real me.

I know and love the real me.

Keep inhaling and exhaling for a count of five and gradually return your breathing to normal. Become more aware of the space you're in: Tune in to the sounds, scents, and sensations. When you're ready, slowly open your eyes.

Asé.

2 | Know Your Values: Align

Invocation

Most High,

Please sow seeds of strength within me:
Strong boundaries, strong beliefs, strong values

Please sow seeds of goodness within me:
Good thoughts, good deeds, good character

I pray for the blessing of honesty:
May I mean what I say and say what I mean

I pray for the blessing of dignity:
May I carry myself with honor and pride

I pray for constant integrity:
May my thoughts, words, and actions always align

I pray for unshakeable consistency:
May I always be true to myself

May my mind and my life be in alignment with The Light
May my actions reflect my values
And may my values be of the highest order
May my values serve as a constant north star
Guiding and easing my way through life

Forever and ever

Amen

~ ~ ~

I Shall Not Be Moved

It was a stare down.

My boss towered over me, glaring, trying to physically intimidate me as I sat in my office chair.

But I was not the one.

Intimidated? Nah.

Not my mother's child.

Not me, born in Jamaica.

Not me, bred in Barbados.

Not me, who my father had nicknamed "Dreaddos" because from a tiny, tiny age I took no nonsense.

They stared. I stared back. Deadpan.

It was a corporate "This town ain't big enough for the both of us" moment. I thought to myself, "If this is how you want to play this, I can do this all day. All. Day. Trust."

The issue was that someone on the team had been discovered plagiarizing. We were all shocked, though not surprised, when we found out. When we thought about it, it kind of made sense as the person in question had joined the company under dubious circumstances, misrepresented their credentials, and made mistakes that someone at their purported level of expertise should not be making.

They were not merely taking other people's words and doing a lazy or uncredited rephrase—which would be bad enough—but actually engaging in wholesale, outright theft. Just lifting entire paragraphs that someone else had written and attempting to pass them off as their own. And, though there were several other writers on the team, my boss was trying to force me, and only me,

Know Your Values: Align 31

to co-write with that person. To "train" them how to write original copy. At my big age I was supposed to teach a fully grown human to not steal? Seriously?

No sir, no ma'am. Won't be happening.

That's not how I said it, but that was the spirit of my response.

My boss was not pleased. They resorted to threats.

"I won't promote you."

"You'll become obsolete."

"You won't have a future with this company."

I was like "Okay."

Mentally, I shrugged.

I would not be moved.

For me, this was a "let the chips fall where they may" moment. Because what we were not about to do was get Mrs. Hurley's second child involved in this griminess.

I already knew how this would play out if I let it. The other person would continue to plagiarize, and if we collaborated, the blame would ultimately be ascribed to me. This is how they set up Black people in corporate America.

Instead, I proposed a solution that meant that I would never have to go anywhere near the plagiarizer's projects. There was more than enough volume for there to never be any overlap. They would be free to steal copy to their heart's content, and I would be free to ... not.

They stared. I stared back. Deadpan.

Stalemate.

Eventually they gave up and stormed off in a huff.

Checkmate.

I swung around in my chair and got back to writing non-plagiarized copy. I knew my days at that job were numbered, but so be it. I also knew that there would be other jobs.

There are some principles on which one cannot compromise. As a writer, there are few things that disturb my spirit as much as plagiarized copy. As a creative, deliberately plagiarized art gives me agita too. I refuse to associate myself with content of dubious origin.

My boss was more upset that I, the lone Black person on the team, was being "uppity" and not following orders rather than that a mediocre, minimally melanated person was putting the department and company in legal and reputational jeopardy. Because priorities.

32   Know Yourself

Gotta keep the negroes in line after all. If nothing else, white supremacy sticks to its script.

I never touched the plagiarizer's projects again.

How they chose to produce their copy was between them and whatever god they served. Not my circus; not my monkeys.

Everybody won't agree with my handling of the situation, and that's okay. I'm good. My conscience is clear. I went home and slept in peace. Sometimes in life you have to agree with yourself and keep it pushin'. Be a committee of one. Be unanimous with *you*. Know who you are and act accordingly. Stand firm in your values.

Years later, I hired one of my LinkedIn connections to contribute to an editorial project I was leading. They did not have a lot of writing experience, but I decided to give them a shot. Having so frequently been gatekept out of opportunities, I did not want to be a gatekeeper.

As soon as I opened their submission, I knew something was off. The "voice" didn't read like theirs. The vocabulary was more sophisticated than anything I had seen from them before. There was a lot of mismatched formatting. My spidey senses started tingling. One simple search later, I found the article they had plagiarized. It was from a publication of record. A major one. I was gobsmacked. Paragraphs on paragraphs on paragraphs. They had made some small changes—"however" to "but" and "Black people" to "people of color"—and truly thought I would be fooled.

Nope.

Situations like this are usually cases of "where there's smoke there's fire," so since I had time that day I went through several of the person's long-form posts. All of them were plagiarized. Every last one. Oof. I emailed them back to let them know that there were numerous "anomalies" in their content, and that it was therefore not publishable—at least not by me.

I allow grace for humanness: Nobody is perfect. Sometimes one is in a rush, or one forgets to do a rewrite. There are times when one truly cannot find the source of a piece of content. At times, there might even be operator error or a system glitch that removes citation information. But it takes multiple decisions and sketchy intent to *repeatedly* copy-paste, change "and" to "plus," then not cite or tag the original writer. Folks who have a lot of energy when copy-pasting other people's content, but who can't keep that

Know Your Values: Align   33

same energy when it comes to citing their sources make my blood boil. I also give major side-eye to people who publish multi-paragraph posts—with nary a quotation mark to be seen—and then bury a citation at the end in .0000001 font. Whole time, you thought the words were theirs. Not cool. Imagine reading an entire book and then at the very end the "author" goes, "Thanks to [robbed writer's name] for providing these words." See how that lands? Exactly. It's weird.

Quotation marks are free.

That said, just throwing on quotation marks is not where it ends. You should also cite your sources appropriately.

Being a writer is a fundamental part of who I am; of who I have always known myself to be. As such, "Cite your sources" is one of my core values when it comes to writing.

"Do your own work" is another. That's a value in which I stand firm. Now before y'all come for me, this does not apply to ghostwritten copy—as long as the ghostwritten copy is not, itself, plagiarized. (Yes, I have seen that happening wholesale out on these dusty social media streets. Clients are paying some of these "ghostwriters" big money for stolen content. Lawd have mercy.)

I have nothing against ghostwriting. As a former writer-for-hire, I've ghostwritten more than my fair share of content for clients. I also know of several authors whose books have been ghostwritten. There is absolutely nothing wrong with that because there is clarity from the outset. There are contracts involved. Sometimes people have great ideas but lack the time or temperament to express them in written form. That's what ghostwriters are for. However, as a career writer, it would be dubious at best for me to have someone write my book on my behalf.

While we're here, indulge me in a mini-rant. I know we're in the age of AI—that horse is out of the barn never again to return. It's galloping happily on the range, eating hay to its heart's content. But bear in mind that AI is trained using other people's intellectual property. Do with that information what you will.

To paraphrase a post I once wrote: In terms of AI, there is nothing wrong with using it, but your readers can often tell when you do. If you don't make any effort to spice it up with your own flavor, all we're thinking is, "Wow, AI did an okay job."

Please add seasoning. A condiment or two. And please go beyond the basics. Salt and pepper alone will not suffice; neither will mustard and ketchup. Try Old Bay. Lawry's. Adobo. Pesto. Drop in a dollop of Bajan pepper sauce. Sprinkle on some of Auntie Tab's Sunshine mix. Do *something* with it. Unseasoned AI copy is flavorless—and obvious. There are ways to make it your own.

My achy hands can attest that I typed these 90,000 words myself. Like with the ghostwriting example, it would be … weird … if as someone who's been a professional writer for decades, my book was written by ChatGPT.

Not everyone will agree with me, and that's okay. These are some of *my* core content creation values, and I stand by them. Knowing your core values in life is a big part of knowing yourself and living your life in alignment.

I've been on this earth longer than I care to admit, lol. But honestly, it's a blessing. Every day above ground has the potential to be an awesome day. One of the great parts about having lived, having gone through the crucible, having been tried and tested, having been blessed again and again is that you get very clear.

Clear about who you are. Clear about what you cherish. Clear about who you love. Clear about what you stand for and why. Clear about what you will and will not tolerate. You also get better at holding true to your principles; at cleaving to your values. That clarity makes life easier, and that ease gives you more space to exhale.

When you can stand firm in your values, peer pressure has little effect; often none at all. Your cache of effs to give grows smaller daily. Eventually, it dwindles to zero. You care less and less whether people like you … because YOU like you.

We've all done silly things in our youth. In our adulthood too, if we're honest. We've all made questionable decisions. I've done my fair share of foolishness, so I'm definitely not out here trying to pass myself off as any kind of arbiter of perfection. (Thank goodness there was no social media back in the day to capture every cringey moment I wish had never happened.) But as we learned from ancestor Maya Angelou: When you know better, you do better. The longer I live, the better I do.

These are the Values that Help Me Do Better.

Integrity

Based on the story I shared at the beginning of this chapter, I'm sure this comes as no surprise. Integrity is supreme. Trustworthiness is such a

Know Your Values: Align 35

wonderful quality. The ability to be in private who you claim to be in public. The ability to be honest. To have your word be your bond. To keep your commitments. To honor boundaries and confidentiality. Will we always get it right? No. We're human. But one should at least aim for this as a north star. And if we slip up, take accountability, and then do better: Make actual behavioral changes. I love that with my close circle there is mutual trust, because we operate based on this fundamental principle. Here's to integrity.

Generosity

"Everybody can eat" is one of the teachings with which I was raised. In other words, there is room for us all to thrive. There's no need to act like crabs in a barrel. No need for selfishness. Folks are really out there trying to hoard resources, gatekeep opportunities, and win at other people's expense. It's as if they believe that if someone else gets something—a job, a contract, an interview—then there is nothing left for them. Rather than embracing collaboration and abundance, they have a mindset of competition and lack. It doesn't have to be that way.

Everybody needs support, so I give. Time. Energy. Money. Attention. Resources. Expertise. I share. I do unto others as has been done unto me. God has been good. People have been good. So I give back and pay forward. I truly believe that there is enough for us all. What is meant for me will never ever pass me, and what is meant for you is yours. People tend to think that sharing divides, but I believe that sharing multiplies. Generosity is a loving, expansive energy. Growing up in Barbados we shared, especially among family, friends, and neighbors. If you have coconuts and I have mangoes, then we *both* have coconuts and mangoes. Simple so. Let's rebuke the scarcity mindset. Here's to generosity.

Kindness

I am grateful to have received lots of kindness in my life. People who have helped, supported, blessed, and protected me—just because. I still remember my "big brother" Stephen Smith giving me my first job to help me get on my feet when I returned to Barbados from France. He's also the person who offered to take me to the police when someone I was dating assaulted me. I also remember a former co-worker who let me stay at her house for a few days when I was on the run from an abusive ex. Neither of them ever asked me for a solitary thing in exchange. I'm forever grateful. Because of experiences like these and because it's who I inherently am, I do my best to lead with kindness, to see people's humanity, to extend grace, show empathy, and offer a helping hand if it is wanted, needed, or requested.

Being on the receiving end of agendaless, non-transactional kindness is a top-tier life experience that everybody deserves to have. The sort of kindness that gives with an open hand; that doesn't say "Now that I've done this for you, I require your first-born child, your 401K, and the deed to your home in return." Life can be hard. Kindness makes it easier. Here's to kindness.

Presence

I show up. Whether IRL or virtually; whether with a phone call or a text message, I show love to the people in my life by being present. There is so much joy, so much resonance in being a part of people's big moments. Nothing beats being in the midst of a landmark occasion in your life—one of those rite of passage moments—and seeing your loved ones out in the crowd supporting you.

There's also so much fulfillment in being there to share the daily mundanities of life. There is magic in the minutiae. Sometimes, folks just need someone to be there with them when they have to go to the doctor or when they have a day full of errands to take care of. There are few things as sweet as a "chores date" or supermarket run with a good friend. Let's commit to showing up for our people. Consistently. Here's to presence.

Consistency

I'm a "what you see is what you get" kind of person as well as a "you can depend on me" kind of person. I love being someone that my family and friends can rely on. They know they can because they have always been able to: I show up for them consistently. They know that if I say I'm going to do something, in 99 percent of cases I will. And the one percent is because I truly cannot.

My mom knows I am going to call her twice a day every day. My sister knows that I will amplify any initiative she's a part of. My friends know that if they need to talk, I'm there. My niece knows that I'm there for her as a safe adult and also as a friend. She can call me anytime. She can stay in my home anytime as well. She has a key. She is always welcome to just show up. As her auntie, I offer love, shelter, life advice—and

I also try to get her to eat a few more vegetables. As her friend and occasional partner in crime, I'm also up for our inside jokes and long conversations about all the things, sometimes while indulging in a shopping spree in New York.

My people all know I'm in their corner and never have to doubt it. They know what to expect from me because there's no Jekyll and Hyde energy. They can relax into our relationship rather than walking on eggshells, and I can do the same with them. Reliability is a beautiful thing. My close relationships work because positive, consistent behavior goes both ways: I am able to depend on them too, and I love it.

Since I value consistency, I have no time for flakers and sometime-ish people who flip on you like a light switch. I have no patience for people who repeatedly pull the rug out from under you. We all need folks in our circle who we can truly depend on. Here's to consistency.

Directness

This might be a neurodivergent thing, but I say what I mean and mean what I say. Also, my face has no filter, so even if I were to try to dissemble, it wouldn't work. I don't believe in brutal honesty—honesty doesn't have to be violent—but gentle honesty is a vibe. It is always my goal to be honest, but with grace.

If you have spinach in your teeth I'm going to discreetly tell you, and I appreciate people who do the same for me. This is about spinach, but it's also not about spinach.

I'm from a generation that used to wear half slips. Thankfully, they're mostly a thing of the past, but I always appreciated it when someone would let me know that my slip was showing. To me, it shows generosity of spirit. It demonstrates solidarity. It says to me that they care about me showing up at my best; that they do not want me to be embarrassed. It's direct—but kind.

Same for if I was about to submit an important document with a huge typo: I would not feel attacked by someone pointing out the mistake. I would feel relieved and grateful that they had spared me some embarrassment. When I was in the editing phase of this manuscript, I asked my early readers to just be honest with me. Thankfully, they were, and the book is the better for their efforts—and their directness.

38 Know Yourself

If I have made a mistake or am about to, I truly want to know. Don't snack on your popcorn, wait until I mess up, and then have something to say after the fact. When I was writing this book, a couple of my friends said to me—with love—"Lis, you're losing focus. That distraction is not serving you right now." They gently snatched my edges and got me back on track. I was like "You know what? You're right. Thank you."

Let me know the truth, so I can handle it and adjust. I like it when people are honest with me; when they are politely direct; when I don't have to read tea leaves and consult an oracle to try to figure out what they mean. Be open. Just say the thing—kindly. Here's to directness.

Privacy

I respect people's privacy, and really appreciate it when people respect mine. In the age of social media, people truly seem to be confused about this, but you can be transparent *and* maintain privacy at the same time. It's called boundaries. As an introvert and as someone who came up in a pre-internet world, I value privacy—my own and other people's—very highly. I am skilled in having long, but nonrevelatory conversations. People don't need to know all your business.

These days folks seem to imagine that they are entitled to insight into every detail of people's lives. That is not the case. When I'm in Barbados and I go out with certain friends of mine, the moments remain among us even if we even take photos. Everything does not need to be posted.

If you're a "poster" (raises hand), get in the habit of asking people if it's okay to publish photos in which they appear. We probably all need to work on this. I've definitely gotten better at this over time. Just because *you* like a group photo doesn't mean everybody in it will. Just because a picture is in your phone doesn't mean you own it. Just because you have access to someone else's photos doesn't mean you get to decide what to do with them. Ask. And a good rule of thumb is when in doubt, don't.

I am the picture taker in my family, but I get permission before publicly sharing private moments. My life partner is a "please don't take or post any photos of me" kind of person, so even though I never met a camera I didn't like, I honor his wishes. He prefers to be private, so I treat that preference with respect. If my good gorgeous sis Cassandra and I are at the same

Know Your Values: Align 39

gathering, we take 5,000 selfies together since like me, she also loves a camera. But we still check with each other before posting anything publicly.

On the topic of sharing things publicly: We all share screenshots in the group chat—but the group chat needs to remain sacrosanct. It's supposed to be a safe space. No one should have to worry that screenshots, photos, and conversations shared in private will become public fodder. Exposing private communications? Just ... NO. That is such dusty behavior. This does not apply to mean or threatening DMs from strangers on the internet. Those sometimes need to see the light of day. Exposing trolls and bullies can be a good thing. But everything else? Mum's the word.

And finally, let's talk about safeguarding people's secrets. Not that kind of secret: Your sketchy uncle who can't keep his hands to himself should absolutely be called out. I'm talking about non-sketchy scenarios. I'm talking about respecting confidentiality. As we say back home: Don't talk out other people's business. Assume that every conversation starts with "Please don't share this," and act accordingly. Behave like you signed an NDA.

Also, frankly: We don't want to know all of your business either. Truly. We're not interested. Let there be a veil. Here's to privacy.

Peace

Why is peace one of my values? Because I have frequently experienced its opposite. From childhood chaos to adult agita, I have too often swum in murky, muddled waters that have wreaked havoc with my equilibrium. So I go out of my way to seek peace. Give me calm. Give me serenity. Boring is beautiful to me. (I'm sure my therapist is writing down "TRAUMA RESPONSE" in all caps as they read this, but so be it.) I have brunch energy, not club energy. Nothing is wrong with the club; it's just that I've had my club days, and now my spirit and knees are tired. I'm in my rich, rested, relaxed Auntie era, and I love it here.

I come in peace and I therefore seek out peaceful people. I try to be a person that folks feel safe around, and I love myself enough to remove unsafe people from my orbit—or myself from theirs. If folks bring unrest, gossip, discord, drama, and disrespect to my door, I politely escort them back out, literally or figuratively. Yes, I have absolutely made someone leave my home because they were being loud and disruptive. A few minutes (and some sage) later, order was restored.

40　　　　　　　　　　Know Yourself

If folks are committed to seeing the worst in me, they gotta go too. I will not spend time and energy trying to convince people of my value, or feeling like I need to beg for approval. I walk away. I refuse to engage. I revoke access. I choose peace.

Scrapping with strangers on the internet is also a no. There's no need. Debate? Absolutely. Argument? Absolutely not. I decline. People will write a whole nonsensical screed in the comments section, call you everything except your given name, and then act surprised when you disengage. If I respond at all—I usually don't—it's just to say "okay" and be done. They get blocked, and I stay blessed.

Over the years, many of my friends have told me that my home feels like a spa. It's serene. It's quiet. It smells good. Nag champa vibes. Palo santo. Sandalwood and lavender essential oils, with a hint of peppermint for clarity. So relaxing. Life can be chaotic. Cultivate calm. Here's to peace.

Joy

Yes, joy is a value because who doesn't need more happiness? I do what I can to make the people in my circle feel joyful; to lighten their load and bring a smile to their face. I take the same approach with my wider community. I post #FootwerkFriday and #StandupSaturday videos on LinkedIn because we all need an end-of-week energy cleanse to make us feel better. Inside The Great Exhale there is a space called The Healing Power of Laughter because laughter truly is one of the world's best medicines. We share jokes, memes, and spend time kiki-ing together. One of my awesome community members once left this testimonial that warmed my heart: "The Great Exhale is a vibe, a balm, and an amazing collective ... The healing, laughter, and collective compassion is black joy in a bottle." It makes me happy to know that my sistas are happy. Happiness is high-vibrational. Elevate the energy. Here's to joy.

Community

This might come as a surprise from a known introvert, but I truly believe in community; in the value of, and necessity for, the village. We cannot do this thing called life alone, and I don't believe we're meant to. Everybody needs

Know Your Values: Align 41

a village to celebrate or mourn with; people with whom we mark big moments and rites of passage; kinfolk and skinfolk to help us muddle through the mundane days and make sense of life. We need each other to help when times are hard and to share the easy times with as well.

My awesome neighbors (I call them "the boys," but they are fully grown men) check in on me all the time. They even check on my fur baby King. If they don't hear from us for too long, rest assured a text is coming my way: "Hey Lisa, are you and Kingie ok?" They also pet sit for me when they can. My mom and I bring them presents from Barbados, and when she's visiting me, they bake her the most delicious cookies.

Of course, I check in on them too: See if they're okay after a storm, or if they need help with anything. If they need a stick of butter or a cup of sugar, they just text me and I take it down. I lend them my tools and extra-tall ladder. We rescue each other's Amazon packages from the elements—and the porch pirates. If I get any super-heavy deliveries, they take them upstairs for me. They're the absolute best. We're our own mini-community. That's how it's done.

Similarly with The Great Exhale. We all check in on each other and provide a container of safety. We lovingly support each other and bless each other with sisterhood that feels like a sanctuary.

I appreciate when my community shows up for me, and I do my best to show up for the communities of which I am a part. I am honored and grateful that there are people who count me as a member of their real world or virtual village. Here's to community.

As a Reiki Master there are additional values I hold dear: The five precepts of traditional Usui Reiki. I'll come right out and say that I'm still working on them all, some more so than others. That's the goal. To move forward, sometimes falter, try again. Progress, not perfection. The work is continuous. The precepts are simple, but not necessarily easy:

Reiki Precepts

Just for Today, Do Not Worry

This one is for all the overthinkers, myself included. Worrying achieves nothing. The tricky thing is that when you're busy worrying, it *feels* like you're doing something—but you're really not. Worry has treadmill vibes:

Motion but no progress. All that energy could be better used either addressing what you're concerned about, or shoring up your faith. Let go and let God.

Just for Today, Do Not Anger

This is one of the more challenging precepts to adhere to because, honestly, there can be a lot in life to feel angry about. Sometimes people see your last nerve out there struggling and choose to jump on it, repeatedly, with both feet. Naturally, you're allowed to feel your feelings—that is healthy—but if we can get into the habit of at least taking a breath before *reacting* in anger, it can be very helpful indeed. Many a relationship (or job) has been saved by people choosing to practice the pause in fraught situations.

With this precept, sometimes I hit, sometimes I miss. All I can say is my Scorpio energy is fierce, and God ain't done with me yet. I'm a work in progress.

P.S. I don't think anger is necessarily a "bad" emotion. Anger can be your friend, but that's another topic for another book.

Honor Your Parents, Teachers, and Elders

None of us got here alone. This precept is about acknowledging the people in our lives who have laid the groundwork for us; those without whom we would not be here today. Those who have nurtured and guided us. There's no need to bow and scrape or kiss the proverbial ring; no need to put people on a pedestal. Just show appreciation. Lead with respect.

Something that truly warms my heart is to see my niece and my mom interacting. There is so much mutual love and respect. There's an energy of adoration. They take care of each other. They enjoy each other's company. Taryn treats her grandmother with honor and solicitousness, and I love to see it.

Speaking of respect, I know I'm going to get some "respectability politics" comments about this one, but I was brought up to greet certain people with their honorific, for example: Mrs. Alleyne, Colonel Beckles, Mr. Clarke, Reverend Forde, Dr. Holder. Actual blood relatives or adults who were close to the family were addressed as Auntie or Uncle. In

Barbados, I never heard the adults in my circle tell a child, "I ain't one of your little friends," because it wasn't necessary. That was made clear by the forms of address. Similarly, when I took ninjutsu classes with my good friend Greg, a Hall of Fame martial artist and founder of the Way of the Winds Martial Arts System, once we were in the dojo I addressed him as Shihan. It's a mark of respect.

Of course, the caveat to this is that you are not obligated to respect people who treat you disrespectfully or bring harm to your doorstep, no matter who they are. Yes, that includes family. If they harm you, you owe them nothing.

Earn Your Living Honestly

In its most reductive form, this can mean "don't steal the paperclips," but it also has a deeper definition. Are you earning your living honestly by staying in that job you hate? Are you earning your living honestly by hiding your talents? Are you earning your living honestly by not going after that promotion? Are you earning your living honestly by taking credit for someone else's work? Are you earning your living honestly by overworking to the point of burnout? There's more to ponder here.

Obviously, there is nuance. If you are in survival mode and you need to make money to pay your bills, then the most honest thing you can do is get a job. But even in cases like these there are probably gigs that you know are just not for you. I once walked off a job after one day because my spirit said "Nah." It was a bad fit. Never regretted it. I went home and sent out some more applications for roles that were better for me. That was the most honest thing I could do in that circumstance.

Show Gratitude to Every Living Thing

Nothing increases abundance like expressing gratitude to and for the people who make your days feel lighter; like being grateful for all you've been blessed with. Having a regular gratitude practice will change your life for the better and attract more experiences to be grateful for.

P.S. When you're expressing gratitude for the good people in your life, remember to include yourself.

How to Identify Your Values

Take a look at this values list and see what resonates with you. Choose your top 10.

Know Your Values

Abundance	Expressiveness	Presence
Accomplishment	Fairness	Privacy
Accountability	Faith	Productivity
Assertiveness	Family	Professionalism
Attentiveness	Foresight	Prosperity
Awareness	Freedom	Reflectiveness
Balance	Friendship	Relaxation
Beauty	Fun	Respect
Belonging	Generosity	Responsibility
Boldness	Genius	Rest
Bravery	Giving	Reverence
Brilliance	Goodness	Sacredness
Calm	Grace	Safety
Candor	Growth	Self Love
Centeredness	Harmony	Sensitivity
Clarity	Health	Serenity
Cleanliness	Humanitarianism	Sharing
Comfort	Humor	Significance
Commitment	Honesty	Silence
Common Sense	Honor	Simplicity
Community	Hopefulness	Sincerity
Compassion	Imaginativeness	Sisterhood
Competence	Ingenuity	Stillness
Confidence	Innovation	Softness
Consciousness	Insightfulness	Solitude
Consistency	Inspiration	Spirituality
Contentment	Integrity	Spontaneity
Contribution	Interdependence	Structure
Control	Intuitiveness	Success
Courage	Joy	Support
Courtesy	Justice	Sustainability
Creativity	Kindness	Thankfulness
Credibility	Liberty	Thoughtfulness
Curiosity	Learning	Tolerance
Decisiveness	Logic	Tradition
Dedication	Love	Tranquility
Dependability	Loyalty	Transcendence
Determination	Mastery	Transparency
Devotion	Maturity	Trustworthiness
Dignity	Meaning	Truth
Discipline	Mellowness	Underdrive
Drive	Moderation	Understanding
Ease	Motivation	Uniqueness
Efficiency	Openness	Unity
Encouragement	Optimism	Vision
Empathy	Order	Vitality
Enjoyment	Originality	Warmth
Enthusiasm	Peace	Wealth
Ethics	Persistence	Winning
Excellence	Playfulness	Wisdom

Elevation: Vibrate Higher

Exhalation: Breathe Easy

Spinal Breath

Sit comfortably, with your back straight but not stiff.

Breathe deeply and slowly through your nose, with your belly and chest rising as you inhale; your chest then belly falling as you exhale.

Inhale, belly and chest rise.

Exhale, chest and belly fall.

Inhale, belly and chest rise.

Exhale, chest and belly fall.

Inhale, belly and chest rise.

Exhale, chest and belly fall.

Repeat this a few times, and when you are comfortable, gently close your eyes.

Bring your attention to the base of your spine.

Inhale deeply, imagining your breath moving up your spine all the way to the base of your skull.

Exhale slowly, visualizing your breath moving down your spine all the way to your tailbone.

Repeat this three more times:

Inhale, breath moves up your spine.

Exhale, breath moves down your spine.

Inhale, breath moves up your spine.

Exhale, breath moves down your spine.

Inhale, breath moves up your spine.

Exhale, breath moves down your spine.

(continued)

Know Yourself

(continued)

Continue breathing like this for as long as you are comfortable, remembering not to rush or strain.

When you feel ready, return your breathing to its normal cadence, and slowly open your eyes.

Affirmations: Speak Life

- I am choosing to live in integrity.
- I am giving myself permission to do better.
- Today and every day, I am holding myself in the highest light.
- I am grateful to be living a peaceful, principled, productive life.
- I am blessed with good values, good thoughts, good deeds, and good character.

Introspection: Journal & Heal

- What matters most to you?
- Who and what inspires you? Why?
- What would you fight for, and why?
- What are your spiritual beliefs, if any? What philosophies resonate with you?
- What principles could you stand firm on even if you were offered a lot of money to veer from them?

Curation: Do the Work

Conduct a values assessment. From your top 10 values, choose your top 3. These are the ones that you think you can adhere to for years.

Answer these questions:

- How can my actions align with these values?
- How can I build habits that support these values?
- How do these values add ease to my life and career?

(continued)

(continued)

Appreciation: Express Gratitude

What are you grateful for? Count your blessings:

- I am grateful ...
- I am grateful ...
- I am grateful ...

Celebration: Razzle Dazzle

Flex on 'em, sis! What are you proud of? Celebrate yourself:

- I am proud of myself for ...
- I am proud of myself for ...
- I am proud of myself for ...

Meditation: Think Blissfully

Sit or lie down comfortably. Your back should be straight and neutral. To begin, breathe gently and easily, without straining or changing the cadence of your breath. Inhale and exhale a few times, gradually feeling more relaxed.

Now turn your attention inward and gently close your eyes.

Slow down your breathing a little, making your exhales slightly longer than your inhales. Inhale for a count of three and exhale for a count of five.

Inhale: 1, 2, 3; exhale: 1, 2, 3, 4, 5

Inhale: 1, 2, 3; exhale: 1, 2, 3, 4, 5

Inhale: 1, 2, 3; exhale: 1, 2, 3, 4, 5

Keep breathing at this cadence and as you feel more and more relaxed, bring to mind a value, principle, or quality that you hold dear. Focus on it and as you breathe, imagine that this quality is permeating your entire body.

(continued)

Know Yourself

(continued)

If you can't bring to mind what you would like to focus on, let's choose the principle of love. Imagine love indwelling and surrounding your entire being.

As you inhale, the quality of love infuses every cell in your body.

As you exhale, the quality of love enters the world as you uniquely express it.

Inhale, blessing yourself with the love you need.

Exhale, sharing love and light with the world.

Inhale, sending love to the parts of your body that most need it.

Exhale, sending love to the parts of your life that most need it.

Inhale, sending love to the parts of your mind that most need it.

Exhale, sending love to the people in your life who most need it.

Continue this for as long as you're comfortable, and when you're ready, let your focus word drift away. Gradually allow your breathing to return to its usual pace.

Bring your attention back into the room and, when you're ready, slowly open your eyes. Before you fully return to reality, give yourself a few moments to relax and enjoy the vibes.

Asé.

3

Know Your Strengths: Focus

Invocation

Most High,
You have made me unique, and for that I am thankful
It is wonderful to be me

Thank You for my natural talents
Thank You for my special genius
Thank You for Your guidance on using my gifts for good

May my mind be fertile
May my hands be productive
May my passion and my purpose align

May I respect my rarity
May I celebrate my selfhood
May I always stand securely in my strengths

May I amplify my abilities
May I create with confidence
May I express my excellence with flair

May I evolve in the direction of my innate ingenuity
Flourishing like a forest toward the sky

May I see and celebrate my strengths
May I see and celebrate my strengths
May I see and celebrate my strengths

Amen

Riding the Struggle Bus

I will never forget failing my CXC maths* mock exam in 5th form.† Like **total fail.** I came second from the bottom in class.

It was an uppercase moment, and I showed up with lowercase energy.

This was a big deal because, as every West Indian high school student knew, maths was one of the exams that would DECIDE YOUR FUTURE. (Yes, the melodramatic all caps are necessary.) These exams—the real ones—would set the tone for whether one would be a respected, contributing member of society, or a shameful failure. Yes, that is how it felt and how it was communicated to students by Caribbean society at large.

The pressure was real.

---

*Informal explanation: In the Caribbean, there is a series of examinations that one must take in order to move up to the more senior classes in high school. They're called the CXCs and they are a BIG DEAL. Especially for core subjects like maths and English. And yes, in Barbados we pluralize maths, or at least we did back then.
Formal explanation from the Caribbean Examinations Council (CXC) and World Education Services (WES): "The CXC® is a regional examining body that provides secondary and post-secondary examinations in 16 English-speaking Caribbean countries and territories. The examination for the Caribbean Secondary Education Certificate (CSEC®) is designed to be taken after 11 years of elementary and secondary education and constitutes the standard secondary school leaving qualification in the CXC® member states and territories. WES considers this certificate equivalent to a high school diploma in the US and a secondary school diploma in Canada. The official language of instruction in the 16 countries is English; the examinations are conducted in English."

†At the time, Barbados used the British school system. In 5th form, students were 15 years old on average.

Know Your Strengths: Focus

But anyway: Nobody who knew me could honestly say they were surprised I had flunked. I had never been good at maths. Never. Not for a nanosecond. All my eggs were nestled fully in the artistic / creative / linguistic basket. However, because of the way the Barbadian education system was set up, I had no choice but to spend hours upon hours of my life trying to be good at something I knew I would never master. Super annoying. Numbers enter my brain in perfect order but immediately get scrambled into an incomprehensible white noise, like an old-school TV with a broken rabbit-ears antenna. Numerical static.

Nowadays I would likely be diagnosed with dyscalculia, but back then there was little information available about learning disabilities of that type. And to be honest, even if there had been, the Black community in general did not acknowledge issues of that nature. Some folks did, but most didn't. For that kind of stuff, my era was rough. And don't come for me, y'all. Y'all know good and well that Black people will say things like an elder has "bad nerves" and "a little sugar" when the truth is they're depressed, diabetic, and in need of medical attention. It's as though we think that if we euphemize a condition, it doesn't really exist. Thankfully, as a community, we have gotten better at this and continue to improve.

Multiple things can be true at once, and in this situation, these are my truths:

Truth 1: I am forever grateful to my mom, my sister, and "the village," including Auntie Sylvia, her older daughter Angela, Auntie Jackie, Mr. Phillips, my various maths teachers and tutors, and all the people who believed in me. That's the beauty of being raised in a majority-Black country. That's the power of growing up in an environment where you are seen as innately worthy, smart, and investable-in. They never once gave up on me even when I gave up on myself. It encourages one to keep trying. It imbues one with a sense of confidence when the people you love and respect reciprocally see value in you and view you through a positive lens.

Truth 2: Every single day I felt like a failure. As the saying goes: "If you judge a fish on its ability to climb a tree, it will live its whole life believing it is stupid." I felt like the proverbial fish trying to climb a tree. I felt stupid. I also felt sad. I wanted to dance, and write, and act, and twirl through life but could not fully devote my energy to the things I was naturally good at. I was allowed to dance, thank goodness, but it was made very clear that there was no way it could be my actual profession, so instead I met most days feeling heavy-hearted and like I had already lost at life.

By some miracle, I got a passing grade in the final exam. To this day I have no idea how I passed. Actually, I take that back. I *do* have an idea: I was driven by complete desperation and fear of shame. I knew I could not bring dishonor to my family name. I guess it worked. Motivation by any means necessary, I guess?

I will always remember the moment when I got my CXC math results, or more accurately, the day after. Y'all … the joy!! The full-bodied relief I felt from knowing that I would never ever again have to open a mathematics textbook. I ran across the Queen's College quadrangle to my maths teacher Mrs. Cummins-Williams and all but jumped into her arms screaming "I passed!! I passed!!" She smiled, hugged me, and said, "Of course you passed! I never had any doubt." (Sidenote: Good teachers are angels. We need to treat them better and pay them more.)

From Struggles to Strengths

In contrast to the struggle energy I experienced with mathematics, dance was my thing. So was writing. I was naturally good at them both.

I was introduced to the performing arts when my family moved from Trinidad to Barbados. My new school, Hindsbury Primary,[‡] helmed by Mrs. Campbell, was ever-present at NIFCA[1], Barbados' National Independence Festival of Creative Arts.[§]

Mrs. Campbell entered the school into every category possible. I still remember us all learning our parts for an excerpt from the A.A. Milne play *The Toad of Toad Hall*, practicing our choral speaking, getting our costumes and uniforms ready, rehearsing our exits and entrances.

[‡] I ask for grace from my Hindsbury schoolmates if I got any of these details wrong. It was such a long time ago.

[§] NIFCA was conceived in the seventies by two noted Barbadian creatives, the husband and wife team of Arden Clarke and Jeanette Layne-Clarke, and it is still going strong today. At the festival's inception entrants competed in dance, drama, speech, music, fine arts, and literary arts. The categories have since been expanded to include film, photography, crafts, culinary arts, and more.

Know Your Strengths: Focus   53

One year, we performed the classic Bajan folk song, Gerdine:

> Sweet-sweet leather coat and cou-cou [**]
> Sweet-sweet leather coat and cou-cou
> Sweet-sweet leather coat and cou-cou
> Gerdine I going marry to you
> Gerdine leh muh see yuh fing-fing
> Gerdine leh muh see yuh fing-fing
> Gerdine leh muh see yuh fing-fing
> Dah fing-fing going wear my ring

So much fun.

While I enjoyed the acting and singing, my favorite thing to do every November during NIFCA season was learn Barbados Landship choreography. [††2]

Like actual Landship crews did, our student group dressed in nautical-themed costumes that represented various ranks in the British navy, got into double file behind our "captain," and followed her "commands" as she called out the maneuvers that we in turn enthusiastically executed. One of our favorites was the wangle low: Arms akimbo, waist rotating, [‡‡] knees bend as you dip closer to the ground. Doing African-inspired moves like these to the rhythms of tuk band [§§] music was one of my personal highlights from my school days.

[**] Leather Coat, formally known as Leather Jacket, is a species of fish. Cou-cou is a part of Barbados' national dish: Flying fish and cou-cou. Cou-cou is made of cornmeal and okra, and is similar in consistency to porridge or grits. In this courtship song, a suitor is promising to marry a young lady (Gerdine), asking her to show him her ring finger, and declaring that she will soon be wearing his wedding ring.

[††] The Barbados Landship is a kind of friendly society similar to the Freemasons. As the name suggests, the community-based organization, founded by former seaman Moses Wood, brings naval traditions onto terra firma, representing ships on land. Working-class communities form groups known as ships, and the members (aka "crews") gather at club centers (aka "docks") to enjoy camaraderie, entertainment, and support. One thing Bajans love to do is dance, so of course, there is dancing in the mix as well. Landship groups also provide crew members with mutual financial aid inspired by the Ghanaian susu tradition. Initially only men were allowed to join landships, but by the early 1900s, women were permitted to become members. The Landship (and the dances or maneuvers that are a part of it) is a crucial element of Barbados' intangible cultural heritage.

[‡‡] Not too much because we are well brought up young ladies with personal and familial reputations to uphold, lol.

[§§] In keeping with the naval theme, each Landship has an "engine" that powers it, i.e., the music to which the dances are performed. A musical genre unique to Barbados is Tuk. Similar to the Landship, tuk bands are an artistic creolization of African and British traditions. Each tuk band is composed of a bass drum, a kettle drum, a flute or penny whistle, and sometimes a triangle.

The experience of presenting these dances on stage revealed a talent I had not known I possessed and unlocked a lifetime love for the creative and performing arts.

My school friend Michelle Hinkson (may she rest in peace) and her mom, realizing that I had caught the dancing bug, reached out to my mom to persuade her to let me start dance classes. Fortunately, she didn't need much convincing.

Michelle was taking dance lessons at the YMCA—they were good, and better yet they were free. My family didn't have a lot of extra money lying around, so this was a great thing. Feeling reassured that I would be in decent company, in good hands, and gainfully occupied, my mom said yes. From then on, for years, I spent hours every Saturday afternoon in choreography heaven.

I did not have the language for it then, but now I know that I enjoyed dance so much because I was in a flow state. There was no struggle. I had an almost photographic memory for choreography, and my body had an innate kinetic intelligence; a spatial awareness that made it easy for me to pick up and execute new steps. I became one of the people who was frequently called to the front of the class to demonstrate how steps should be done. I was one of the dancers who was often placed at the front of the stage for performances because I knew the choreography cold, my execution was crisp, and when needed I could turn on a kilowatt smile.

There were only a few of us children in the YMCA class: Michelle and I were around 11 years old. Most of the other participants were adults, probably in their 20s, though I'm not totally sure. One of them, my friend and guardian angel Shelley Worrell, took me under her wing. Once she realized how good I was, she made it her business to nurture my talent and give me opportunities to improve, gain confidence, and shine, whether in dance or in other areas.

She invited me to join another dance troupe that she was a member of, led by iconic Barbadian creative Tyrone Trotman (may he rest in peace), so I would have access to even more classes—for free. She also found opportunities for me to perform. She secured me a part in a local musical called Bimshire, and later in life she got me involved in pageants.*** It is thanks to her that I danced on Barbados' hotel circuit for years. And yes, she made sure I got paid.

*** I had won the Miss Cave Hill pageant while attending the University of the West Indies, and later went on to win the Miss Barbados-Independence pageant and to represent the island as Miss Barbados at the Jaycees Caribbean Queen pageant. It is thanks to Shelley that I participated in the latter two.

Know Your Strengths: Focus

55

One of the awesomest things Shelley did when I was in my early teens was encourage me to audition for a scholarship from the Barbados Dance Theatre Company. She told me about it one Saturday after class at Tyrone's studio, and auditions were being held in the middle of the following week. I did not know what to expect, and didn't feel fully prepared, but decided to go for it based on her confidence in me. She said I could do it, and I chose to believe her. I told my mom that I was going to try out for the scholarship, and in her usual way, she fully supported me. She drove me to the audition and waited patiently till I was done.

The instructors put us through our paces and then did the sorting process, dividing us into groups. (Yes, the whole "If I call your name step forward" thing really happens.) To my surprise and delight, I was awarded a full scholarship. Of course, being me, I ran out to the car screaming and jumping up and down with excitement to tell my mom. Good times.

From then on, for several years, my life revolved around dance. African, ballet, Caribbean folk, jazz, modern ... the works. I went to school because I had to, but I danced because I loved it. Even though I was relatively new and young, I was also invited to take classes with the company—the actual pros. What an honor. I was completely in my element. Such joy.

I could—and did—dance for hours without ever feeling tired. Dance made me feel happy, and worthy, and capable. It boosted my self-esteem. Whereas maths made me feel bad about myself, dance made me feel good about myself.

Dance was my nirvana.

I felt similarly about writing.

When I think of Who I Am, a few key words come to mind: Introvert, creative, fashionista, chocoholic. But the most resonant one is writer. I have been writing since I can remember myself. Writing is life. Writing is joy. Writing is oxygen.

I wrote my first song when I was very young: My big sis says I might have been around three. Lyrics, melody, and of course choreography. Later in life I caught the songwriting bug again, and I still have hundreds of songs and poems hidden away in my archives.

At primary school English was my strongest subject. I had a knowledge of how the language worked and how it should sound. This is probably because I started reading at a very early age. Unlike in maths, in English class when my teachers asked for a student to answer a question, I would be one of the first to raise my hand. I still remember them saying, "That's the right answer, Lisa, but how do you know that?" I would reply, "I'm not sure, ma'am. I just know."

One of my proudest accomplishments in primary school was winning a prize in the national Pine Hill Dairy Essay Contest. And honestly, the pride was not so much because I did well, although that clearly mattered; it was more because the prize made me a provider. My writing helped me make a positive difference. My family was going through some lean times financially, so the weekly deliveries of Pine Hill Dairy products—milk, cheese, juices, and other staples—meant that we could live, and eat, a bit more richly without spending any more money. For the months that it lasted, it was amazing. I would sometimes just go over to the fridge, open the door, and smile with pride. And with relief. Tears would come to my eyes. Being able to help my family in a concrete way because of something I wrote meant everything to me.

At high school, I continued excelling in English—especially in English Composition. This carried over into the other languages I studied. My high school French teacher Ms. Williams once told me that she could tell that writing was my thing: "You are happiest when you are left to your own devices to write and express yourself in unique ways. That is when you shine."

Thank you for seeing me, ma'am. Thank you.

How I Leveraged My Strengths in My Career

When I graduated from the University of the West Indies (UWI) with a BA in French, Spanish, and Linguistics, I went to Nice, in the south of France, to be a teaching assistant at a high school. Once I returned to Barbados, I decided that I wanted a career in the hotel and tourism industry. (I had always known that I absolutely did not want to get into teaching, and spending a year as an ESL teacher only confirmed my decision.) I figured since I was semi-fluent in French and Spanish, and I loved to travel, it would be a good fit.

I worked at Sam Lord's Castle briefly and then at Almond Beach Club. At both, I had responsibility for a float.

Lawd Jeezus. When I tell y'all I struggled to get it to balance. Close-of-shift was an utter nightmare. Everything was there—cash, vouchers, credit

Know Your Strengths: Focus

57

card slips, traveler's checks (remember those??)—I just couldn't make heads or tails of it. Thankfully, my co-workers were extremely patient with me. They realized I was smart—just not with numbers. They helped me balance my float, and they also got me involved in other activities that did not involve computation. They made it easy for me to focus on my strengths.

At Almond Beach Club especially, I directed my energies elsewhere and was eventually able to draw on my talents for writing and dance. Firstly, as soon as I could leave the Front Desk & Reservations rotation of my management training programme, I did. The cash drawer was not my ministry.

My next stop was the Guest Services department. Once there, I gravitated toward projects that involved writing, like creating the hotel's Guest Services Manual. I also conducted orientations for new visitors and took them on island tours. That was fun because it was not a "sit down in the office staring at your calculator" kind of activity. Fresh air. Sunshine. Beach vibes. Camaraderie. Jokes. Snacks. Teaching people about my island. What's not to love? In addition, I helped organize some of the weekly floor shows, and I also performed in them as a dancer and model. I appreciated the opportunity to razzle and dazzle. It was a welcome break from the mundane.

Finally—thankfully—I moved into marketing, where even more of my natural talents could shine. I finally felt like I could breathe. I was promoted to the position of Marketing Officer: UK, Europe & LATAM. Because I am not a natural extrovert and this role required me to be one, I drew on my experience in the performing arts and was able to "switch on" when necessary. For years, I represented the hotel at World Travel Market in London, ITB in Berlin, and BIT in Milan.* I was also part of national delegations sent to Brazil and Peru.

One of my favorite trips was the one to Peru where I wrote and delivered my presentation on Barbados in Spanish. If my luggage was overweight it was not only because I packed an outfit for every second of every day— I'm a founding member of Overpackers Anonymous—it was also because of the ginormous Collins Spanish dictionary that I took with me so I could quadruple-check my work. I guess the presentation went well, because afterward the attendees approached me excitedly and started speaking to me in rapid Spanish all at the same time. They were definitely not expecting

---

*ITB is the Internationale Tourismus Börse Berlin. BIT Milano is the Borsa Internazionale del Turismo. Like the World Travel Market, both are annual travel fairs.

58   Know Yourself

someone from the English-speaking Caribbean to present to them in their
native tongue, so it was a pleasant surprise for them. I had to explain that my
flawless Spanish was only for the speech, lol. Fortunately, they all spoke
English fluently.

When the hotel's management team entered a few of us into a national
public speaking contest held by the Business and Professional Women's
Club of Barbados, I was honored to be selected as one of the competitors,
and I participated with enthusiasm. Now *this* was something I could do.
I knew I could write a great speech, captivate an audience, and deliver a
dazzling performance. Shout-out to my mom and my English teachers at
Queen's College for always insisting on good diction, and to the Cavite
Chorale[†††, ‡‡‡] and my dance tutors who taught me so much about
stage presentation: "Cover the stage!" "Project!" "Connect with one
person in the audience!" It all came in handy. On the night of the
semifinals, my speech wasn't even finished, but somehow I still
managed to deliver it convincingly, and the judges voted me on to
the next round.

Once I moved forward to the finals, I started working with a wonderful coach, John Graham, and spent several hours after my shifts editing,
refining, and rehearsing my speech. Many a night I finished work at 11:00,
and then my Mom would drive me over to John's home so we could all
continue whipping the speech—and my delivery thereof—into shape. I
knew that this time around I couldn't wing it. Oratory is an art. On competition night, I nailed my speech and emerged victorious as Barbados'
Young Career Woman.

Thank goodness there was no math involved.

Later in life, once I had fully resigned myself to the fact that I would have
to be an upstanding adult, i.e., hold a job, earn my keep, and contribute to

---

[†††] The Cavite Chorale is one of the student organizations of the University of the West
Indies. Based in Barbados at the Cave Hill campus of the university, the Chorale is made up
of current students and alumni. The choir performs a variety of genres: Sacred and secular,
classical and contemporary, including madrigals, motets, and negro spirituals. Of course,
Caribbean genres such as folk, calypso, reggae, and spouge[‡‡‡] are also an important part of the
Chorale's repertoire.

[‡‡‡] Spouge is a genre of music that is indigenous to Barbados. It was created by Barbadian
musician Jackie Opel in the 1960s and is a blend of Jamaican ska and Trinidadian calypso. In
its brief heyday, spouge was popularized by Bajan artists including The Draytons Two,
Richard Stoute, Wendy Alleyne, The Escorts, and Cassius Clay (né Winston Yearwood).
Unfortunately, the genre has largely faded into obscurity.

society, I decided that my jobs would focus on writing. Ergo, my 9–5s have mostly been in the copywriting space. I moved away from the world of "pure marketing" that I had been immersed in while in the tourism industry and pivoted to something I more fully enjoyed. Life and work are hard enough. It's good to have something you love doing to look forward to every day.

Outside of the 9–5 world, for example, with my activism and community building, I use my writing as a vehicle to inspire change. Everybody can contribute to the cause but in different ways. In all honesty, I will probably never be the person to be out marching in the street. But I march with my pen and my keyboard. That is where my strength lies. My words put in the miles. Like back in the day when I won that essay contest, being able to use my writing to help people, and hopefully change lives, is incredibly fulfilling.

Lessons I've Learned from Being a Writer and Dancer

Talent Matters

There is nothing as sweet as using the gifts God gave you and operating in the flow. **Lesson: Embrace your strengths.**

Discipline Matters More

Talent is great, and inspiration is wonderful, but discipline beats them both every time. On the tough days at work or in life, discipline is one of the qualities that help you keep going. Sometimes, you just have to buckle down and get things done. When I was writing this book, the talent made it somewhat easier to accomplish; however discipline and consistency are what helped me meet my deadlines and complete the manuscript. **Lesson: Be consistent.**

Fundamentals Are Key

In most dance forms, like ballet for instance, there are foundational positions that every student of the discipline must learn. Many people today want to "skip steps" and achieve a celebrity lifestyle (or whatever goal they have set their sights on) without doing the basics or putting in the work. It's like wanting to be a surgeon without going to med school. Whether it's with dance, music, writing, acting, whatever; it's important to master the fundamentals.

60 Know Yourself

Learn your positions. Practice your scales and arpeggios. Grasp the rules of grammar. From there, you can riff and adlib to your heart's content. The basics are what prepare you to shoot into the stratosphere. The shortcut is the longcut. **Lesson: Do the work.**

The Background Work Is the Main Work

When I used to dance, rehearsals were my favorite part. I loved the discipline of making incremental improvements and mastering the moves. From there, the performance was easy. With this book project, I loved working on my website, social media platforms, and all the public-facing proof that the book was real. But none of it mattered if the manuscript was not completed and the editing was not done. The unsexy "background stuff" is actually the main stuff. **Lesson: Prioritize intelligently.**

Be Yourself, Whether People Understand It or Not

A lot of people used to ask me, "How come you say you're introverted, but yet you're on stage all the time?" I honestly didn't see the contradiction, because that was just my norm. When I was dancing, I knew the choreography and didn't have to talk to anybody. I could do what I had trained to do and then be gone. Immediately after every performance, I would go straight back home to my bubble. Introverts unite separately. **Lesson: Do you.**

Why You Should Focus on Your Strengths

So, knowing what you now know, can you imagine me working as an accountant?

Exactly.

Not saying it couldn't happen (although I can't imagine a universe in which it would), but if it did, I would probably be the most stressed out, mistake-prone accounting professional there is. For that matter, my clients would probably be stressed and unhappy too. Their books would be in a complete and utter shambles.

Imagine working day in, day out, coping with regular office shenanigans, and then on top of that having no clue what you're doing. Or worse yet, outright hating it. Imagine the constant strain, the struggle, the continuous feelings of frustration, of being a failure.

Just ... why?

There's no need to do that to ourselves.

I believe that while it's important to be aware of your weaknesses and compensate where necessary, it is even more vital to focus on your strengths. Fake it till you make it has its limitations.

There's nothing wrong with identifying areas for growth and improvement of course. One should want to evolve and be a better human. However, we should not look at ourselves as inherently broken and in need of repair. We should not spend our lives fixated 24 / 7 / 365 on what's "wrong" with us and trying to compensate for real or imagined deficiencies. That's not healthy.

Instead, we should allocate our energy toward activities that we have a hope of mastering or improving; toward topics that we have a real interest in; toward endeavors that bring us joy. We should build on what is naturally there; expand on the innate.

We've got limited time on this earth—might as well spend it shining. We need to move in our magic.

Focusing on your strengths will help you to:

Experience Ease

Life is already hard enough. Why add orders of difficulty? Rather than constantly struggling and berating ourselves for not being or doing what "they" say we should be or do, we can instead elect to saunter down the path of least resistance. We can decide to align with our A game rather than engage in daily fisticuffs with our spirit. We can opt to compliment, rather than criticize, ourselves. We can choose to treat ourselves with gentleness. A soft life with lots of space to exhale must be steeped in ease.

Manifest Abundance

I mean, who *doesn't* need more abundance? Focusing on your strengths means that you are operating from a spirit of prosperity and overflow rather than from an energy of scarcity and deficit. Instead of being mired in the tension that can result from constant self-criticism, you invite room to enjoy life by focusing on the positive—about yourself. From a position of positivity, you can then attract more expansive experiences into your life. Big up yuhself, focus on your blessings, and prosper.

Increase Joy

I haven't gone into it much, but suffice it to say that there was considerable upheaval, and at times outright chaos, during my childhood. Dance is what helped me cope. It helped me escape. It helped me process some of the tension and trauma out of my body. It helped me feel happy. I found solace in the steps; transcendence in the training; comfort in the choreography. Dance is what brought consistent joy into my life even during times when happiness was otherwise hard to find. Since I danced almost daily, there was always something to look forward to. Yes, life can be tough, but if we actively carve out pockets of positivity, it can be a bit easier to deal with. Despite everything, life can still be filled with joy. And heaven knows we all need more of it.

Find Your Comfort Zone

I'm a fan of the phrase "get comfortable with being uncomfortable," but you don't have to be uncomfortable *all the time*. It's okay to take a break. It's okay to seek solace. It's okay to relax. You are deserving of comfort. Growth and healing come not only from stretching ourselves, but also from allowing ourselves a little room to breathe. Like elastic, if you keep stretching with no release, you will snap. Discomfort is not the only avenue to elevation. Embrace soothing energy. Claim comfort. Explore activities that you love, and that also help to regulate your system. During the 2024 Olympics in Paris, it was great to see so many athletes prioritizing their comfort and mental health. Remember Tom Daley, the British diver who spent his downtime knitting? That's what I'm talking about.

Move Beyond Competence to Calling

My brilliant niece, one of those people who is great at everything she puts her mind to, thankfully did not inherit my aversion to maths. She's a "straight A's in every subject" kid of chick. More importantly, she's an all-round cool and awesome person. And beautiful too, inside and out. (Yes, I'm an unabashedly proud, healthily obsessed Auntie. Best. Niece. Ever.) That said, although Taryn is good with numbers, that is not what she wanted to dedicate her considerable brain power to. Competence and calling are not the same. Just because one *can* do something doesn't mean that one *should*. Instead, she chose to lean on the linguistic side of her talents since that brings her more joy. As of this writing she's at the University of Manchester pursuing a PhD in Linguistics—and she's truly happy. Words and language

Know Your Strengths: Focus 63

are part of her calling. I'm fully expecting a book or two from her in the future.

Boost Self-Esteem

Of *course* you're going to feel good about yourself if you're engaged in activities that you're talented at. Of *course* you will thrive in spaces that welcome your greatness. In a world that actively tries to drain us of confidence, it is empowering to deliberately engage in self-directed counter programming. Leveraging your strengths—the ones that bring you joy—can help you feel energized and accomplished. You'll feel smart, secure, and self-assured. You'll remember that you are indeed THE ONE. This is important for us all, but especially for Black women who are so often criticized simply for existing; so frequently treated like imposters and ignoramuses in our fields of expertise.

Improve Mental Health

Relatedly, boosting one's self-esteem can also help support a positive mental state. Feeling better helps you feel better. As someone with multiple mental health diagnoses, I can attest that the battle, and the stigma, can at times feel overwhelming. However, focusing on what I'm good at puts me in a more positive frame of mind and reduces the frequency and severity of depressive episodes. In addition, having a creative outlet can help one excavate existential angst and process it out of one's psyche. Our minds and bodies should not be mausoleums for housing trauma. Chase away the gray days by taking stock of—and using—your talents.

Maximize Motivation

Maybe it's just me, but I confess that I have an uncomfortably close relationship with procrastination. I know it achieves nothing—quite literally—yet and still I persist in putting off simple tasks for months that would take mere minutes to complete. But this is in part because the to-dos I procrastinate on are either not in my wheelhouse, too overwhelming to manage on my own, or completely uninteresting. That said, nothing cures the "do it laters" like interest and enthusiasm. Sometimes, it even flows over into other areas of my life that I'm neutral about. If there's a task I've been putting off (that can't be outsourced to someone else), sometimes I'll make a deal with myself to

64 Know Yourself

complete it first and then reward myself with something I'm actually interested in doing. Fold some laundry, then write. It's like our parents saying, "You can't go out to party until you clean your room." Centering one's strengths boosts motivation, which then energetically creates more of itself. It feels wonderful to move from inertia to alacrity.

Find Your Flow

Effortless efforting. Frictionless focus. There are few things as sweet as being in the zone and experiencing flow. Coined by Hungarian-born psychologist Mihalyi Csikszentmihalyi (pronounced Me-High Cheek-Sent-Me-High), the term "flow" refers to an altered mind state where everything comes easily and we perform at our peak.[3]

As I explained earlier, in my youth I frequently experienced a state of flow when I was dancing. (Now, unfortunately, my hips, back, and knees won't let me be great.) These days, I often slip into a flow state when I am writing. Time simultaneously speeds up and slows down. My surroundings slip away. I change mental gears and move into hyperfocus. My ADHD brain is able to collect itself from confusion into coherence. Divine downloads abound. I enter into a semi-meditative state in which I become a conduit for inspired action. It is absolute bliss.

We've covered the why of focusing on your strengths; now let's get to the how.

How to Leverage Your Strengths

When my family moved to Barbados from Trinidad, life changed dramatically—at least that's how it felt. There definitely appeared to be more strain, financially and otherwise. We weren't poor, but things were definitely tight. Smaller house, sometimes smaller meals, no more housekeeper. Our poor piano lived outside on the patio. That broke my heart. We thankfully still had a car, but it had seen better days.

My mom did everything she could to make sure that we remained afloat and enjoyed life as much as we could in our new home. I learned directly from her how to leverage one's strengths and seek joy—both at work and beyond.

Since sharing is caring, let me share with you a few lessons that Mama Bear taught me:

Know Your Strengths: Focus 65

Be Practical

Ever the Taurean, my mom is extremely down to earth. Practicality is one of her strengths. With two children to raise, she couldn't afford to be shilly-shallying around trying to find herself. She needed a job, so she got a job. In fact, she made arrangements to be interviewed even before she left Trinidad for Barbados. As a language major and former librarian, she looked for a role that was semi-related to those areas. She stayed in her lane. That way, although she was adjusting to life in a foreign land (she's Trinidadian by birth), at least there would be minimal struggle at work. She got a position at the Delegation of the European Commission and was able to draw on her existing competencies. She started as the receptionist, it being the rule at the time that anyone starting at that office had to learn the ropes at the front desk. She was soon promoted to archivist and was later promoted to information officer.

Now I doubt that anybody ever said, "When I grow up I want to be an archivist," but adulthood makes demands of us that must be met. I'm pretty willing to bet that it was not her dream job (at least at the beginning), but that's okay. The truth is, most of us don't have the luxury of landing our dream job and doing "flow-state work" all day every day. We have adulting to do, responsibilities to take care of, bills to pay. These companies don't care about whether or not we're inspired. Our creditors don't care if we enjoyed earning the money with which we pay them.

I don't know if my mom experienced her job as flow-state work but at least (a) she knew what she was doing, and (b) it paid the bills. She put her foundation in place so she could live her life and take care of her family from a position of stability. You know what else puts you in a flow state? Feeling stress-free because your bills are paid.

Lesson: Sometimes, staying in your lane is the best thing you can do. Know what you're good at. Do what you're good at. Stick to your strong suit.

Be Creative

For many of us, focusing on our strengths and finding our joy just might have to take place after working hours. It's great if you can blend job and joy, purpose and payment, but if you can't, that's okay as well. There are alternatives. It's perfectly acceptable to have a job just to pay your bills.[§§§]

I've always thought of my mom as an artist who, like so many adults, was forced to be practical. So she handled her business at work, but let me tell you, once she was off the clock, all her creativity was expressed. Interior design, macramé, gardening, singing, flower arranging, leathercraft: You name it, she did it. Necessity is the mother of invention, but Mama Bear is definitely an aunt. Honestly, she was a mini Etsy microindustry before Etsy existed.

And did I mention the sewing? Because THE SEWING!! She made everything from bespoke bridesmaids' dresses and intricately embroidered dashikis to curtains and cushion covers. She spent hours in front of her Necchi sewing machine whipping up outfits for herself, my sister, and me to wear. Whenever we wore them, people would ask us where we had bought them. Her work was impeccable. She also designed a couple of my pageant gowns that I still have to this day.

She made creativity an equal priority with practicality. Not all of us know what we want to be when we grow up. It's okay to keep searching.

P.S. We really need to bring back the arts patronage system, because adulting is truly the enemy of artistry. Artists need opportunities to be able to create without being burdened by practicalities. Nothing blocks creativity like bills.

P.P.S. It's okay to be interested in all the things.

Lesson: Two things can be simultaneously true. It's okay to stay in your lane AND give yourself permission to switch over to other lanes. Drive the whole highway. Play. Create. Explore your interests.

[§§§] Let me just answer this interview question for us all: "Why do you want to work here?" "Because I have bills to pay and you're hiring."

Be Multifaceted

My mom is the original multihyphenate. In addition to her 9–5 and numerous creative endeavors, over the years she's also owned a couple of businesses. Her first foray into entrepreneurship came after she took an early retirement: Silks & Things, her flower arranging company. She created silk flower arrangements for weddings, product launches, and other special events. She also designed commissions for some of the hotels on the island, as well as a few pieces for cruise liners. She and I spent many a heavenly hour in the New York Flower District sourcing supplies.

Her second company is the Touch of Light Reiki School & Healing Centre. In the mid-1990s, she became interested in Reiki, so she dived right in. She got her first and second degree, and a few years later became an Usui Reiki Master. She launched Touch of Light in 2006, and it's still going strong: She is an active practitioner and teacher.

Speaking of her being a teacher, my sister and I are very proud to have been trained as Reiki Masters by none other than Mama Bear herself. Lineage is one of the nine core elements of traditional Usui Reiki, so it's very cool that we share this spiritual lineage as well as our genealogical one. In my mind, I refer to us as RM I, RM II, and RM III. As a Reiki Master Teacher she leads in-person classes in Barbados, along with my sister, about once a quarter.

But wait, there's more, lol. She's also one of the founding organizers of the Barbados Reiki Association's Open Day, which has evolved into their annual Holistic Health Fair.

Additionally, she's a past president of the Barbados Reiki Association, and is still an active member.

Remember the "Move from Competency to Calling" part of leveraging your strengths? That's what my mom did, and I'm super proud of her. Her career was based on her competencies. Reiki is part of her calling. She feels fulfilled and is living her best life.

By the way, did I mention that she's in her 80s? She truly is my shero.

Lesson: Embrace the side quest. You never know ... it could become your main quest.

Be Curious

"I'm going to Dubai." This was Mama Bear's opener to one of our daily conversations a few years back. I was like "Wait … what?! Going where?!" One thing my mom absolutely loves to do is travel, so I guess it should not have been a surprise that she had signed herself up for yet another epic trip: She's always ready to hop on a plane. If there's a flight to be caught, rest assured she's gonna catch it, even now that she's in her 80s. Her passport stays ready. Exploring new territory is one of her favorite things in the world. It keeps her inspired.

Even if there are no planes involved, she's always up for an adventure. Back in the day when she was a teaching assistant in the south of France, she took the opportunity to hitchhike through Europe. She and a girlfriend backpacked from where they were based in Nîmes, and went on to Nice, Cannes, Genoa, Milan, Lake Como, back to France, crossed over the Alps, Dusseldorf, Hamburg, Brussels, Antwerp, Amsterdam, Strasbourg, Paris, and finally Le Touquet-Paris-Plage. From there, her friend went back to England, and Mama Bear took a ship back to Jamaica where she was a student at the University College of the West Indies. Just … wow. I aspire.

I've moved often, but wherever I am, my mom always flies in to visit. She ends up knowing my neighborhood better than I do. She loves outside as much as I love inside. She takes a walk or hops into an Uber and off she goes exploring. When she gets back home, we do a debrief where she tells me about her adventures and all the cool stores, restaurants, or resources she's discovered.

She always wants to know, see, and experience more. She has a curious mind. This not only makes her an interesting person to talk to, but it also nourishes her inner artist. This is how she stays inspired. Her curiosity feeds her creativity. And her creativity is one of her strengths.

Lesson: Seek inspiration. Expand your horizons. Feed your inner artist.

Be Yourself

Of all the lessons I've learned from Mama Bear, this might be the most important one. In a world that insists that we be as strident and extroverted as possible, she demonstrates the power of quietness. She fully embraces her introversion. She is not a boisterous, belligerent, broadstrokes person. She is serene, soft-spoken, and stately. Oasis vibes. She is never the loudest person in a group, but rest assured she will make the biggest impression. Instead of sucking all the air out of a room, she elevates the energy.

She does not chase; she attracts: Good people, good experiences, good fortune. She stands tall, radiating dignity and positive vibes, and folks are naturally drawn to her. She does not do drama; she vibrates at a level where drama never even enters her ambit. She embodies the energy of peace.

Her stillness is one of her strengths.

She refuses to be swayed by who anyone else thinks she should be. She shows up, unapologetically, as herself. Quiet or not, she definitely has main character energy.

By modeling the beauty of being calm and quiet, she gave me permission to embrace my introversion and lean into pursuits that align with that trait.

Lesson: Do you. Be true to yourself. You don't have to be loud to be a leader.

Elevation: Vibrate Higher

Exhalation: Breathe Easy

Alternate Nostril Breathing / Nadi Shodhana

For this breathing exercise, you'll be breathing through your nose only, and using the thumb and ring finger of one of your hands to close alternating nostrils. Let's start with our left hands. Keep your inhales and exhales even; about 5 counts each.

(continued)

70 Know Yourself

(*continued*)

Let's begin:

Sit comfortably and close your eyes. Place your ring finger on your right nostril

Inhale through your left nostril for a count of 5, then close it with your left thumb

Exhale through your right nostril for a count of 5, then close it with your ring finger

Inhale through your left nostril, then close it

Exhale through your right nostril, then close it

Repeat this a few more times:

Inhale on the left, close your left nostril

Exhale on the right; close your right nostril

Inhale on the left for 1, 2, 3, 4, 5; close

Exhale on the right for 1, 2, 3, 4, 5; close

Inhale: 1, 2, 3, 4, 5; close

Exhale: 1, 2, 3, 4, 5; close

Inhale: 1, 2, 3, 4, 5; close

Exhale: 1, 2, 3, 4, 5; close

Now, let's reverse directions and start our inhales with our right nostril:

Place your thumb on your left nostril

Inhale through your right nostril for a count of 5, then close it with your right ring finger

Exhale through your left nostril for a count of 5, then close it with your thumb

(*continued*)

Know Your Strengths: Focus 71

(*continued*)

Inhale through your right nostril, then close it
Exhale through your left nostril, then close it

Repeat this a few more times:

Inhale on the right, close your right nostril
Exhale on the left; close your left nostril

Inhale on the right for 1, 2, 3, 4, 5; close
Exhale on the left for 1, 2, 3, 4, 5; close

Inhale: 1, 2, 3, 4, 5; close
Exhale: 1, 2, 3, 4, 5; close

Inhale: 1, 2, 3, 4, 5; close
Exhale: 1, 2, 3, 4, 5; close

Continue for as long as you're comfortable. When you're ready, return your breathing to its normal cadence, and open your eyes.

Affirmations: Speak Life

- I am brilliant, gifted, and talented.
- I am that girl, and I love being me.
- I am a wise and worthy steward of all my gifts.

(*continued*)

(continued)

- I am choosing to see and celebrate my strengths.
- I am giving myself permission to express my innate genius.

Introspection: Journal & Heal

- What is your calling?
- What do you KNOW you're great at?
- What accomplishments are you proud of and why?
- What activities make you happy and induce a state of flow?
- What are your strengths? Personally? Professionally? Creatively?

Curation: Do the Work

Do an ikigai assessment.

Ikigai is a Japanese concept that, loosely translated, means life purpose. Using the graphic below as a guide, identify your ikigai.[4] Note that even though "what you can be paid for" is included here, not everything that brings you joy or makes you feel fulfilled needs to be monetized.

(continued)

(continued)

Appreciation: Express Gratitude

What are you grateful for? Count your blessings:

- I am grateful ...
- I am grateful ...
- I am grateful ...

Celebration: Razzle Dazzle

Flex on 'em, sis! What are you proud of? Celebrate yourself:

- I am proud of myself for ...
- I am proud of myself for ...
- I am proud of myself for ...

Meditation: Think Blissfully

Sit or lie down comfortably. Breathe normally and become aware of where your body is touching the surface beneath you. Gently relax your eyelids and flutter your eyes closed. Gradually slow down your breathing, inhaling through your nose and exhaling through your mouth for equal counts of five.

Inhale for a count of 1, 2, 3, 4, 5; exhale for a count of 5, 4, 3, 2, 1

Inhale: 1, 2, 3, 4, 5; exhale: 5, 4, 3, 2, 1

Inhale: 1, 2, 3, 4, 5; exhale: 5, 4, 3, 2, 1

Continue breathing at that pace. Feel the coolness of your breath in your nostrils with every inhale, refreshing and inspiring you. Feel the warmth of your breath with every exhale, grounding and relaxing you.

Smile gently and focus your attention on your third eye.

(continued)

(continued)

Silently, repeat this phrase to yourself:

I am gifted.

I am gifted.

I am gifted.

Focus on that affirmation for as long as you wish, releasing it when you feel ready.

Continue inhaling through your nose and exhaling through your mouth for a count of five. Now silently repeat this phrase to yourself:

I am a conduit for Divine creativity.

I am a conduit for Divine creativity.

I am a conduit for Divine creativity.

Focus on that affirmation, feeling your connection with your higher power growing stronger and clearer. When you feel ready, gently let go of the affirmation.

Next, mentally repeat this phrase to yourself:

I have everything I need to fulfill my unique purpose.

I have everything I need to fulfill my unique purpose.

I have everything I need to fulfill my unique purpose.

Focus on that affirmation for as long as you wish, and when you feel ready, gently release it from your mind.

When you're ready, return your breathing to its normal cadence, slowly open your eyes, and smile softly.

Asé.

PART II

Love Yourself

4

Curate Your Thoughts: Manifest

Invocation

Most High,

I come to You, as always, with a pure heart and an open mind

I am ready to
Claim my Divine birthright
Fulfill my highest potential
Manifest my unique purpose
Amen

I am calling in
Divine Love and Divine Favor
Divine Wisdom and Divine Courage
Divine Abundance and Divine Alignment
Amen

I am grateful for
Divine Provision and Divine Intervention
Divine Guidance and Divine Inspiration
Divine Expansion and Divine Elevation
Amen

A Manifestation Testimony

"Where's my book deal?"

In early 2022, this question was constantly on my mind. It was on my sister's mind too. As activists, we had both been showing up daily on LinkedIn, on our other social media channels, on our blogs and newsletters for more than two years, and we were ready to go to the next level. A few of our peers had published books, but for the most part the book deals seemed to be going to those of a paler persuasion.

We were annoyed.

We knew we were just as talented, just as visible, and just as worthy. Not to mention, in most cases, way more experienced. Apart from anything else we are both professional writers—writing is literally what we do in our day jobs. We did not begrudge anybody *their* book deal; we just wanted *ours*. We wanted us *all* to get book deals.

This was on our minds so much that we recorded an episode about it on our podcast *The Introvert Sisters* called, unsurprisingly, "Where's My Book Deal?" My sister, always one to forge ahead independently, decided not to wait. (I so admire her for this.) As an essayist, educator, and professional journalist, she is amazingly prolific. She moved ahead with her plans, opting to self-publish. She had lots of material and could easily produce more since she was in the habit of writing to meet precise word counts and tight deadlines. By the fall of 2022 she had published her second book, *I'm Tired of Racism*.

On my end, I decided that self-publishing was not an option for me. You gotta know yourself, and I was clear that I, alas, don't have the laser focus that it takes to self-publish. I knew that I needed structure—the structure I believed working with a publisher would provide. I pushed the book deal idea to the back of my mind and continued living life. I semi-resigned myself to the possibility that I might never publish a book at all, and I let it go. I delved deeper into my activism and got busy with myriad projects.

For a while, I truly forgot about my dream of being published, but by January of 2023, I started thinking about it again. I actually began writing my book proposal but got distracted by daily life.

Did I mention that focus is not my strong point? For me, a typical sequence of events looks like this: Let's say I have a goal of folding some laundry. An hour or two later, I might have dusted my baseboards, cleaned my windows, posted on socials, mopped my floors, done the dishes, stalked my Amazon deliveries, recorded some affirmations, and checked my email. But what would remain untouched would be the task I had initially set out to do: Tackle the mountain of unfolded laundry. Shout-out to ADHD.

In addition to general adulting, I had also started the pre-launch process for The Great Exhale. That took all my time and energy, so between balancing that and my 9–5, I was at max capacity.

But then the universe intervened.

I am a long-time follower of Luvvie Ajayi Jones. Yes, *that* Luvvie. Four-time *New York Times* bestselling author, pop culture commentator, and my sista-friend in my head. In the summer of 2023, I came across a post of hers promoting her latest venture: The Book Academy (TBA). She created TBA to teach authors-in-waiting about the publishing industry and provide guidance on how to get published. I felt like the heavens had thrown me a lifeline. I saw it as a clear sign that my time was coming. I gathered my coins, paid sis her fee with gratitude in my heart, and got ready for what would become a life-changing experience.

As Black women do, Luvvie underpromised and overdelivered. The Book Academy was amazing. Gems on gems on gems. Education. Inspiration. Motivation. Validation. It was exactly what I needed. Each module was a masterclass. All meat, no bone. The vibes vibed. The energy was elevated. The community was supportive. It was all Luvv.

Luvvie followed up The Book Academy's inaugural cohort with her first-ever Book Proposal Power Program (BPPP). This would be implementation time. We had been taught the theory, and this would be our opportunity to put our lessons into practice. Writing our book proposals would bring us one step closer to being published authors. Having had such a positive experience with The Book Academy, I registered for the BPPP with indecent haste. I might have been the first person to sign up. As soon as they dropped the link, I hopped right on it. It was a no-brainer.

This was the structure I was looking for. I knew that it would be a step-by-step how-to guide. I wanted to complete my book proposal, so I availed myself of the Divine assistance that had been sent my way.

And then the magic happened.

80 Love Yourself

This was the sequence of events:

- 09 / 19: Registered for the Book Proposal Power Program
- 10 / 09: Victoria Savanh from Wiley (WILEY, y'all!!) emailed me
- 10 / 10: The first BPPP session began
- Gems
- Support
- Inspiration
- Motivation
- Cheat codes
- Occasional, but much-needed, edge snatching
- 10 / 10: Started writing my book proposal again
- 12 / 12: BPPP course ends
- Procrastination
- Procrastination
- The holidays
- More procrastination (Hey, at least I'm honest)
- 01 / 08: Victoria followed up with me to see where I was with the book proposal
- 01 / 31: Submitted my book proposal
- 02 / 07: Project greenlit
- 03 / 05: Signed by Wiley!!

So, approximately five months after starting the Book Proposal Power Program, I officially became a signed author, and now here we are. Published, y'all. God is good. Thanks and praises.

This is one of the best examples from my own life of how the manifestation process works, but over the years I have been inspired by people like Oprah, Iyanla Vanzant, Deepak Chopra, and another sista-friend in my head: Ciara. I mean … if Ciara's prayer isn't an example of manifestation, I don't know what is.

But back to why this manifestation of a book deal worked. There are multiple ways to manifest: **Think** it into existence, **visualize** it into existence, **write** it into existence, **speak** it into existence, **behave** it into existence. I had done them all.

Over the course of several months, one of the repeated thoughts in my mind was that I was ready for, and deserved to have, a book deal. That kickstarted everything. I also believed that it could happen for me. In addition, I started visualizing my book on bookstore shelves.

As the thoughts coalesced and I got serious about publishing my book, I created some affirmations and wrote them out daily for a few weeks. And then I spoke it into existence on my podcast. I asked the question, "Where's my book deal?" and the Universe said, "Here you go."

"Behave it into existence" means taking inspired action. Faith without works is dead. You have the faith on one side of the equation and the works on the other side. The faith part was believing that the Universe would support my heartfelt desire. It was knowing that the help and resources I needed would show up in the perfect way at the perfect time. It was believing that authorship was possible for me and that I was worthy of having my dream come true. Coming from a family of writers—my father and sister are both published authors—I knew that being published could happen. Gotta love that DNA.

My works or actions included honing my craft daily, signing up for The Book Academy and the Book Proposal Power Program, and completing my book proposal. In other words, getting prepared for the blessing I wanted and acting as if success was guaranteed. As the saying goes: Luck is what happens when preparation meets opportunity.

Manifestation 101: Intro to Alchemy

So what is manifestation? Manifestation, also known as the law of attraction, is not new. It has been written about by Louise Hay, Abraham Hicks, Florence Scovell Schinn, and many others. It was also popularized by the book *The Secret*, by Rhonda Byrne. It is the art of bringing a thought to reality. It's the "Ask and it shall be given" of it all.

So: What do you want?

No, really. What do you want for yourself, your life, and your loved ones? What do you want for your health, your relationships, your home? What do you want your days, career, and lifestyle to feel like? Do you even want a traditional career? And do you love yourself enough to ask for what you want? Do you believe that you are worthy of having your wishes fulfilled? Give it all some thought.

Also ponder: What do you *not* want?

That's important to consider too. Curation is a two-fold exercise: Keeping what is needed and discarding what is not. It's like sculpture. You must chip away at (and dispose of) the unwanted material in order to reveal the masterpiece.

82 Love Yourself

As you go through the process of curating your experience and creating more space to exhale in your life, these are some of the questions you'll need to answer for yourself.

Manifestation and the law of attraction are often associated with gaining material objects, financial abundance, and worldly achievements. There is nothing wrong with that per se, but I want to make sure that we expand our framing.

Abundance is more than money, and material items aren't the only things that matter. Currency, cars, jobs, and houses are great, and we welcome them; but love, ease, health, peace, joy, rest … these are all priceless and can improve one's quality of life immeasurably.

When I went through what was essentially a breakdown in 2024 (you can read all about it in the "Rest" chapter), one of my requests to the Universe was for support. I didn't need another "thing." I didn't need more clothes, or shoes, or jewelry.* What I needed was love, hugs, and care. I needed rest, comfort, and a soft place to fall. My family, friends, and community showed up for me in exactly the ways I needed.

My sister and niece called and texted regularly to check in on me. If I was silent for too long, I knew a WhatsApp call would be imminent. My friends who are like family checked in on me as well. Sometimes, it was as simple as a text saying, "You okay?" That is all I needed to bring a smile to my face. It means a lot to be thought of.

I spent some time in Philly with my father, stepmother, and stepsister just hanging out. There was nothing I needed to do, and little I felt capable of doing, so I did absolutely nothing—except enjoy the delicious vegan dishes they prepared for me, dance in the kitchen just because, and watch some good Nollywood movies. Heaven.

My mother, angel that she is, very literally showed up as well. She made the trip from Barbados to New Jersey and spent three months with me. Her baby was in trouble, and she swooped in to handle things. It was very cuddly but determined "Not on my watch" energy. It was so lovely. We hugged, we laughed, we chilled. We gave each other Reiki treatments. We binge-watched *Bridgerton* (gentle reader) and a few other series as well. She helped me get more organized and feel more settled. It was absolute perfection.

---

*That said, if someone gifts me with them, I'll never turn them down, lol. To whom it may concern, I love FeNoel and Tiffany. Just sayin'.

Curate Your Thoughts: Manifest 83

My TGE community, which I consider part of my extended family, came through for me too. They embodied the saying "Love is a verb." Clearly, community is a verb too. A few of them stepped up and started posting more so that I could take a break. They blessed me with texts, gifts, and sista-friend Zoom calls. They extended me so much grace, y'all. I had initially been planning to have a big IRL party to celebrate the one-year anniversary of the community, but I just couldn't. My tank was below zero. Everyone was very understanding, and we kept the vibes low key. I literally did one "Happy anniversary" post, had our monthly community check in, and that was that. Less was more. The blessing was that I felt free to show up or not show up, and had no fear of being judged. I am eternally grateful.

All of this is to say: It's okay to ask for non-material blessings too.

How to Manifest

Let's delve into the manifestation process. As I mentioned earlier, there are five steps:

1. **Think** it into existence.
2. **Visualize** it into existence.
3. **Write** it into existence.
4. **Speak** it into existence.
5. **Behave** it into existence.

Think It into Existence

Every human-made thing on the planet started out as a thought or idea. One of my favorite lines from *A Course in Miracles* is "There are no idle thoughts."[1] None of our thoughts are neutral. All of our thoughts are creative. Thoughts are like seeds: Whatever you sow, that is what you will reap. Not in a doomsday or karmic kind of way, but in terms of logic. You cannot plant a mango seed and get a coconut tree. "As above, so below" and "As within, so without" are expressions of this fundamental tenet.

When you know how powerful your thoughts are, you become very careful about the ones you allow to germinate in your mind. Are you using your mental power to your benefit or to your detriment? Are you dreaming about the kind of life you want to enjoy, or ruminating on possible failures? Are you fixating on all the obstacles, or focused on all the wonderful possibilities? Are you preoccupied by what could go wrong, or focused on what could go right? Since all thoughts have creative power, you will manifest whatever you repeatedly think about, good or bad, positive or negative, whether you're conscious of your thoughts or not. So the key is to deliberately direct your thoughts to help you manifest the life you want.

I have been blessed to manifest many positive experiences. Like the time I needed money, did a manifestation meditation, and an inheritance I hadn't even known about came through out of the blue. Or the time I urgently needed a house to live in short term, and a friend of my mom's just happened to have one available. Or the time I needed an apartment, told the Universe what I was looking for, and got exactly what I wanted—and even a little more—at the perfect price for me.

Another example that's dear to my heart is how I got my fur baby. Two of my previous pups had been named Sultan and Czar, so I decided that my next dog would keep up the "royalty" tradition with their name. Sultan was a Rhodesian Ridgeback and Czar was a Golden Retriever-Doberman mix; in other words, they were big boys. I decided I wanted a dog that I could easily lift if necessary. Fast forward a few years. My mom and I were walking through Union Square in Manhattan and came across an adoption drive outside of PetSmart.

I swear to you the world went still, and in the midst of all the barking and brouhaha this tiny little white pup with a brown spot over one eye, lying down quietly in his cage, stood out as if a spotlight were shining on him. I had found the one!! I asked the people in charge what breed he was (not that I cared, honestly, at that point), and they said they thought he was a Jack Russell Terrier. Small and liftable: Check! "And does he already have a name?" I asked. "Yes he does," they replied. "His name is King." Regal name: Double check. Mummy and I happily took him home on the PATH train, and 15+ years later, he's still the sweetest, goodest boy.

Being clear and staying true to your vision counts too. It's okay to want what you want how you want it. Case in point, several years ago, when I was in the market for a new car, I decided to get a Volkswagen Beetle. The salesperson asked what color I wanted, and I told him green. He was like … we don't have any in stock, so you might have to choose another color. Just write down three other color options for me. So, I did. When he looked at the paperwork, he laughed, because I had written Green, Green, and Green. And y'all already know: I got a green Beetle with a pink flower. Exactly what I wanted. And I named her Sweet Pea. She was adorable. I still miss her.

Curate Your Thoughts: Manifest

Be aware, however, that the universe can be very literal.

I remember once going through some friend drama. The kind where one day you and this person are tight and then the next? Ghost like Casper. It completely unsettled my spirit, and I confess that I started to obsess about it, trying to figure out what had happened. The schism was such a surprise to me because it came out of nowhere. The recurring thought about it was "That came out of left field, and it's hit me really hard."

Well guess what? A few weeks later, I was crossing the street (yes, I had the walk signal; yes, I was on the crosswalk) and a car came out of nowhere and slammed into me—you guessed it—on my left side. It literally came out of left field and hit me really hard. Apparently I flew up in the air, then on my way down hit the roof of the car, then the bonnet, then the road.

Ouch.

So yeah. Discipline your mind. Guard your thoughts.

You must seed your subconscious with what you want to manifest. Anytime my life starts feeling like it's going haywire—it happens to us all—I check in with myself about what I've been habitually thinking. If there are any self-sabotaging thoughts that are not serving my highest good, I replace them with better ones.

If you want a soft life, if you want time and space to exhale, you must consistently set aside time to track your thoughts, set your intentions, and from there, create your goals.

One sure-fire way to determine what your overriding thoughts are is by looking at your experiences. What does your life look like right now? Are you stressed out or zenned out? Are you burned out or in balance? The likelihood is it's a mix of both. For the parts of your life that are serving your highest good, choose more of those thoughts. For the parts of your life where you're riding the struggle bus, choose different thoughts.

This is not to say that thinking differently is easy. There are times when it will be decidedly difficult. We're only human. It takes practice. It takes focus. It takes commitment. It is also not to say that the results you desire will be instantaneous (although in some cases they can be). If I'm having a mental health moment, it definitely gets more challenging to focus and keep my thoughts positive. The point is to keep trying daily. That's why meditation is called a practice.

If you find yourself in a negative thought spiral, do your best to interrupt it, calm your mind, and think differently. By way of example, when I was writing this book, there were definitely times when I felt overwhelmed.

The writing was, of course, the biggest part of the project, so nothing else mattered if the book wasn't finished. However, while completing the manuscript was the main thing, there were also all the other subprojects to take into account: Managing the permissions process for quotes, doing the developmental edits, securing blurbs, organizing a shoot for my author photo, updating my bio, writing the copy for my Amazon page, securing my URLs, getting my websites built, updating and expanding my social presence, planning my launch strategy and book tour, figuring out the bulk buys process, marketing, marketing, and more marketing ... you get the picture. It was a lot.

At one point, I found myself repeatedly thinking "I feel like I'm drowning." But realizing that that was not helpful, I took measures to change my thinking. I went for a long walk, did some breathwork, and got myself feeling less panicked and more regulated. I then changed my thought to "I have more than enough time, and I have all the help I need. All is well." I repeated it to myself a few times and started feeling better. And help showed up. A trusted friend hopped on a Zoom call with me, and we brainstormed some solutions.

Visualize It into Existence

The mind loves pictures. That's why movies are so powerful. It's also why vision boards work. If you're a visual person and you have a good imagination, visualization can be a powerful manifestation modality.

Visualization, also known as mental rehearsal, is used by many elite athletes as a performance enhancement methodology. Basketball legend Michael Jordan, Olympic sprinter Usain Bolt, iconic tennis champion Serena Williams, and Olympic gymnast Simone Biles are all the G.O.A.T. in their respective sports. Interestingly, they all credit their success not only to their physical prowess and tenacious work ethic but also to the power of visualization. If it works for these world champions, it can work for you too. It might be on a smaller or less visible scale, but that's okay.

For example, when I was leading the rebrand for The Great Exhale, part of the exercise was to provide my awesome graphic designer Rose Reynolds with a creative brief. Among other details, the brief needed to include a mood board—a pictorial representation of what I wanted the logo and brand identity to convey—so, I put a lot of time and thought into

Curate Your Thoughts: Manifest

visualizing what that would be. I had to be clear so that Rose would be clear. I also visualized the project going smoothly and successfully. In addition, I told Rose to "make the logo look like a gentle breath."

Fast forward to the first concept review and Rose nailed it in one. Can anybody say #BlackExcellence? She was able to pick up what I had put down and leverage her expertise to capture the vibe. This is the beauty of clear communication and aligned collaboration. She ran the brief through that brilliant brain of hers, and the output was the gorgeous logo and visual identity for The Great Exhale. The key? Clarity of vision.

Whether you're designing a logo or designing your life, clear vision matters.

If you are one of the lucky people who can easily create detailed pictures in your mind, then dedicate part of your meditation time to visualization. If making mental pictures is challenging for you, then try guided meditations to help you focus. Another option is to make your visualization an external rather than an internal process.

Create vision boards; put pictures of what you want to manifest on your bathroom mirror or fridge; design a Canva or PowerPoint slideshow and look at it repeatedly; or hop on to Pinterest and create a few boards themed around what you want to bring into reality. I have often used an old-school corkboard for my vision boards. I would cut pictures out of magazines or catalogs, put them on the board with pushpins, and then place the board in a place where I would see it several times a day. It can be useful to place it in your bedroom, so you see it first thing in the morning and last thing at night.

Once, I was looking for matching tables to go on either side of my sofa. I had seen a gorgeous table on Pottery Barn's website and immediately thought, That's the one. It had a white marble top and a black base. Simple, elegant, classic. When I clicked, an "out of stock" message popped up. Bummer. However, I decided to have faith in the unseen since I answer to a higher power than man-made logistics. I put a picture of the table on my vision board, and every time I passed next to it, I smiled. I mentally welcomed it into my home. For months, every time I checked back, it was still out of stock until one day the skies parted. It was finally back in stock! I hastily added two tables to my cart and completed my purchase. As soon as I was done, the status reverted to out of stock. The Universe came all the way through.

Write It into Existence

"In the beginning was the word." There are many ways to interpret this famous line from the Bible, one of which is that, like thoughts, words are creative. Harnessing the power of the written word is another highly effective manifestation method. Many people get powerful results by writing out what they plan to manifest.

How many times have we heard about people writing a wish list for a new job, home, or relationship and having it come true? It has definitely worked for me.

At one point, I was about to give up on relationships forever. The dating pool seemed more like a putrid swamp: All frogs, no princes. I was resigned to being a "crazy cat lady," albeit with a dog. But I decided to give it one more chance. I wrote a list of the kind of person I wanted, including both character traits and physical attributes. At first I felt like it wasn't working. Patience is not my strong suit, y'all; I'm still a work in progress. But then I revisited the list, refined it a little, and in short order my person appeared. Handsome, smart, and with all the great qualities I wanted. Yay!

For writing things into existence, your journal is your best friend. The first step is to create your intention or mantra. Then, working in sprints of 7, 14, or 21 days, write it out daily three times in the morning, six times in the afternoon, and nine times at night. This is known as the 3-6-9 method. For this exercise, it's best to focus on one goal at a time.

The beauty of this approach is the consistent repetition, which cements your goal into your subconscious.

Speak It into Existence

When putting the law of attraction into practice, the spoken word is just as effective as the written word. The way it's usually done is by using mantras, affirmations, and oríkìs.

Mantras: One of the best ways to improve your life is to have a consistent meditation practice. Getting your mind and energy right is one of the keys to achieving your goals more easily and living the life of your dreams. A form of meditation that has served me well is chanting mantras.

I first learned about mantras when I watched the Tina Turner biopic *What's Love Got to Do with It*. When she was going through one of the

Curate Your Thoughts: Manifest 89

lowest times in her life, she discovered Buddhism and was introduced to the chant "Nam Myoho Renge Kyo." Queen Tina chanted it daily to help change her life for the better, which included safely leaving an abusive marriage and successfully relaunching her music career.

I rediscovered mantras a few years later when I was searching for ways to enhance my meditation and manifestation practices. As synchronicity would have it, I was led to the book *Healing Mantras* by Thomas Ashley-Farrand. I have since worn out my first copy and bought another one. The book breaks down the history behind Sanskrit mantras, suggests ways to incorporate them into your daily practice, and of course, provides a comprehensive list of mantras and their meanings. You can also find a multiplicity of mantras on YouTube.

These sacred phrases originate from Hinduism, and call upon Hindu concepts of divinity. The great thing is that most of them are pronounced phonetically, so they're easy to learn. These are some of the ones that have worked for me, and I am setting the intention that they will work for you as well:

- **Bliss:** Ananda
- **Love:** Aham Prema
- **Peace:** Om Shanti Om
- **Insight:** Om Namah Shivaya
- **Health:** Om Hiranyagarbaya Namaha
- **Transformation:** Om Mani Padme Hum
- **Luck:** Om Sharavana Bhavaya Namaha
- **Success:** Om Eim Saraswatyei Namaha
- **Removing Obstacles:** Om Gum Ganapatayei Namaha
- **Prosperity:** Om Sri Rama Jaya Rama Jaya Jaya Rama

These mantras are usually repeated 108 times. To help yourself keep count, get a set of mala beads, which are easy to find on Amazon.

Affirmations: Affirmations are another powerful means of bringing about positive life changes. I first encountered them years ago via Louise Hay's famous book *You Can Heal Your Life*. Since then, I have used affirmations as part of my self-care system. Repeating affirmations helps me manage my mood, stay focused on the positive, and bring my dreams to reality.

Composed of two of the most powerful words in the English language, the invocation "I am" acts as a master key to unlock your blessings and highest potential. It is thought that any statement that follows the words "I am" will come to fruition. The phrase "I am that I am" connects you to Source and ignites your innate power. And who doesn't need extra power?

To use "I am" affirmations, simply say (or write) "I am ..." and insert the quality, state, feeling, characteristic, or mood that you want to embody and experience.

Some popular ones are:

- I am safe.
- I am loved.
- I am happy.
- I am worthy.
- I am grateful.
- I am abundant.

Of course this is not the only way to create affirmations, but it's one of the most effective.

When I started my journey as an activist, I found the work very fulfilling but also extremely draining. The sheer volume of content I was creating, combined with being subjected to keyboard bullies, online trolls, and constant caucacity, led to burnout. (You can read all about it in the "Rest" chapter.) To help myself cope, I decided to do some conscious counterprogramming. I launched my TikTok channel in the summer of 2021 and dedicated it solely to affirmations. It is a soft, healing corner of the interwebs designed to help myself and others focus on the positive. There's no anti-racism content at all—I save that for LinkedIn—just high vibrations and affirmations for manifestations.

Affirmations have made such a positive difference in my life that when I was designing The Great Exhale, I included a space in the virtual community that is dedicated solely to affirmations. As Black women, we are used to being berated, talked down to, gaslit, and verbally attacked. The misogynoir is real. The micro- and macroaggressions are real. Unfortunately, many of us internalize these negative messages. The affirmations space in TGE is designed to help us consciously and continuously to push against that; to shower ourselves with positivity and speak to ourselves with love. As my community members scroll through that section, they are met with a wave of positive messages

Curate Your Thoughts: Manifest

91

affirming their beauty, talent, intelligence, and innate #BlackGirlMagic. It's so healing to see us all focus on uplifting ourselves and each other.

I'm such a big believer in the power of affirmations that (as you've already seen) I included several at the end of each chapter to make it easy for you to incorporate them into your daily self-care practice. Imagine the wave of positivity and high-vibrational energy we can co-create by consistently choosing to speak lovingly to ourselves and about our lives.

This is definitely not a call for toxic positivity. Nor is it a call for us to deny our difficult experiences or suppress our challenging emotions. It is a call that recognizes that, as the Donnie McClurkin gospel song goes, "We fall down, but we get up."

In creating affirmations, we are acknowledging that the "fall down" has happened—but the "get up" is possible.

Use mine or create your own, but either way, affirm yourself daily. It will change your life for the better.

Positive Self-Talk: Have you ever received a compliment and blocked it? As in, someone compliments you on your outfit, and you immediately respond, unironically, "This old thing?" Or you reply by saying that you don't really like what you're wearing? Or you start talking about how self-conscious you are about your belly, arms, butt, hips, or thighs? What about if someone raves about your complexion, and instead of thanking them you immediately point out some supposed flaw on your face? (Btw: You're beautiful. ♥)

Why do we do this?

We reject words of affirmation because we deem ourselves unworthy. We counter a compliment with a self-directed insult because we were taught that speaking highly of ourselves is arrogant. We believe that in order to be liked and accepted we must appear humble. We have residual self-hatred, so we look in the mirror and hyperfixate on everything we do not like, which makes it hard for us to believe it when someone calls us beautiful.

For Black women especially, this is a huge issue. Everybody wants to be us. Everybody wants to appropriate our look, our lips, our hair, our hips, our glow, our magic, our vibe. Our natural beauty and characteristics are revered—once they're not on a Black body. As Black women, we receive an awful lot of criticism about our natural melanin from pale people slathered in self-tanner. This can wreak havoc on our self-esteem.

92   Love Yourself

Maybe we reject compliments because our achievements were never celebrated when we were growing up, and now we find it almost impossible to see ourselves as the accomplished, fabulous superstars we are.

It's beyond self-deprecation; it's self-degradation. Yes, it's that deep. No, it's not okay.

Our internal dialog would make our enemies rejoice.

It's bad enough that some sorry souls take time out of their day to minimize us. Let's not join in and minimize ourselves. There should be no hateration in our personal dancerie. And any holleration should be of the celebratory variety. (Shout-out to our sis, iconic singer Mary J. Blige, who is all we need to get by.) We must embrace positive self-talk. We must big ourselves up. We must speak life over ourselves. How we talk to and about ourselves is a crucial element in the manifestation process. Because how can you manifest greater abundance or live the life you want if you don't even think you're worthy of it?

Oríkìs: One of the best ways of speaking positively about ourselves is via oríkìs. I was first introduced to this West African form of praise poetry by author Luvvie Ajayi Jones. She has been creating oríkìs online for years and wrote about them in her book *Professional Troublemaker*.

> What is an oríkì? It is a Yorùbá word that combines two words to mean "praising your head / mind." Orí is "head" and kì is "to greet or praise." An oríkì is a greeting that praises you through praising your kinship and speaking life to your destiny. It is your personal hype mantra.[2]

Oríkìs are traditionally chanted or sung to pay tribute to a person, family, or tribe, but for now, we'll focus on the personal. They are typically created when children are very young and are used throughout their lives to:

- Remind them of their lineage and heritage
- Express their parents' hopes for their future
- Connect them spiritually with their ancestors
- Celebrate life milestones and rites of passage
- Capture their personality and positive qualities
- Proclaim what they have achieved, or hope to achieve
- Encourage and uplift them when they need motivation or are experiencing self-doubt

Curate Your Thoughts: Manifest

I love all the oríkìs that Luvvie has writen. She has immortalized in verse greats such as Oprah, Toni Morrison, Issa Rae, my Bajan sis Rihanna, and my forever POTUS and FLOTUS Barack and Michelle Obama. However, although I'm a fan of the oríkìs she's created for others, one of my favorites is the one she wrote for herself:

Luvvie Ajayi of House Jones
First of Her Name
Assassin of the Alphabet
Bestseller of Books
Conqueror of Copy
Dame of Diction
Critic of Culture
Sorceress of Side-eyes
Eater of Jollof Rice
Rocker of Fierce Shoes
Queen of the Jones Kingdom
Taker of Stages
Nigerian Noble and Chitown Creator

I'm such a fan of oríkìs that when my sister launched her book *I'm Tired of Racism*, I included one as a part of her intro since she had asked me to emcee her launch event:

Sharon of House Hurley Hall
First of Her Name
Avatar of Anti-Racism
Viscountess of Vocabulary
Wrangler of the Written Word
Sorceress of Scrabble
Curator of Content
Teller of Truths
Maker of Good Trouble
Polymathic Prodigy
Wakandan World Traveler
Empress of Equality
Author with Authority
The Great Implementor

94   Love Yourself

I mean, who wouldn't want to be introduced, *Game of Thrones* style, with pomp and circumstance? With honor and respect? With accolades and acclaim? And isn't this more impactful than a regular list of accomplishments? Who wants a dry-biscuit intro when you could have a fully flavored buffet of amazingness? I like to think of oríkìs as introductions—but with more seasoning. Because as we know, Black people season everything.

While it's wonderful to have someone create an oríkì on your behalf, the great thing is you don't have to wait for that to happen. You can create your own. A few years ago, I delivered a playshop for a women's organization, and I included an oríkì creation exercise as one of the activities. Of course, I gave full credit to Luvvie, and to the ancestors, for having taught me about oríkìs. I asked the participants to write their oríkì as an affirmation, starting with the words "I am," as if they were introducing themselves. To give them an idea of what I wanted them to do, I created my own oríkì as an example:

I am Lisa, Jamaica-born, of House Hurley
First of My Name
Empress of Energy
Liege of Lexicons
Baroness of Breathwork
Slayer of Style
Barbadian Beach Lover
West Indian Writer
Vegan Viscountess
Avatar of Abundance
Peace-loving Phoenix
Alchemist of Affirmations
Goddess of Good Vibrations

I had the attendees write their oríkì in the first person because there is so much power in proclaiming your own magnificence. Why do you think Muhammad Ali's catchphrase was "I am the greatest?" It wasn't "I'm kind of okay." It wasn't "I guess I can hold my own." It was "I. Am. The. Greatest." Unabashedly definitive. He wanted to be legendary, so even before he became the greatest, he spoke as if it were already accomplished. And it came to pass.

So now it's your turn, sis. Write your own oríkì. If there was ever a time for superlatives, it's now. Let hyperbole abound. Show up. Show off. Show out. If after you've written it the critic in your head whispers, "Girl, who do you think you are?!" that means you did it right.

Flex. Glow. Twirl. Hype yourself up. Put some respek* on your own name. Shine on them so hard that they need sunglasses just to be in your presence.

Sing your own praises.

Salute your own spirit.

Speak life over yourself.

P.S. It's not bragging if it's factual.

Behave it Into Existence

Sometimes, you have to smile till you feel happy. Yes; it really works. According to Verywell Mind:

> "The physical act of smiling activates pathways in your brain that influence your emotional state—meaning that by adopting a happy facial expression, you can "trick" your mind into entering a state of happiness ... A simple smile can trigger the release of neuropeptides that improve your neural communication. It also causes the release of neurotransmitters such as dopamine and serotonin, which can boost your mood. Think of smiling as a natural antidepressant."[3]

In other words, there are times when you have to fake it till you make it. In manifestation work, "acting as if" can be a powerful catalyst for change. It's not a matter of denying reality, it's knowing that another, better reality is possible. It's finding a way to bring your desired future state into your present experience. It's putting out the energy that you want reflected back—matching energy with yourself. It's the concept behind the saying "Dress for the job you want, not for the job you have."

When I started thinking about writing a book, clearly I didn't have a book deal at the time—but I could envision a future where that would be possible. So, I acted as if it was already accomplished. If I had a book deal, I would obviously need to write a book, so I started writing. If I had a book

---

*"Respek" is the Bajan word for "respect."

96 Love Yourself

deal, I would need an author bio, so I wrote my bio for the back flap. If I had a book deal, I would need to create an online presence for it, so I bought my URL and started mentally wireframing my book website. I had the faith and I did the works. I took inspired action.

If you want a happier, more easeful life, what would you be doing right now if you already had it? What actions can you take today to behave your desires into existence?

The Manifestation Process

Now that we've covered the concepts, let's put them into practice. Here's an easy-to-follow process for manifesting your intentions.

Breathe: Focus on your breath. Slow down your breathing, making your inhales and exhales twice as long as usual. Get yourself into a serene state. This is important because if you do manifestation work when you are angry, upset, or dysregulated, the results might not be pleasant. You don't want any cosmic smoke. Use the breathwork exercise at the end of this chapter, or choose one of your favorites from throughout the book.

Meditate: Now that you're in a calm, meditative state, focus on your heart's desires. Ask yourself questions like "What do I really want?" "What would my 'dream life' look like?" and "What does a soft life mean to me?" Tune in to your thoughts to get the answers.

Ideate: When the initial answers come to you, go a bit deeper. Get out your journal and your favorite pen and write down what you would like to bring into your life. Don't edit yourself. Even if it seems crazy or out of reach, write it down. Actually, *especially* if it seems out of reach. Remember back when the phrase "delulu is the solulu" was trending on TikTok? We're bringing it back. Delusion is absolutely the solution. This is the time to dream big and ask audaciously. We are given our dreams and hearts' desires for a reason. Ask for more.

Create: Once you have identified your desires, state your intentions. Ask for what you want in the present tense. Place your order to the Universe. Writing (and then speaking) your affirmations in the present tense is vital, as it tells your subconscious that your desire is already manifest and

Curate Your Thoughts: Manifest 97

makes it easier for the Universe to bring your wishes to pass on the physical plane. Start your affirmations with "I am ..." or "I intend that I am ..." and fill in the blanks from there. So, rather than "I want a new job" (which creates the reality of wanting rather than having), write "I intend that I am loving my new job where I am happy, fulfilled, and paid what I'm worth." The latter approach is much more effective.

Identify Your Why: Once you have stated or written the first draft of your affirmations, ask yourself "Why?" Why do you want more money, why do you want a new home, why do you want that relationship, why do you want more space to exhale? How is this desired experience, item, or state of being going to improve your life? What problem will it solve for you? What will you do with your blessings once you receive them? Dig deeper. The answers could surprise you—and help you further refine your requests. Keep rewriting and refining your affirmations until they capture exactly what you desire.

Specify: Do you want to "work in construction" or to be an architect? Either is okay; just be clear. Are you in search of "a little more money" (which could result in you finding two pennies on a random sidewalk), or would you prefer to receive multimillions? Specificity is key. Once, a work buddy of mine was looking for another job and decided to use the law of attraction to help them do so. A few months into their search, they came to me, expressing frustration. They were getting lots of interviews, but every time they reached the final round, the job would fall through. I asked them to share their manifestation script with me, and as soon as I read it, I saw the problem: They had asked for lots of job opportunities, which is exactly what they were getting.

So I asked them, "Do you want opportunities, or a job? Do you want interviews, or employment? If you want a job, you need to ask for a job." Shortly after they made the switch in what they were requesting, they secured a full-time role with a great company. As with writing a book, the editing process is crucial when you're writing your affirmations. Revise them until they capture what you intend.

Give Yourself Permission: Sometimes our subconscious can work against us. Say for instance you create an affirmation that says, "I am a millionaire." Depending on where you are in life, your mind might be looking at you with full zero-balance energy like, "Girl, no you are NOT." Or you

98   Love Yourself

might be knee deep in depression, repeating an affirmation that says, "I am happy." In both instances, it might be too much of a leap for your subconscious to accept. In cases like that, use the permission workaround. Try phrasing your affirmation as follows: "I am giving myself permission to be a millionaire." or "I am giving myself permission to feel happy." Those are statements that your subconscious can easily accept.

Watch Your Thoughts: I've mentioned this before, but it bears repeating: Your subconscious thoughts matter. In *Eat Pray Love* by Elizabeth Gilbert, her love interest Richard kept asking God to open his heart … and he ended up having open heart surgery.

Several jobs ago, I was feeling quite worn out. It had been a season of months of intense focus and extremely long hours. I was completely frazzled. I realized that I needed a break. Instead of taking time off (I didn't have any PTO left), I just kept thinking over and over, "I really need a break. I really need a break. I really need a break." Well, I got exactly what I (unconsciously) asked for. I got a break. I ended up losing my job and did not get another one for several months. So I was rested—but unemployed.

Take Inspired Action: Once you get the guidances and experience the synchronicities, act on them. Make that call. Apply to that job. Go to that new café. Drive down that street you've never traveled on before. You never know what beautiful miracle is waiting to greet you. In my case, when I prayed for help with publishing my book, The Book Academy appeared, and I moved on the opportunity immediately. Don't let inertia keep you from achieving your dreams. As they say in the church, "Don't block your blessings."

Also remember to "act as if." One of the first things I do when I'm starting an abundance meditation is go and spend some money. It doesn't have to be on anything expensive—I'm not suggesting that you purchase a Mercedes when your bills aren't paid—just buy a small treat like a latte or a lip gloss to signal to the Universe that you are already financially abundant. You already have purchasing power. You're just asking for more of what you already have.

Protect the Energy: Move in silence. Let the vibes incubate in peace. Be very careful about who you share your hopes and dreams with. Everybody doesn't have your best interests at heart. Everybody doesn't have to know what you're working on.

Curate Your Thoughts: Manifest 99

You don't plant a seed and then dig it up daily to see if it's growing. You don't expose the little baby roots to the sun. In fact, that's a great way to guarantee that what you've planted will never flourish. Similarly, you shouldn't publicize your goals and ideas before the time is right. Keep them to yourself, or share them with a tiny circle of people who have proven that they are deserving of your trust. Give the energy space to flow uninterrupted.

Give Thanks: Gratitude is one of the most vital elements. Give thanks for what you already have. Give thanks in advance for what you desire to have. Give thanks when your prayers are answered. Appreciation always reaps rewards and puts you on the path to even more abundant blessings. Having a consistent gratitude practice puts you in Divine Flow. This is one of the reasons why I included an "Appreciation" section in every chapter.

Be Open: Be willing to receive your blessing exactly as it appears. Detach from the outcome.

Make Space for Miracles: Request "this, or better." Ask for "this, or more." I also make sure to request that everything I am asking for is for everyone's highest good. I tack on "with good to all and harm to none, under grace and in perfect ways and timing" to the end of many of my affirmations. Leave room for God / the Universe to bless you above and beyond what you have asked for.

Elevation: Vibrate Higher

Exhalation: Breathe Easy

5-5-5 Breath

For this breathing exercise, you'll be inhaling through your nose and exhaling through your mouth. You're going to inhale slowly for a count of five, hold for a count of five, and exhale slowly for a count of five. While you're holding your breath, smile gently and think of someone or something you're grateful for. Close your eyes, and let's begin:

(continued)

100 Love Yourself

(*continued*)

    Inhale: 1, 2, 3, 4, 5

    Hold, feeling gratitude: 1 2, 3, 4, 5

    Exhale: 1, 2, 3, 4, 5

    Inhale: 1, 2, 3, 4, 5

    Hold, feeling gratitude: 1 2, 3, 4, 5

    Exhale: 1, 2, 3, 4, 5

    Inhale: 1, 2, 3, 4, 5

    Hold, feeling gratitude: 1 2, 3, 4, 5

    Exhale: 1, 2, 3, 4, 5

Continue for as long as you're comfortable. When you're ready, return your breathing to its normal cadence, and open your eyes.

Affirmations: Speak Life

- Everywhere I go I prosper, and everything I do succeeds.
- I have more than enough money and resources to live well.
- I am giving myself permission to have all my dreams come true.
- I am giving myself permission to live a soft, centered, serene life.
- I am a magnet for Divine prosperity: I am easily attracting everything I need.

Introspection: Journal & Heal

- What does abundance mean to you?
- How can you take inspired action toward achieving your goals?
- What material or non-material blessings would you like to experience?
- What can you let go of in order to make room for what you would like to attract? Make a list.
- Think of an area in your life where you are struggling. What does taking the path of least resistance mean to you? What would represent a miraculous solution?

(*continued*)

(continued)

Curation: Do the Work

How would having more space to exhale manifest itself in your life? In your relationships? In your home? In your career? Create a few affirmations to express your goals.

Appreciation: Express Gratitude

What are you grateful for? Count your blessings:

- I am grateful …
- I am grateful …
- I am grateful …

Celebration: Razzle Dazzle

Flex on 'em, sis! What are you proud of? Celebrate yourself:

- I am proud of myself for …
- I am proud of myself for …
- I am proud of myself for …

Meditation: Think Blissfully

Before we begin, let's talk about chakras since they are mentioned throughout this meditation. "Chakra" is a Sanskrit word, pronounced with a hard "ch," which loosely translates to wheel. It refers to energy centers or vortices located at various points on the body along the spinal column. Each energy center corresponds to specific colors, meanings, mantras, and even musical notes. You can refer to Figure 1 for a full explanation. Since the concept of energy centers on the human body is not unique to South Asian yogic practices, I have included the African names for the energy centers as well.

(continued)

102 — Love Yourself

(*continued*)

CHAKRA	SANSKRIT NAME	AFRICAN NAME	LOCATION	MEANING	COLOR	MANTRA	MUSICAL NOTE	AFFIRMATION	SYMBOL
Crown/7th	Sahasrara	Ori	Above the middle of the head	Enlightenment	Violet	Ah	B	I am	
Third Eye/6th	Ajna	Orunmila	Middle of the forehead	Intuition & wisdom	Indigo	Om	A	I am wise	
Throat/5th	Vishuddha	Obatala	Middle of the throat	Self-expression	Blue	Ham	G	I am speaking my truth	
Heart/4th	Anahata	Oshun	Middle of the chest	Love	Green	Yam	F	I am love	
Solar Plexus/3rd	Manipura	Oggun	Solar plexus	Courage	Yellow	Ram	E	I am brave	
Sacral/2nd	Svadhishthana	Yemaya	Sacrum/pelvis	Creativity	Orange	Vam	D	I am creative	
Root/1st	Muladhara	Shango	Base of the spine	Survival	Red	Lam	C	I am safe	

Figure 1 Chakras and Their Meanings

(continued)

And now, let's begin:

Close your eyes and settle yourself into a comfortable position. Take a relaxing breath in through your nose, then breathe out through your mouth. Deep breath in, then out. And one more deep breath in, then out. Gradually slow down the speed of your breathing.

Inhale: 1, 2, 3; exhale: 1, 2, 3, 4, 5, 6

Inhale: 1, 2, 3; exhale: 1, 2, 3, 4, 5, 6

Inhale: 1, 2, 3; exhale: 1, 2, 3, 4, 5, 6

And one more time inhale slowly for 1, 2, 3 ... then a deep exhale: 1, 2, 3, 4, 5, 6

Focus your attention on your root chakra at the very base of your spine. Now inhale deeply, directing love and light toward this energy center, bringing it into perfect balance. With the power of your intention, infuse your root chakra with a radiant red light. Exhale, and release all worry about survival. Repeat silently:

I am safe, secure, and fully provided for.

I am safe, secure, and fully provided for.

I am safe, secure, and fully provided for.

And so it is.

Now bring your attention to your sacral chakra in the lower part of your pelvis. Inhale deeply, directing love and light there, bringing this chakra into perfect balance. With the power of your intention, infuse your sacral chakra with a warm orange light. Exhale, and release all limits to your creativity. Repeat silently:

I am easily expressing my unique creative genius.

I am easily expressing my unique creative genius.

I am easily expressing my unique creative genius.

(continued)

104 Love Yourself

(*continued*)

And so it is.

Next, focus on your solar plexus chakra, a few inches above your belly button. Inhale deeply, directing love and light toward it, bringing the energy center into perfect balance. With the power of your intention, infuse your solar plexus chakra with a glowing yellow light. Exhale, and release all worry about success. Inhale, and make the yellow light of your solar plexus chakra as bright as the sun. Exhale, and release all fear of failure. Repeat silently:

I am already successful.

I am already successful.

I am already successful.

And so it is.

Now move your attention up to your heart chakra, in the center of your chest. Inhale deeply, directing love and light toward your heart, bringing it into perfect balance. With the power of your intention, infuse your heart chakra with a healing green light. Exhale, and release all fear of being unloved. Repeat silently:

I am love and I am loved.

I am love and I am loved.

I am love and I am loved.

And so it is.

And now, bring your attention to your throat chakra. Inhale deeply, directing love and light toward it, bringing it into perfect balance. With the power of your intention, infuse your throat chakra with a soothing blue light. Exhale, and release all fear of expressing yourself. Repeat silently:

(*continued*)

(continued)

I am powerfully expressing my authentic self.

I am powerfully expressing my authentic self.

I am powerfully expressing my authentic self.

And so it is.

Next, focus your thoughts on your third eye chakra in the middle of your forehead, at the midpoint between your eyes. Breathe in deeply, directing love and light toward this energy center, bringing it into perfect balance. With the power of your intention, infuse your third eye chakra with a beautiful indigo light. Exhale, and release all fear of the unknown. Everything you desire to know is revealed to you. Repeat silently:

I am wise.

I am wise.

I am wise.

And so it is.

And now we're at the crown chakra. Move your attention up to a point a few inches above your head. Breathe in deeply, directing love and light there, bringing your crown chakra into perfect balance. With the power of your intention, infuse the chakra with a magical violet light. Exhale, and release any disconnection from your higher self. Inhale and make the violet light of your crown chakra brighter and brighter. Exhale and release all fear of shining bright. Know that you are more powerful than you could ever imagine. Know that the world needs your light. Repeat silently:

I am light.

I am light.

I am light.

(continued)

(continued)

And so it is.

Finally, imagine that you are a beautiful star in the sky, and with every inhale, you glow brighter and brighter, a breathtaking combination of all the colors of all your chakras.

Inhale, and feel your entire body flooding with light. This light is who you really are.

Exhale, feeling blissful, bright, and beautiful.

Inhale, filling your body and aura with light. Know that your glow makes the world a better place. Feel the beauty of Divine alignment. Exhale, and feel your unity with the other stars in the sky.

Inhale, filling your being with even more light; so much light that it cannot be contained. Exhale, happy in the knowledge that your unique light is shining brightly for everyone to see. You know exactly who you are Divinely destined to be. You know that you have all you need. You know that there are no barriers before you. Repeat silently:

I am everything.

I am everything.

I am everything.

Take a couple of minutes to absorb the energy, and when you are ready, open your eyes.

Asé.

5

Curate Your Circle: Connect

Invocation

Most High,

Grant us all good company as we travel through life. Grant us discernment as we select those with whom we navigate this journey. As we choose wisely, may we likewise be chosen by those with good hearts, good minds, and good intentions, who love us in ways we appreciate and understand.

May we also remember to choose ourselves.

Please place your protective mantle around us. May our friendships *feel* safe and *be* safe. May they be healing and not hurtful. May they be reciprocal and not transactional.

May there always be divine alignment. May there always be mutual respect. May there always be authenticity.

May You always be present.

Love Yourself

Please fill our shared moments with joy, and fun, and celebrations. With love, and light, and laughter. With harmless mischief, captionless memes, and wordless glances. With long talks, un-posted activities, inside jokes, and comfortable silences.

Active support. Staunch loyalty. Gracious giving. Grateful receiving. May all this and more form the bedrock of our connection.

Please grant us spiritual kin: Soul-deep connections that serve our highest good. Grant us friends who understand that "gurl" is an entire conversation and that love is a verb. Bless us with folk who ride as hard for us as we do for them.

Surround us with people who, when necessary, defend us loudly in public, but correct us gently in private. Who don't require that we dim our light so theirs can shine. Who love us wholly, though parts of us are broken.

May we be connected with folks who love us whether we live humbly or extravagantly; whether we ride on a bike or in a limo. May we have some ground floor friends to travel up to the penthouse with.

May our friendships be equally yoked.

May there be love, forgiveness, and upliftment.
May there be care, comfort, and commiseration.
May there be good vibrations, fun vacations, and shared libations.

May we receive and give wise counsel. May we transform each other in beautiful ways. May everyone in our personal village speak our love languages and may we speak theirs.

May there be joy.
May there be ease.
May there be peace.

May we have true friends, and may we be a true friend. May our friendships help us rise, and also be a soft place to fall. May our chosen family enthusiastically choose us back.

May our friendships be close yet give us room to breathe.

Curate Your Circle: Connect 109

May we belong.
May we belong.
May we belong.

Amen.

~ ~ ~

Best Friends Forever

"Hey Annie, I have to come to ATL for a few months, and I need someplace to live. Can I stay with you?"

The fact that I felt safe enough to even ask that says a lot. The fact that she responded with an immediate and enthusiastic "Yes!" says even more. To be honest, as soon as I realized I would need a temporary home in Hotlanta, she was the first person that came to mind. We're besties now, so clearly it went amazing.

What made it work? We had a foundation of friendship because we had gone to AIU university together. We had a few classes in common but fully "saw" each other in one of our final exams. The exam took the form of a *Jeopardy*-style competition, and we were on opposing teams. We competed hard, hitting the buzzer and shouting out the answers even before the professor could finish asking the questions. So much fun. I think she was surprised that "the quiet one" had a fierce competitive spirit, a ridiculously loud laugh, and a Bajan accent. I don't even remember which team won—it was probably hers—but we had an absolute blast.

We recognized each other as kindred spirits. There was lots of mutual affection—but there was also mutual respect. In addition, we were both "nontraditional" students: We were the two oldest people in the class. She's a quiet extrovert and I'm a loud introvert, so we complemented each other. There were lots of shared shenanigans; there was fun and laughter galore, but as the Khalil Gibran poem goes, there were spaces in our togetherness. We respected and honored each other's boundaries.

It probably also worked because we're both originally from the Caribbean, so we did our island gyal ting. The rice and peas of it all. The pudding

110 Love Yourself

and souse. The curry and roti. The lime and salt. The patois and dialek.*
Cultural similarities helped. There may or may not have been the occasional wuk up ** session in the sunroom.

Y'all, she made me feel completely at home. Completely. I had my own
bedroom and bathroom and the full run of the house. I never felt as though
I had to hide in a corner and make myself small because she said, "Mi casa
es su casa" and meant it. On my first full day there she handed me the keys
to her car and said, "C'mon, roomie! You're driving." (Internally I was like
"Wait ... I get to use the car too??!!") "You sure?" I asked, already grinning
and walking over to the driver's side. I dropped her off at work, went on
about my business, and that was that. Though she did not ask, and I did not
have much, I paid what I could toward her rent and contributed to the
groceries and other household expenses.

And we just lived good.

We both cooked. We both cleaned. We both drove. We did our supermarket runs together. There was no tallying of who did what and when and
how. There was no fighting over the remote. There was no labeling of items in
the fridge because we both had common sense, common courtesy, and good
West Indian broughtupsy.*** Basic manners and considerateness count for a lot.

She forgave me for using regular detergent in the dishwasher that one
time. One minute I was doing chores, the next I was knee-deep in suds and
bubbles. (Having not grown up using a dishwasher and therefore always
been a handwash queen when it came to dishes, I thought soap was soap, lol.
Lesson learned.) We ended up having a good laugh about it while we waited
for the suds to die down.

Fast forward to now, and we're still good.

We don't talk every day. Sometimes not even every week. But we are
100 percent there for each other.

---

*Dialek is a creolized form of the word "dialect." Caribbean dialects were formed when
people from Africa were enslaved, brought to the West Indies, and forced to speak the language of the colonizers. In the case of Barbados (where I'm from) and St. Kitts (where Annie
is from), the colonial power was Great Britain. The dialects of our islands are therefore
hybrids of various African languages and British English.

**Wukking up is a dance unique to Barbados that features hip isolations and a rhythmic
gyration of the lower half of the body. It is African in origin. It is not the same as twerking.

*** "Broughtupsy" is a West Indian word that means "upbringing." If you were "brought up"
rather than "dragged up," you have broughtupsy.

Curate Your Circle: Connect

Once, when she knew I needed some company, she flew up to NYC to spend a few days with me. Another time, she came up to celebrate my birthday. Both times, we had almost too much fun. It was constant laughter from start to finish. When she broke one of her fingers in a random rock-climbing accident, I flew down to A-town to be there for her on surgery day and stayed to help her out for a few days after. Despite the circumstances, we still had a ball. Somehow, no matter the occasion, we make it fun. And when she was celebrating a milestone birthday, of course I was there for the party and the after-party. Shoot … for the pre-party too!

We honor each other with the gift of presence. We very literally show up for each other.

We've done each other's makeup, worn each other's clothes, seen each other at our best and worst. Told each other "Girl!! Why did you think that was a good idea?!" Celebrated each other's wins. Mourned each other's losses. Kept each other's secrets. Encouraged each other to evolve. Counseled each other through life and career transitions. Asked each other the hard questions—with love. We've both listened on the other end of the phone while the other one bawled incoherently or screamed excitedly. We've exchanged presents, though never at Christmas. It's more of a random "Oooh, I know she'll love this" kind of vibe. If I need money and she has it, it's mine—and vice versa. We share the shekels. There is no ledger of loans, there are only full-hearted gifts.

When I think of new friends to add to my circle, Annie is the template. Most of them don't make it y'all, 'cause people are trifling.

She is a person of good character who oozes integrity. She is kind, loyal, smart, and dependable. Equal parts hilarious and serious, Annie says what she means and means what she says. Like me, she takes no nonsense and has a generous spirit. She's a true gem.

After every conversation we have, I feel better and happier. Hopefully, she does too.

She is someone I can truly relax around. Because of how she shows up, she makes it safe for me to exhale.

When you're thinking of choosing friends—close friends—this is the kind of person you want to have around you. All sun, no shade.

Everybody needs an Annie in their life.

What Makes a Good Friendship?

We tend to prioritize romantic relationships over platonic ones, but our friendships are just as important as our intimate partnerships. It's great to be boo'd up, but it's just as important to be crewed up.

Stop right now and think: Who is in your sister circle? Who are your bros? Who are the people that you know want you to win—and will help you do it? Who are the women that bun fiyah pun mean-queen energy and instead embrace sisterhood, collaboration, and mutual support? Who are the people who make you feel truly included? Who are the folks you can dance, and laugh, and be silly with? In other words: Who are the souls around whom you feel safe enough to exist unmasked?

As you live your life, the people with whom you spend the most time will have a big impact—positive or negative. So choose wisely. Surround yourself with the *right* kind of people.

Your close circle could include members of your immediate family, buddies from school or university, and colleagues-turned-friends, but whoever they are, they should enhance your life rather than detract from it. You should feel better and *be* better by dint of having them in your life.

Friendship should not feel like a struggle. There should be peace, harmony, and energetic concordance. Friendship should flow.

Curating your circle is one of the most important things you can do to manifest a happier life. But how do you determine who belongs in your sanctum sanctorum? How do you divine who will be there for you versus who will betray or abandon you?

We need to start doing friend assessments rather than keeping or letting people in our lives simply because of history or proximity.

On the journey to curating your circle, it can be helpful to know what friendship red flags and green flags to look for. Let's start with the red flags, or the kinds of people to avoid.

Who to Release

Frenemies

Like love, friendship isn't supposed to hurt. Unfortunately, frenemies didn't get the memo.

Curate Your Circle: Connect

What is a frenemy? Frenemy is a portmanteau of "friend" and "enemy," so that tells you most of what you need to know. You probably have a couple of them in your circle without even realizing it. These are the people who (bizarrely) hate you so much that they want to be around you. Super weird. Of course, their intentions are nefarious. The best way to figure out if you have a frenemy in your midst is to tune in to how you feel when you engage with them. If you frequently feel drained, anxious, or hurt after interacting with them, they just might be a frenemy.

The vibes never lie.

The reason that you feel "off" or dysregulated around frenemies is they do not wish you well. They want proximity to your light while simultaneously resenting you for shining. Truth is, they want to snuff your light out. Sometimes, it can be difficult to decipher because if you're not that kind of person, your brain doesn't even work that way. (Raises hand.) Not sure if it's a Scorpio thing, but if I don't like somebody, I don't want to be around them. At all. Because logic.

However, I've discovered to my detriment that everybody does not approach things in that way.

Frenemy relationships often start out seemingly positive. Usually, they approach you, rather than the other way around. It's only later that you realize that you were essentially being groomed and love bombed. They put on a mask so you will let them into your life and start opening up to them. Once they're in, the shady shenanigans begin.

Here's how to tell when you have a frenemy:

They Don't Celebrate Your Wins: Once, I had successfully delivered a major presentation at work and was floating on that post-accomplishment high. I swung by one of my close friends to tell her how everything had gone, and to celebrate with someone I thought would be happy for me. Y'all already know: She wasn't. I had barely gotten a word out when she started talking over me loudly, taking time to mention that what I had achieved wasn't really a big deal. I sat and listened to her for a few minutes and then quietly left, feeling deflated.

These conversational kleptomaniacs are not the kinds of people you want in your life. We all need cheerleaders, and we all need to cheerlead. With good friends, cheerleading duties should alternate: Sometimes you're

114 Love Yourself

the celebrity sometimes you're the paparazzi. The sun shines for us all—but the light might hit us at different times. And that is as it should be.

We must be okay not only with letting folks have their moment but also with being enthusiastic about it. We must be happy to gas our people up, cheer them on, be their hype squad. When the occasion calls for it, we should act like a rich but slightly ratchet auntie at their niece's or nephew's graduation: Proud and boisterous. And of course, when it's our moment, we should receive the same.

If the people in your circle can't be genuinely happy for you, run.

They Try to One-Up You: Frenemies can't celebrate your wins because they are caught up in a one-sided, subliminally expressed rivalry with you. They live in a stringently hierarchical universe in which there can only ever be one "winner." How can you tell? They try to one-up you every chance they get.

Comparison is the thief of joy, and they have been robbed of all of theirs. From this sunken place of misery and low self-esteem they interact with you. Their goal is to aggrandize themselves and diminish you. It's the only way they can think of to make themselves feel good. These are the kinds of folk who would show up fully bedecked in a *Say Yes to the Dress*-level white gown on someone else's wedding day.

For frenemies, every conversation is a competition. Every talk is a tournament. If you say you have an apple tree, they will immediately start telling you about their orchard. You rented an apartment? They just closed on their house. You started working out and walked a mile? They completed a marathon. You're going on a cruise? They only take private jets. Weirdly, some folks do this even with negative news: You caught a cold? They contracted pneumonia. You get the idea.[†]

If by any chance one-upmanship doesn't work to silence you, frenemies will often move on to outright insults.

[†]Note: This is not the same as when people (neurospicy fam, raise your hands) share similar experiences in order to build a connection with someone. That energy is different. There, the intention is positive. The tone is empathetic. In those situations, the goal is to let someone know that you get them; to reassure them that they're not alone. If I'm going through something and someone shares their experience with me, I feel grateful, seen, and understood.

They Minimize and Insult: "With your natural hair you look so cute!" I started to smile, and then the next thing I heard was "Kind of like a troll." (Insert record scratch.) These were the words that a "friend" of mine said to me one day after I had taken my braids out and was rocking my fabulous 'fro.

"A troll???" I asked, head tilted, squinting in confusion. "You mean like under a bridge??? Like a monster???"

I gave them grace, because they tried to fix it: "Well a really, really cute troll. The cutest one."

I've been negged several times, but I must say that was the best (or worst?) occasion. Who in their right mind includes the word *troll* as part of a so-called compliment?

People who act—or rather, attack—in this manner are insecure. They are seeking a level of status that they perceive themselves to lack. They want to feel superior and believe that their only path to doing so is to make someone else feel inferior. So sad. They also believe that reducing your level of self esteem will make you easier to manipulate and control.

(In the manosphere, this looks like mediocre members of the patriarchy insulting a woman with whom they never had a chance anyway. But I digress.)

If minimizers can't one-up you, they'll approach it from the other direction and try to take you down a peg or two. They put effort into diminishing your achievements. It's as if they interpret any success you have as a personal attack on them. Whenever you share a win, an accomplishment, or anything you're happy about, they either perceive it as bragging on your part, or it triggers something in them that believes that there is not enough success to go around. They then go into passive-aggressive attack mode. A clear sign is anytime your frenemy uses the word "little" to describe something that is important to you:

- How's it going with your little podcast?
- How's your little business doing?
- How was your little trip?

116   Love Yourself

Because frenemies want to strip away your sense of self-worth, they are often mean. They are generous with verbal barbs and backhanded compliments like these:

- "You look great … for your age."
- "What a gorgeous photo. Is that really you?"
- "Have you lost weight? You look amazing now."
- "I love your new haircut! It makes your forehead look a lot smaller."
- "Wow, your new home is so cute! I could never survive in such a tiny space."

As with so many things in life, Black women experience this kind of treatment more than most. Having misogynoir and anti-Blackness in the mix adds another layer of disrespect. Many of us are subjected to microaggressive moments such as these:

- "You're pretty … for a Black girl."
- "Your hair looks nice. Is it a weave?"
- "You look so much better now your hair is straight."
- "You have gorgeous skin. What are you mixed with?"
- "You're so articulate. Where did you learn to speak English?"

It's like we can't just be Black and beautiful and erudite and eloquent and amazing.

But anyhoo.

If you object to their insults-disguised-as-jokes or call them out on their haterish comments, they go into full-fledged attack mode. They deflect, redirect, and DARVO: Deny, Attack, Reverse Victim and Offender.

Be prepared for pushback and gaslighting: Very "I'm upset that you're upset that I upset you." They'll respond to you with phrases like:

- "Can't you take a joke?"
- "You're being way too sensitive."
- "It's not that deep. You're being dramatic."
- "I don't let things like that bother me. You're overreacting."
- "Why are you always so emotional? You should be more rational like me."

Curate Your Circle: Connect   117

Bonus points for the classic faux-pology: "I'm sorry you feel that way."

They're Angry and Argumentative: Like a broken toaster, frenemigos tend to have one setting: White-hot anger. In this relationship you are the slice of toast, and they want to burn you to a crisp. Almost everything and everyone annoys them. They pick fights and argue for the sake of it—frequently to a scorched-earth level. These are the kinds of people who when you do some digging you realize they have no close friends. Like … none. Because they're even mad at the folks who tried to befriend them.

Since frenemies love to argue, they spend a lot of time strategizing how to win arguments. Their goal is to verbally or emotionally annihilate you. They will stonewall, lie, manipulate, gaslight and do whatever it takes to make themselves feel like they have "won."

They debate simply because they have a mouth. Just full of chatter and bad intentions. I'm all for healthy debate, but I don't want to spend all my time arguing back and forth over inconsequential matters. Sometimes I just want to relax. If there's too much "Just to play devil's advocate" energy, I'm out. Plus, why are you advocating for the devil anyway? Satan does not need any sponsors.

They're Jealous of You: Frenemies want your life, or what they perceive to be your life. They are guided by a scarcity mindset, believing that there is not enough good to go around. They want your shine, your glow, your magic. They want people to respond to them the way folks respond to you, and in their warped minds, the easiest way to achieve that is by claiming proximity to you, or even taking what's yours. They also think that you are not deserving of your blessings—innate or acquired—and that everything you have should rightfully be theirs.

In terms of categories of people to avoid, if all you do is stay clear of frenemies, you're already ahead. The curation process is twofold. The first part is about who or what to remove. Clearly, with frenemies the recommendation is to cut them off. However, if you think the relationship can be salvaged, remember that verbal apologies are nice, but the only true apology is changed behavior. Listen to what people say, but pay even closer attention to what they do. If you decide to keep the transgressors in your life, as an act of self-love you must require changed behavior that is consistent over time.

118   Love Yourself

In addition to frenemies, there are some other categories of folks from whom you need to keep your distance.

Next up, meet the Extractivists.

Extractivists

One thing about takers: They're always going to take. Energy vampires and emotional leeches want everything from you: Your time, your attention, your money, your light, your connections, your joy. They will try to vacuum the entire life force out of you. They want to siphon your soul. Extractivists are like parasites, and their goal is to use you as a host. These are the kinds of people who only call you when they want something.

I am a natural giver who hesitates to take, and it was years before I realized that so many people are the exact opposite. My mom, no doubt fearing that her big-hearted baby daughter would be eaten up by the world, has often told me, "Lis, I love how generous you are, but you don't have to give away the entire farm. It's okay to keep some things for yourself."

The last time she warned me about this was when I let a (former) acquaintance stay in my house rent-free since they were in a jam. They had been evicted from their previous place and needed somewhere to move into ASAP on a temporary basis for a couple of weeks. (A note: Do your research on people. There was a good reason why that eviction notice had been served.)

Next thing I know, their partner had all but moved in as well (I know, I know.) I couldn't sleep at night because they were extremely ... active; I was scratching around for food in my own fridge—it was *gone* gone; this was the original "no crumbs left"; and every day, more and more of their stuff appeared. It felt like I was being starved, suffocated, and squeezed out of my own home. They even took over the extra bedroom that I had designated for my office. I came home from work one day, and the room was completely rearranged and full of their stuff. One thing they did not hesitate to do was take up *all* the space. They had audacity a-plenty but no manners or considerateness.

The last straw was when I went to my mailbox one day and, lo and behold, there was a stack of mail—for them. They knew they had it good and had clearly made plans to ride the freebie train till the wheels fell off.

One thing about me is I might let a situation slide for a while, but once light dawns and I decide I'm done, then I'm done. Instantly and in perpetuity.

I got them and their stuff out of my house in less than 24 hours, changed the locks, and smudged the entire place with sage. Good riddance.

Now there are multiple angles to most situations, and I'm sure my therapist has big thoughts as to why I got myself into that pickle in the first place. That's another tale for another book. But although the details might differ, I'm sure many of you have gotten yourselves into a similar bind even though you had the best of intentions.

Problems Architects

You know Solutions Architects? Their job is literally to evaluate a corporation's business issues and design technical solutions for them. They are professional problem solvers. Well in friendship terms, Problems Architects are the exact opposite. These chaos mongers **live** to find a problem for every solution. And if there's no problem, they are happy to create one. You have a new idea for a business? Here they come with 10 reasons why it will never work. They pick at it like a sparrow-bird on a ripe mango, extracting all the goodness and all your joy, till there's nothing left but pockmarks and regret. Regret that you ever shared your idea with them. Bonus points if a few months later, they come out with a version of your concept—the same one they repeatedly told you was not strategically sound.

A subset of these are the people who only want to discuss problems (always theirs; never yours) or who spend too much time complaining. Just drowning in eternal pessimism. I love a good venting sesh as much as the next person, but there's a limit. Balance is necessary. There must be something to celebrate and be grateful for. There must be positive conversations. If your convos with these folks are only ever about all the bad experiences and people in their life, then cut your losses and run. I have definitely ended friendships with people who only ever had critical commentary about everybody else. Who has time to swim in an ocean of negativity?

Surround yourself with people who can acknowledge when there's a problem—and also seek a solution.

Flakers

As an introvert there's a big part of me that loves canceled plans. I love my house. I love my space. I love inside. I love doing "nothing" as an activity. When people say "Go big or go home," there's a 100 percent likelihood that I'm going home. Let me snuggle on my couch in peace.

120   Love Yourself

That said, because of how I was raised, if I commit to something, I tend to follow through. If I don't, it's because I truly cannot. Sometimes life is life-ing and we have no choice but to adjust.

With all those disclaimers in place: I am not a fan of flakery, aka habitual and repeated cancellations. We all have to reschedule from time to time, but if we're friends and you cancel 99 percent of the time that we're supposed to get together, then on my end Imma just stop making plans with you. I'm not spending time and energy to get ready and put on makeup only for you to flake out at the last minute. Again. My Fenty costs good money; I can't be wasting it on non-events.

If you consistently disrespect my time by showing up late, that's also a no for me. I'm not talking about the globally accepted 15-minute grace period; sometimes slight lateness is unavoidable. I'm talking about egregious levels of lateness: Folks who repeatedly show up hours late. It truly grinds my gears. I once had a friend who did this frequently. The last time it happened, they once again showed up more than an hour late and called me to come downstairs.

They are still waiting for me to respond.

I looked down at the phone, smiled, and went back to watching my show on Netflix. (Like I said before, I'm still a work in progress, y'all. God ain't done with me yet.)

Similarly, if the relationship is one-sided, i.e., I habitually show up for you, but when I need you, you're a ghost, that's also a heck no. There must be reciprocity and positive consistency.

Boundary Breakers

I'll never forget the neighbor who, the first time I showed her around my house, cannonballed onto my bed. Like literally took a flying leap from the doorway and landed on my brand new comforter. With her shoes on. Eww and double-eww. I was living in the sticks in Pennsylvania, and there weren't a lot of people around who looked like me. I wondered if this was some kind of cultural norm that I had somehow never been made aware of. Strange times. Anyway, suffice it to say she was never invited back.

I just believe in respecting people's space.

As a Black woman, a broken boundary I have had to deal with repeatedly is the hair touching violation. First of all, touching somebody's hair or any

Curate Your Circle: Connect

other part of their anatomy without permission is assault. So now that we've established that, please for the love of all that is holy stop randomly touching Black people's hair. I am not sure how you make it acceptable in your mind to violate a stranger's personal space like that. It is not okay. Please stop it.

I remember standing on a platform once, minding my business and waiting for my train, when I felt the heat of someone's beady eyes drilling into me. Somebody's grandma was staring in glassy-eyed fascination at my 'fro. Next thing I know, she vigorously stretched her hands out toward me to try to put them in my hair. No "Hello." No "How are you." No acknowledgement that I am a human being. I somehow managed to do a *Matrix*-like backbend and elude her grubby grasp. Interestingly, she appeared very annoyed that I had prevented her from putting her paws on me. Apparently, I was supposed to just stand there and let her examine me like an exhibit in a zoo.

On behalf of me and all Black people everywhere: Don't. Touch. Our. Hair.

It must be said: You do have to check in with yourself to make sure you are communicating your boundaries clearly and enforcing them consistently. Blurry boundaries are problematic. You cannot expect people to honor your boundaries if you do not honor them yourself.

Who to Keep

The second part of the curation process is who to keep around. So now that we've covered what to avoid in a friendship, back to the original question: What Makes a Good Friendship? Who should be part of our circle? How do we assess that? Here are some green flags to bear in mind.

Keep around you:

Friends Who Are Likeable

This might seem obvious, but choose people who you actually like! No mean-girls energy allowed. No gossipy weirdness. Many of us drift into community with people without giving it any real thought, and then wonder why our friendships are just "meh." Being friends with people *solely* because of proximity is a setup.

122 Love Yourself

Select folks who make you feel genuinely happy and who have an optimistic outlook on life. Choose people who treat others well, regardless of what they perceive the other person's "station" in life to be. You're going to be spending a lot of time with your friends, so you should enjoy their company. Choose fun, positive people who radiate good vibes.

Friends Who Are Present

A good friend should be there for you. They need to show up for you in good times and bad. The friend who blesses you with the gift of presence is there whether you just want to shoot the breeze or if you have "big stuff" going on: Birthdays, weddings, funerals, surgeries, and graduations. A big part of any good friendship is listening to each other recount your highs and lows. Keep people around you who are willing to be fully present when you need them to. Phones down; ears and heart open.

As we grow older and there are more competing priorities, the ability to be there in person might change, but there should be some form of contact, even if only a text. Something that says: I see you. I'm there with you. You matter to me.

I have some "daily / weekly" friends and some "annual / occasional" friends, but between us, we know that if "the call" goes out, we will 100 percent be there. One Christmas, when my long-time friend Alison and I ended up being in Barbados at the same time, we immediately made arrangements to get together. It wasn't a question of *if*, it was a matter of *when*. Same with my friends Rachael and Stephanie, and, when she was still with us, my guardian angel Bonita (may she rest in peace). We live thousands of miles apart, but once we are in the same place, we do everything we can to see each other. When Annie's mom passed, I flew to Atlanta to spend some time with her. She has done similar for me. It's called the Ministry of Presence.

Friends must show up.

Friends Who Are Confident

People who are self-confident tend to be comfortable with other people shining. They are too happy with who they are to have time to hate on anyone else. They are just as happy when the spotlight falls on you as when it shines on them. I recently learned of a German-inspired word called freudenfreude. (No, it's not a real German word[1], but I love the concept behind it.) Freudenfreude is the opposite of schadenfreude. It refers to the ability to take delight in other people's successes: Our friends' joy becomes ours. Over the course of a friendship, people will take turns being the lead singer and the backups. Make sure the folks in your close circle are happy in both roles. Choose friends who are good are good with both your supporting cast vibes *and* your main-character energy.

Friends Who Are Trustworthy

"Word is bond" is an expression I grew up hearing. It means that if you say something, other people can trust you to keep your word. If you make a promise, people know you will deliver. Let your word be your bond, and choose people whose words and actions you can trust. It can even be with something as simple as being on time. Thankfully, I have lots of people in my life who if they say they're going to be in a certain place at a certain time, then that's where they will be. I can relax and know that they will show up. This carries over to other contexts. Because I can trust them to be on time, I trust them in other ways as well. For instance, the people in my life who are punctual are also the ones who can honor a boundary and keep a confidence.

Friends Who Are Loyal

Neutrality is sometimes necessary, but there are also times when one must pick a side. You need people in your life who will stick by you. (That assumes, of course, that you are not the toxic or problematic person in the scenario. In that case your friends should—firmly, but lovingly—let you know what's what.) Here's a particularly salient example: If you have been harassed, abused, bullied, or sexually assaulted, you don't want someone who's supposed to be your friend "playing devil's advocate," minimizing the level of harm you experienced, sympathizing with your abuser, or making excuses for why the aggressor did what they did.

You want to be believed. You want to be protected. You want to be defended. Out loud. In public. You don't want your friends to be silent. You want them to speak up and speak out on your behalf. Silence, "neutrality," and inaction can signal complicity. In addition, it emboldens abusers to continue abusing others.

124   Love Yourself

You also don't want a close friend asking, "What were you wearing?" or any other victim-blamish questions. You don't want to hear anything along the lines of "They (meaning the perpetrator) have always been good to me." When people fix their mouths to say things like this in such circumstances, it truly boggles my mind. Like … you're saying you want to be friends with the person who raped me? With the person who robbed me? With the person who bullied me? With the person who abused me? You're saying you support them? Please explain yourself. In fact, don't bother.

You don't want someone who is supposed to be a true friend choosing to be on good terms or in close community with someone who they know has seriously and deliberately harmed you. They don't need to villainize the person, but they do need to make their affiliation clear by creating some distance.

For acquaintances, the rules might not be as stringent; however, I distance myself from *anyone* who chooses to maintain closeness with someone around whom I feel unsafe. They now embody secondhand danger to me, so as an act of self-love and self-advocacy, I refuse to share space, time, and information with them.

In cases like these, you want your friend to show up with undiluted "we ride at dawn" energy, ready to go to bat for you in the way you need. In some situations, there is no neutral ground or grey area. We all need people who have our back, front, and both sides.

Friends Who Are Generous

Both materially and energetically, good friends should be generous with each other. With their time, talents, compliments, resources, and more. They should be able to sometimes put others first. A good friendship is grounded in reciprocity and generosity.

Friends Who Are Respectful

We covered this at length in the red flags section, so it's no surprise that it's showing up here too, albeit in the inverse. You need people around you who will respect your boundaries, your space, and your wishes. This is a big green flag. When folks respect your boundaries, you can relax around them and feel safe in their presence. This is important, because a friendship should be a container of comfort. You need to feel safe, and mutual respect lays the foundation for that.

Friends Who Are Emotionally Intelligent

My bestie and I sometimes get super busy, but even during the busy times, we check in on each other. It can be as simple as a text message: "You good?" "Yeah, I'm good." "You good?" "Yeah I'm good too." Just taking the time to touch base, however briefly, builds connection and lets your friend know that they matter to you.

Emotional intelligence in action can also sound like:

- "I completely understand why you feel that way."
- "Checking in on you, sis. How are you feeling today?"
- "Sorry you're struggling. I'm here to listen if you need to talk."
- "Congratulations!! What an amazing accomplishment. Let's go celebrate!"
- "I'm not good company right now, so let's get together when I'm feeling better."

I can't count the number of times that my people and I have said words like these to each other. These moments of caring connection are a beautiful part of the human experience. It feels so good to be seen, supported, celebrated, and understood.

Friends should be able to empathize with you. When asked, they should be able to suggest solutions. They should treat you with kindness, compassion, and considerateness. Emotional intelligence wins the day.

A part of emotional intelligence is being able to speak each other's love languages. The concept of love languages was first developed by Gary Chapman PhD, and he introduced it to the world in his bestselling book *The 5 Love Languages*.[2] Although the book focused mostly on romantic relationships, the theory applies to all close relationships, including friendships. The five love languages are:

1. Acts of Service
2. Receiving Gifts
3. Quality Time
4. Words of Affirmation
5. Physical Touch

126 Love Yourself

With Annie and me, Acts of Service is a love language. Love is a verb, and we demonstrate our affection for each other by our actions. She picks me up from the airport when I come to visit, she cooks food that she knows I'll like, and she checks in on me frequently. When I was looking for a home in Atlanta a while back, she drove me around all day, took pictures, and offered suggestions for what would work best for me. Once, when she was drowning in work and was expecting houseguests, I cleaned the house for her as a surprise. She didn't have time and I did, so I took care of it. Anytime she needs help with her resume, I write it for her. I know she prefers calling to texting, so for long conversations I call, rather than subjecting her to an everlasting text string. If she's sick and needs some extra care, I'm there.

So what are the overall lessons?

1. **Listen to your gut:** If something feels off, it usually is.
2. **Believe the evidence:** As the saying goes, when people show you who they are, believe them *the first time*.
3. **Seek reciprocity:** Your relationships, whether close or distant, should be grounded in reciprocity. To paraphrase my friend Alexis Mobley: Friendships should be bi-directional and mutually beneficial. There should be an equal exchange of energy and effort. If it's one-sided, that's a no. If you're having to do too much "chasing," that's a no. If you're doing all the giving, that's also a no. If people only reach out to you when they want something, that's another big no.

At the same time, one cannot CFO one's friendships, doing a daily tally of debits and credits either. There is no room for pettiness.

Speaking of pettiness, can we stop doing mathlete-level calculus with the brunch bill? Obviously, there is nuance. If you show up late and only order one drink, then you shouldn't have to pitch in for the full meal. Conversely, if you order two steaks and everybody else only has a salad, just do the right thing. Apart from that, let's just divide the bill equally and stop losing brain cells, patience, and goodwill calculating the coins to the nth degree. For the love of gawdt. Please. I beg you. I don't want to spend 45 minutes doing forensic accounting at brunch. Let's just enjoy our mimosas and keep it moving.

4. **Trust, but verify:** Better yet, verify first. The same way that computers and websites insist that we prove our humanity before proceeding, we should confirm authenticity, honesty, integrity, and other positive qualities before letting people fully into our lives. Everybody cannot and should not be our friend. We can be friend*ly* without being bosom buddies. The word *friend* should be reserved for the few tried and true people in your life who have proven themselves over time. Quality over quantity. Normalize keeping people at a distance until such time as they truly belong in your inner circle. Normalize running at the first sign of a red flag. Normalize using words like colleague, acquaintance, neighbor, classmate, associate. Be discerning.

5. **Check the vibes:** If you say "sim simma" and they don't respond with "who got the keys to mah bimma," you don't need that kind of negativity in your life.

Above all remember:

You deserve to have good friends. Make sure that everyone in your circle knows that and acts accordingly.

Elevation: Vibrate Higher

Exhalation: Breathe Easy

Bhramari Pranayama (Humming Bee Breath)

Sit comfortably in lotus or semi-lotus with your spine straight and your mouth closed. Close your eyes.

Now, gently close your ears using your thumbs or forefingers.

Inhale deeply through your nose into your belly for a count of five.

Exhale slowly for a count of seven, making a humming sound. The humming sound should be amplified since you have your ears closed.

Inhale: 1, 2, 3, 4, 5

Exhale: 1, 2, 3, 4, 5, 6, 7

(continued)

128 Love Yourself

(continued)

Inhale: 1, 2, 3, 4, 5

Exhale: 1, 2, 3, 4, 5, 6, 7

Inhale: 1, 2, 3, 4, 5

Exhale: 1, 2, 3, 4, 5, 6, 7

Repeat for seven cycles, or as long as you like, and when you're ready, open your eyes.

Affirmations: Speak Life

- I am a good friend to myself and to others.
- I am worthy of having great friends in my life.
- I am blessed with loyal friends whom I can trust.
- Every person in my circle is raising my vibration.
- I am easily attracting positive, lasting friendships.

Introspection: Journal & Heal

- Who is in your inner circle and why?
- How have you shown up as a friend to yourself?
- What are the top qualities you look for in a friend?
- What do you do to cultivate and maintain your friendships?
- Do you and your friends speak each other's love languages? If so, describe how.

Curation: Do the Work

The people we spend the most time with can affect our mental and physical health, emotional well-being, and even how much money we make. It's called social contagion. Conduct a friendship assessment to get a clear picture of how your friend circle is set up.

Make a list of the 10 people closest to you.

(continued)

(continued)

- How do you feel around them?
- What do you like most or least about them?
- Are your interactions generally positive or negative?
- Whom do you spend the most or least time with? Why?
- What is the ratio of criticism versus praise in your communications?

(Tip: Please destroy or delete the assessment once you're done with it. The goal is for you to get clarity, not to inadvertently hurt people's feelings. You don't want someone coming across this by accident. It is for your eyes only.)

Appreciation: Express Gratitude

What are you grateful for? Count your blessings:

- I am grateful …
- I am grateful …
- I am grateful …

Celebration: Razzle Dazzle

Flex on 'em, sis! What are you proud of? Celebrate yourself:

- I am proud of myself for …
- I am proud of myself for …
- I am proud of myself for …

Meditation: Think Blissfully

Find a comfortable position, sitting or lying down. Gently close your eyes. Become aware of where your body is making contact with the surface beneath you.

(continued)

(continued)

Breathe normally for a few cycles, then when you are ready, gradually slow your breathing down. Inhale through your nose for a count of three and exhale slowly through your mouth for a count of five:

Inhale: 1, 2, 3; exhale: 1, 2, 3, 4, 5

Inhale: 1, 2, 3; exhale: 1, 2, 3, 4, 5

Inhale: 1, 2, 3; exhale: 1, 2, 3, 4, 5

As you get more relaxed, move your attention to your heart chakra in the middle of your chest. Gently place your hands there, right hand over left.

Keep inhaling for a count of three and exhaling slowly for a count of five. With every exhale, feel more and more relaxed.

Now bring to mind someone with whom you are good friends; someone you feel very positively about. Picture them standing in front of you. Smile. Imagine them smiling back at you. Feel a warm, loving glow in your heart center.

Mentally tell them:

I am grateful we are friends.

I am grateful we are friends.

I am grateful we are friends.

Breathe. Keep inhaling and exhaling slowly through your nose.

Stay there for a few moments, enjoying the exchange of love and gratitude between you and your friend.

Continue inhaling for a count of three, and exhaling for a count of five:

Inhale: 1, 2, 3; exhale: 1, 2, 3, 4, 5

Inhale: 1, 2, 3; exhale: 1, 2, 3, 4, 5

Inhale: 1, 2, 3; exhale: 1, 2, 3, 4, 5

(continued)

(continued)

Now replace the image of your friend with the image of yourself as if you're looking into a mirror. Smile.

Mentally tell your Self:

I am grateful we are friends.

I am grateful we are friends.

I am grateful we are friends.

Bask in the glow of self-love for as long as you like.

When you're ready, gradually return your breathing to its normal cadence.

Move your hands away from your heart center and down to your sides.

Bring your awareness back into your body, becoming conscious again of where it is making contact with the surface beneath you. Tune in to the sounds around you as well as any scents and sensations.

Gently rock your head from side to side. Wiggle your fingers and toes, and when you're ready slowly open your eyes.

Asé.

6

Curate Your Capacity: Rest

Invocation

Most High,

I come to you, exhausted, praying for relief
My body's been feeling tired
My mind's been feeling tired
My spirit's been feeling tired

And I am tired of feeling tired

Yet and still
I have hope

For though my soul is weary, I have not given up
I have faith which keeps me standing even when I feel to fall

This is my vow: I will carry on

I turn to You now, as always, praying for You to:
Grant me relief from all that burdens me, so that I can thrive
Grant me Divine solutions to earthly problems
So I can be free from stress
Grant me a peaceful mind
That I might have a respite from these scurrying thoughts

134 Love Yourself

Grant me Divine Relaxation, a daily sabbath
So I can replenish my soul

Grant me rest
Grant me rest
Grant me rest

It is in the restful moments that I find You
It is in the restful moments that I find myself
It is in the restful moments that I remember the meaning of life

Help me remember that
The ability to rest is mine
The right to rest is mine
The gift of rest is mine

I honor myself when I rest

Help me remember:
That I can rest fully and still live well
That gifting myself with rest is a beautiful act of self love
That my replenishment is in service of my humanity
Not in service of greater productivity
That my rest is not for others, it is for me

And that is as it should be

Bless me with rest for my Inner Child
Who still loves to play and enjoy life
Bless me with rest for my Inner Genius
Who needs a space of serenity from which to create
Bless me with rest for the fully grown Me
Who just wants to be happy, healthy, and fulfilled
Bless me with rest
That I can in turn bless the world with the fullness of my being, if and
when I choose to

Grant me rest in the bosom of my community:
May I find communal sanctuary; soft, safe spaces of shared respite
Grant me rest from emotional turmoil:
May I have peace and harmony
In all things, in all ways
At all times, with all people

For all eternity
Grant me rest for my spirit, mind, body, heart, and senses

I am open to receive this, for it is my Divine birthright
I claim all this and more for myself, and for all who are weary

Please refresh, replenish, and restore us all

May we rest
May we rest
May we rest

Amen

My Relationship with Rest

I have always been a fan of naps.

I still am.

Like many good things in my life, I came to my love of nap time via my Mom. She worked hard and rested just as hard. She set a great example.

Growing up in Trinidad, my sister and I knew that every Sunday afternoon we would be left to our own devices for a couple of hours because it was Mummy's dedicated rest time. She got to sleep and replenish herself for the week ahead, and we got to enjoy unsupervised play time. It was a win-win. Once we moved to Barbados, the tradition continued. I didn't realize it at the time, but we were being taught that there is no shame in being still. There is no shame in "taking a little lie-down." There is no shame in resting.

My mom taught me that rest is its own activity.

My Caribbean culture taught me that as well. Wayyy back in the day in Barbados, the island's capital city, Bridgetown, used to close down from about noon on Saturdays, and not a single store would reopen until Monday morning. It was like an island-wide siesta. People would conduct their business early, go home, and spend the remainder of the weekend restfully, focused on family. (Well, except for a good Saturday night dance-up, but that is its own form of relaxation.) Nowadays, things have changed; the stores and banks keep longer hours, and the island's main mall is open on Sundays. However, because of the tradition in which I was raised, to this day I keep my weekends—especially Sundays—as quiet and restful as possible.

136   Love Yourself

As an introvert, I've always been a fan of inside. I like my house. I like my couch. I like my bed. Most of my evenings and weekends are a combination of lounging and napping. Sweats, snacks, snuggly cushions, mindless movies, and I'm good to go. "Doing nothing" is a line item on my to-do list, and I give it my all.

Unfortunately, however, this is not always the case. Life is not linear, so my relationship with rest has had its ebbs and flows.

The first time I felt the effects of overwork and inadequate rest, I was employed at one of the island's top all-inclusive hotels. I was young, and trying to prove myself. I often worked long hours and back-to-back shifts. An average double-shift day could include everything from manning the front desk and leading island tours during the day, to hostessing in the restaurant and performing in the floor show at night. It was a lot. Wake up at 6:00 a.m to start at 7:00 a.m., then back home by around midnight after a shift that ended at 11:00 p.m. One day, I fainted at work as a result of exhaustion and overwhelm.

One night, on the way home from work after another grueling shift, I fell asleep at the wheel. The car flipped and ended up in a ditch on the side of the road. I still remember hanging upside down dazed, strapped in by my seatbelt, hearing Anita Baker singing "Caught Up in the Rapture" on the cassette player. It was an eschatological moment if there ever was one: "Wow, being dead doesn't hurt," I thought. I truly believed I had passed away, and that Anita Baker music was on the playlist in heaven. As it should be. Clearly, I was completely disoriented. To this day I am not sure how I made it out of the car—but thank goodness I did.

I stood up shakily and started calculating my odds of making it home unscathed. All I saw on either side of me were cane fields, and the road was pitch black. I could only see a few feet in front of me. (Could a girl get a streetlight? A sidewalk? Something? Apparently not.) I was sure that some ne'er-do-well was going to attack me. I kept thinking: Imagine surviving a car crash only to get assaulted.

Thankfully, a helpful stranger came driving along just as I had decided to try my luck shuffling along the roadside, and he took me home. I asked him for his name, so I could thank him properly later, but he said it was not necessary. Sir, whoever you are, thank you for being an angel when I needed one. I am forever grateful to you. May you and generations of your family be blessed. The next day my mom went and looked at what used to be her car and burst into tears. Not about the car, but because she was so grateful that I had survived. She had no idea how I had gotten out of the vehicle, because it was completely flattened. To God be the glory that I escaped relatively unscathed.

After that happened, I focused on having a more balanced approach: On not working full out, on resting more. If I needed time off, I took it, unapologetically. Because guess what? While I was recovering, the hotel kept on running just fine without me.

Rest as Activism

Fast forward to 2020: I started including a call to rest as part of my activism work. We all need more rest, but especially Black people. Whole empires and nations have been built on our ancestors' backs. My people are still, generally, overworked and underpaid. Our enslaved ancestors did not toil, revolt, and claim their freedom only for us to continue slaving away, albeit on a different kind of plantation. They gave enough, and we have also given enough. When we're talking about reparations, rest must be included in the computation of what we are owed.

We dishonor our ancestors when we don't rest.

As I started exploring the topic of Black rest more deeply, I came across the Nap Ministry on Instagram. I knew that I had found my people. The Nap Ministry was founded by Tricia Hersey, author of *Rest Is Resistance*.[1] The Nap Ministry views rest as a core component of liberation work, and believes that the lack of rest is one of the isms affecting marginalized communities, in particular Black people.[2]

Full honor and respect to Ms. Hersey, bell hooks, the Black Panthers, and all those who for years have been preaching the gospel of self-care and restoration for the Black community.

Even if you don't consider yourself an activist, I would posit that existing in Black skin lends itself to activism by default. Everything we do is political, whether or not that is our intention. That includes our rest. As Audre Lorde states: "Caring for myself is not self-indulgence; it is self-preservation, and that is an act of political warfare."[3]

There is a deficit of rest that we must recoup. Since rest has been stolen from our ancestors and from us, every time we rest, in addition to restoring our bodies, we are also reclaiming that of which we were robbed. Currently and retroactively.

The revolution will be rested. We must #DivestAndRest.

In addition to the historical context, the reason why I focus on promoting rest is because almost every Black woman I know is weary. Including me. Tiredt, I tell you. Epigenetically exhausted. We carry in our genes the fatigue our ancestors felt. Many Black women are either currently on sabbatical, planning to take extended leave, or they've recently taken time off from work to recover from burnout. Or, even more likely, they're struggling, barely making it from one day to the next because of years-long, bone-deep fatigue. This is because, among other things, Black women work more and earn less. According to the US Department of Labor, Black women have the highest workforce participation rates of all women but earn a mere 64 cents for every dollar earned by white men. That means we must work longer hours than other communities in order to gain financial parity.[4]

Part of what drives us to overperform, and therefore burn ourselves out, is the experience that we must work twice as hard to go half as far as our non-Black counterparts. Just ask former presidential candidate Kamala Harris. How many of us have credentials on credentials, degrees on degrees, and years of experience, only to have to report to (and train!!) people whose only qualifications are mediocrity and nepotism? Many of us are busy working hard, while others are working smart. It is an unwinnable game.

This phenomenon is so entrenched that Janelle Benjamin, founder and principal consultant of the Canada-based management consulting firm All Things Equitable Inc.,[5] created a YouTube series called *Twice as Hard*[6] to tackle the topic. In this vodcast, Benjamin interviews Black women who have lived experience with giving twice the effort and receiving half the reward. She was inspired to create it after noticing that she and other professional Black women in her circle were undergoing a treadmill-like experience, constantly moving, constantly working, but making little forward or upward progress:

> I was first introduced to the concept that Black people (especially Black women) must work twice as hard as white people to get half as far by my mother. She was trying to prepare me for the realities of life. As I progressed in my career—or sometimes did not progress—I discovered that what she had warned me about was true. Black women are caught in a thankless cycle where we are required to be excellent just to get in the door, and yet often punished, excluded, and moved from pet to threat because of the very same qualifications we were hired for.

Black Girl Magic is real, as is Black excellence, but there is a place for Black averageness as well. There must be. We should not spend our entire lives in the stranglehold of struggle, trying to prove our worth to people who are committed to seeing us as inferior. I said as much when Ellen Wagner, CEO of Cross Cultural Bridges, was gracious enough to interview me for Black History Month:[7]

> What is equally vital is the path of least resistance. That path includes Black joy. Black self-care. Black rest. Black averageness.
>
> Black excellence is a necessary celebration of what we have achieved in spite of the systemic obstacles placed in our path. However, Black averageness—showing up as ourselves, rested, happy, carefree, without the need to overperform and prove our worth—is the ultimate resistance flex.

The Burnout Epidemic

We have become a society that actively campaigns against rest, and instead glorifies busyness, especially for deliberately marginalized identity groups. I suppose that is to be expected from nations that rose to dominance as a result of people—*my* people—being enslaved; being forced to work at an inhumane pace to build the economy and generate wealth that we would be excluded from. Continued dominance demands continued output, and in societies that view humans as resources to be exploited, people's bodies are seen and used as fuel for the capitalistic machine.

The drive to be always on, always working, always going, always scaling, always producing, always at max, is a recipe not just for fatigue, but for compete burnout. The American Institute of Stress reports that 83 percent of workers experience daily job-related stress, which is often a precursor to burnout.[8] And Black Women Thriving reports that 88 percent of professional Black women experience burnout.[9] Those are staggering statistics. And yes, I am one of the 88 percent.

What Is Burnout?

The World Health Organization (WHO) defines burnout as an "occupational phenomenon." They view it as a non-medical condition that can influence one's need for health services, and which is a result of extended work-related stress:

140　　Love Yourself

Burnout is a syndrome conceptualized as resulting from chronic workplace stress that has not been successfully managed. It is characterized by three dimensions:

- feelings of energy depletion or exhaustion;
- increased mental distance from one's job, or feelings of negativism or cynicism related to one's job; and
- reduced professional efficacy.

Burnout refers specifically to phenomena in the occupational context and should not be applied to describe experiences in other areas of life.[10]

Causes of Burnout

Burnout is the result of extended periods of mental, emotional, and physical fatigue. According to Calm, a popular sleep and meditation app, burnout can be triggered by overwork, toxic work environments, and misalignments between your job and your values.[11] Indeed.com lists nine causes of burnout:[12]

1. Experiencing challenging workloads
2. Having a lack of control
3. Earning scarce rewards
4. Having a lack of community
5. Experiencing unfair treatment
6. Having values that don't align
7. Experiencing a toxic environment
8. Working with unfair expectations
9. Working with challenging leadership

Psychology Today agrees with the WHO's definition but adds that burnout can be the result of factors other than work:[13]

Burnout is a state of emotional, mental, and often physical exhaustion brought on by prolonged or repeated stress. Though it's most often caused by problems at work, it can also appear in other areas of life, such as parenting, caretaking, or romantic relationships.

Curate Your Capacity: Rest

I co-sign. When I experienced burnout, work was a large part of the reason why, but life life-ing also had an effect. It wasn't just one thing. It was all the things. Burnout can also be caused by stress related to finances, relationships, and caregiving, as well as grief, compassion fatigue, chronic pain, long-term illness, and traumatic life events such as moving house, losing a job, or getting divorced. For me personally, "entrepreneurial stress" was also a factor. If all or many of these experiences are occurring at the same time, it can be overwhelming.

Autistic Burnout

One's intersecting identities increase the likelihood and effects of experiencing burnout. In my case, as someone who is Black, a woman, Gen X, and neurodivergent, burnout hits harder, and takes longer to bounce back from. Although I took a six-month short-term disability leave to help facilitate my recovery from burnout (more on that later), at the end of the six months I was better, but still far from 100 percent. Having autism adds another layer of complexity: Autistic burnout is a real thing. Samantha-Rae Dickenson, EdD, CEO of DSRD Consulting, explains why:

> Black women are conditioned to push through overwhelm, making burnout feel like a normal part of life. This is even more intense when you're autistic. While workplace burnout disproportionately impacts Black folks—especially Black women—autistic burnout takes it up a notch. It's not just physical exhaustion; it's emotional, mental, and sensory overload, and it takes more than rest to recover.
>
> True restoration comes from understanding our unique needs, restructuring our lives to honor our boundaries, and creating spaces where we can thrive without constantly masking. We also need community support because so many resources were designed for young white males and often exclude people of color.

Part of the issue with autistic burnout is that folks are not inclined to believe what they can't see, and therefore people who are in the throes of burnout often don't get support until it's at level 12: Complete mental and physical collapse.[14] Few people believe we're struggling because *to them*, it doesn't look like we are. I call this phenomenon "Swan Theory: A

Capacity Paradox," because sometimes the easier something looks, the harder it actually is.

Swan Theory is especially relevant for high-masking, "high-functioning," late-diagnosed autistic adults. Burned out individuals with autism often appear to be gliding effortlessly across the pond of life, but (a) we're kicking underwater at speed, (b) we have residual exhaustion from kicking, unsupported, for decades, and (c) because of our neurological differences, and in some cases disabilities, we must kick harder. For us, gliding takes exponentially more effort than it would for a neurotypical, non-exhausted person. For Black women in this subgroup like myself and Dr. Rae, there are additional weights, so to speak, attached to our legs. So we still appear to be gliding, but it takes all our capacity and then some to stay afloat. No wonder we flame out.

Time Frame for Recovery

Burnout typically takes a while to develop, so it will therefore take a while to heal. One cannot expect a three-day long weekend to help one recover from burnout that has been building for months or years. On average, it takes one to three years to fully recover from burnout.[15]

My Battle with Burnout

I woke up crying. And not a subtle, ladylike, one-poignant-tear-down-the-cheek cry. It was the big, blubbering cry. What Oprah calls "the ugly cry." I've always been a crier, but the intensity of this belly-deep bawling surprised me. It was 6:00 in the morning, and I had literally just opened my eyes. What could be so bad? What had happened?

It was January of 2024, and I was exhausted. My entire spirit was depleted. My tank wasn't just empty, it was below "E." Worse yet, I could not seem to find a gas station of any kind to fill myself up again.

My entire body hurt. My scalp. My hair. My eyelashes. My teeth. My insides. The soles of my feet.

My brain.

My brain ached.

It hurt to think.

I could barely move.

My entire system shut down.

I had known for a while that I was deeply fatigued but, like so many of us do, had tried to push my way through. I burned my candle at both ends till there was only the tiniest frazzled stub left in the middle.

Burnout was complete.

But back to the "What could be so bad?" question. If I was honest, I knew. I had been going all out for years. This moment was inevitable.

So the short answer is: Existing and working while Black can be dangerous—and utterly exhausting.

Here's the longer answer:

Life life-ing plus racial weathering had led inexorably to this juncture. Burnout and exhaustion don't spontaneously manifest overnight. It takes time. It takes weeks, months, years of operating within the capitalist matrix and battling white supremacy culture, combined with exposure to various isms and (let's be honest) a tendency toward self-abuse. Here's a little taste of what had led to my soul-weary state.

2019

My journey to burnout had started in December of 2019 when I lost my job as a result of racism. By way of context: A white woman on the team was racist toward me in front of others and (surprisingly) was made to apologize. Of course, she was unhappy that she had been held account-able for her actions, so she consulted the playbook (iykyk) to determine her next move. She threw a strategic tantrum. Short story shorter, she Karened, cried, leveraged her contacts in the Beckyverse, and I was left unemployed. I got an email from HR two days before Christmas and that was that. Two days before Christmas, y'all. I was officially out of work. Again.

Since this was the umpteenth time that I had lost my job, I became very focused on building my own brand and business. The goal was (and still is) to be self-employed so that I would be less subject to the vagaries of corporate America. The build toward greater freedom exacted an onerous price.

2020

Then 2020 happened to us all: The COVID-19 pandemic. Daily rising death counts. Alarming Fauci updates. Lockdowns, paranoia, maskless

144 Love Yourself

coughers, science deniers, bizarre toilet paper hoarding … it was wild. And terrifying. Those of us who were paying attention suspected that there would likely be a widespread post-pandemic mental health crisis resulting from forced isolation, collective grief, and the trauma of trying to survive a global health scare. Our suspicions turned out to be true. The Mayo Clinic reported that:

> At the start of the COVID-19 pandemic, life for many people changed very quickly. Worry and concern were natural partners of all that change … Worldwide surveys done in 2020 and 2021 found higher than typical levels of stress, insomnia, anxiety and depression. By 2022, levels had lowered but were still higher than before 2020. Though feelings of distress about COVID-19 may come and go, they are still an issue for many people.[16]

In a scientific brief published in the spring of 2022, The World Health Organization revealed that the COVID-19 pandemic had triggered a 25 percent increase in anxiety and depression across the globe.[17] I am one of the many people who experienced an adverse impact on my already tenuous mental health.

Concurrently with the pandemic, the racial reckoning precipitated by the brutal murder of George Floyd was taking place. The violence perpetrated against Black bodies, which had started with the transatlantic slave trade, continued for centuries, and kept going through post-emancipation and Jim Crow, had morphed into its latest savage incarnation. Like so many of my peers, I was heartbroken at seeing news report after news report of people who looked like me being murdered with impunity.

I decided that I could no longer stay silent. I started advocating for Black rights and protesting against all the isms that adversely affect Black and Global Majority people. As a writer, it made sense to deploy my words and keyboard as tools to promote awareness and inspire change. This was the beginning of my journey as an activist.

Activism is purpose-driven work. Fulfilling? Yes. Easy? No. Every year since 2020 I grew more and more exhausted. The demands of activism, along with its concomitant bullying, harassment, and online vitriol, took a toll. As a means of coping with the constant negativity I started my affirmations channel on TikTok. The goal was to help myself and others focus on the positive, and experience relief—however temporary—from the unrelenting onslaught of life.

Oh, and let's not forget that I was also unemployed and looking for work. Anybody who has ever conducted a job search knows that looking for a job is its own job. After countless applications and interviews, I eventually found one by the middle of the year. Naturally, I was grateful to be employed once again. What I did not appreciate, however, were the microaggressions that came along with being the only Black person on the team.

2021–2022

Between 2021 and 2022 I went into overdrive. My photo was right there in the dictionary to define "doing too much." (This is why I encourage members of The Great Exhale community to live life in *under*drive. Overdrive is overrated. And unsustainable.)

I had so much going on that many people didn't even realize I had a 9–5. My side hustles had side hustles. I was the co-founder and co-host of *The Introvert Sisters* podcast and co-host of *The Tea on Tap* podcast. I did editorial and social media management for an online platform, my blog, and both podcasts. I also started as host and producer of *Real Talk on Racism*, a public affairs TV show that focused on amplifying the voices and experiences of people of color. And yes, I was still showing up on LinkedIn daily as an activist. Each of those could easily have been a full-time job.

Sis was busy.

I was so busy that I did not initially stop to ask myself: Is this the goal?? Just to be busy?? Um … no.

Speaking of LinkedIn, let's add that I was sexually harassed in the most graphic, egregious of ways by someone on the platform. Alas, it would not be the only time.

To add insult to injury—or more accurately injury to insult—I broke and fractured my right foot. Broke the right pinkie toe and fractured the metatarsals. Instead of taking six weeks to heal, it took six months. The agony, y'all. Lawd. It was next level. I could barely think. I could barely sleep. I could barely cope.

146   Love Yourself

This acute discomfort was added to chronic pain from an old car accident. Yes, another one. Several years prior I had been hit by a car while crossing the street. Injuries were to C4–C7 and L2–S1. So, yeah … constant back and neck pain, basically. Plus, there was also chronic pain from eye surgery gone awry. Thankfully, it improved my vision, but it unfortunately left me with uveitis (ouch!) and photophobia, which is why I now wear sunglasses almost all the time.

Wait … did I mention menopause? Because that was going on too. It had started a few years prior, and I was still experiencing symptoms. Night sweats are the devil. And morning sweats. And random middle-of-the-day sweats. For that matter, all of it felt like an abomination. The highs, the lows, the feelings—SO MANY FEELINGS—all at 150 percent intensity. The hot flashes, the cold flashes, the insomnia, the brain fog, the exhaustion. Many a morning during the team standup I almost blacked out. The only thing that stopped me from crumpling onto the corporate-chic carpeting was my tight-knuckled grip on the top of the cubicle divider.

Between life stress, job stress, being bullied at work and online, overwork, and excruciating pain, my blood pressure spiked. I had been experiencing severe headaches for a while, but with everything that was going on, I did not pay enough attention. My foot hurt more than my head, and that is what I was focused on. (Don't judge me, y'all. I was in so much pain that I wasn't thinking straight.) My mom swooped in from Barbados for a visit, found me a doctor, and (rightfully) insisted that I go immediately. Thank goodness I listened to her. When they took my BP, the doctor told me I was "pre-stroke." Whew. Needless to say, he started me on BP meds. The day after I began taking them, the headaches reduced in intensity.

As if this wasn't enough, there was also some heartbreaking family drama that truly shattered my spirit. To cap it all off, I finally caught COVID over Christmas of 2022. Zero stars. Do not recommend.

2023

At one point, I had understandably dubbed 2022 *The Year That Almost Ended Me.* Then 2023 flew in on dragon wings of chaos and said, "Hold my beer."

Y'all, when I tell you I nearly didn't make it.

It was ROUGH. Very high highs and subterranean, middle-of-the-earth, hellish lows. By the end of the year, I was completely burned out.

Curate Your Capacity: Rest

Burnt to a crisp like that one arson-black piece of plantain that had been sliced too thin and fried too long.

Life was life-ing HARD.

I had already taken steps to reduce how much I had on my plate. I stepped away from hosting *The Tea on Tap* and *Real Talk on Racism* and put an end to the uncompensated work I was doing for a couple of companies. My sister and I also decided to put *The Introvert Sisters* podcast on hiatus.

But being me, I couldn't just leave it at that.

So in addition to still working at my 9–5, which to be honest was more than enough to keep me busy and stressed, I also launched not one but *two* companies (The Great Exhale was one of them), and navigated, not very successfully, business- and family-related drama. And that wasn't even everything. Not even close.

My brain broke, as did my heart. I was constantly feeling depressed, exhausted, anxious, overwhelmed, and suicidal.

And alone.

Let me take a little detour to chat briefly about entrepreneurship. Envisioning and launching The Great Exhale is one of the accomplishments of which I'm most proud. Sometimes, I just scroll through the platform and smile to myself. I see the beautiful Black women posting and interacting with each other, and it makes me happy. It's such a positive space. It's doing what it was designed to do. It's giving what it's supposed to give. I am grateful to the Most High for trusting me with this assignment. To see an idea in your head come to full fruition—there's nothing like it. So fulfilling. To know that Black women are enjoying and benefitting from the soft, safe space warms my heart.

But babyyy …

Nobody tells you how hard entrepreneurship is. Solopreneurship to be precise. Nobody tells you how tough it is to wear all the hats. All. Of. Them. Nobody tells you about the struggles. I had a little support, especially at the beginning, and it was *still* tough. I built a soft space but felt like the building process was hard on me. Daily I dealt with abuses and abandonments; betrayals and bad mindedness; reversals and raggedyness. Even outright theft.

I won't go into details—those who know, know—but it felt like I was simultaneously traveling on two divergent tracks. One was relaxation, meditation, affirmations, and high vibrations. The other was tears, depression, struggle, and suicidality. Whew. You cannot thrive while serving two masters.

When I advise my community members to do less, this is why. It's not theoretical; it's because I know, experientially, what doing too much leads to. I don't want anyone to ever have to go through that. And I don't want anyone to ever feel alone if they are struggling.

This is not to discourage anyone from embracing entrepreneurship. I would still choose it over life on a corporate plantation any day. But if you're going to run your own business, go into it with your eyes wide open. It is not for the faint of heart.

As I've shown, my burnout did not begin in 2023. That was simply the year that my body, mind, and spirit finally all screamed, "ENOUGH!!!" It wasn't one thing. It was the confluence. It was the combination of all the things. I limped through Christmas, honestly just trying to make it to 2024.

2024

By the time I got to 2024, I was *done*-done. I just didn't have anything left. In January, the company I worked for had yet another reduction in force—they had laid off a big percentage of the staff the previous January as well—and I was so exhausted that I literally prayed that they would let me go. (I know, I know, I wasn't thinking straight.)

I felt myself "circling the drain." Every day I thought of ending my life. There were many issues at play. Everything I mentioned above, plus:

I felt irritated with the world. And saddened by it.

Disillusionment.
Despair.
Ennui.

Every day there was some new horror. War. Famine. Genocide. Economic and ecological devastation. The "old horrors" also continued, in the form of all the isms, and relentless misogynoir.

There was also the ongoing horror of the open season on Black women. The year began with Claudine Gay, president of Harvard University, resigning. She submitted her resignation on January 2nd. Her tenure had lasted a mere six months, the shortest ever in Harvard's history. Inside The Great Exhale, on LinkedIn, in group chats, wherever Black women were gathered in community, we expressed the same thoughts: We understood exactly what Dr. Gay had been going through. She was us and we were her. We were sympathetic—and triggered. We understood why she stepped aside and declined to fight.

Approximately a week later, on January 8, Dr. Antoinette "Bonnie" Candia-Bailey, former vice president of student affairs at Lincoln University in Missouri, died by suicide.*

Collectively, our hearts broke.

The Black community mourned for our sister, who had been so mistreated, had reached out for help, and been cruelly ignored.

May she rest in eternal peace.

We don't exist in a vacuum, so we are all affected by events that occur in the wider world. For me personally, probably because I was feeling suicidal myself, Dr. Candia-Bailey's death hit me hard.

How I Handled My Burnout (and How You Can Handle Yours)

I have shared my experience to help normalize talking openly about mental health issues, and to demonstrate that like mine, your burnout did not start today, or a week ago. It's the result of harmful systems that actively make it hard for us to thrive. Capitalism does not want us rested. The system wants us tattered, tired, and traumatized. It wants us to be too depleted to do anything else but drag ourselves drone-like through life. Burnout is also the result of months or, more likely, years of experiences, traumas, and decisions. Think back over the past few years and be honest with yourself. Things happen to us, without a doubt, *and* we also sometimes contribute to our own undoing.

Since burnout does not develop overnight, you should not expect it to disappear overnight. We cannot hustle our way to good health. Healing cannot be rushed. To battle my burnout, I started with small steps. Hopefully my approach can help you too.

Be Honest with Yourself: First, I admitted the truth to myself that I could not go on any longer. I needed a break. I was not and am not the "Strong Black Woman." I am delicate and in need of support.

---

*If you are struggling or in crisis, or you know someone who is, call 988 or visit the American Foundation for Suicide Prevention at www.afsp.org.

150 Love Yourself

Be Honest with Others: Next, I spoke to my boss and told them exactly how I was feeling. They had a positive response and suggested that I take some time off work. They're good people. To be honest, navigating the short-term disability process and wending my way through the mire that is the US healthcare system was an absolute nightmare, but I did what I had to do. The alternative was to continue working, and I simply couldn't.

Ask for Help: I also started reaching out for help and being honest about what I was going through. I asked my close circle and wider community for support. Instead of answering "How are you doing?" with "I'm fine," I started telling people that I was struggling. Yes, I became that person, lol. When people asked if I was okay, I replied, "No I am not." My thinking was that if I flamed out and didn't make it, nobody would be able to say, "I didn't have any idea." I gave people an idea, a very clear one, of what I was going through.

My LinkedIn community came all the way through and helped me find THE BEST doctor. Eminently qualified, of course. But also empathetic, proactive, and culturally competent. (Very different from the so-called doctor who had told me I was "too well dressed, too smart, and too well spoken to be ill." I kid you not.) This doctor, thankfully, gave me some time off work so that I could rest and heal. Dr. Hinds, thank you for being the voice of reason. I did a hard stop. As soon as I spoke to the insurance company, I shut down my work computer, shut off my work phone, and that was that. Being able to take an official sabbatical and remove myself from the scene of the crime, so to speak, was immensely helpful. It started out as a three-month short-term disability leave and then it was extended to six months. Praise the Lord.

Seek Medical Support: I started therapy and also began seeing a psychiatrist. Shout-out to Dr. A., Dr. I., and LPC. W. I was diagnosed with major depressive disorder, generalized anxiety, PTSD, severe ADHD, and a few other conditions to boot. No wonder I was feeling like I was in a sunken place. Side-eye of all side-eyes to the "doctor" who dismissed my cries for help because my blazer was cute. Ridiculous. Side-eye also to the "leader" at my job who, when I had asked for exactly 1.5 days off maybe like a year prior to this, refused my

Curate Your Capacity: Rest

request, instead insisting that I had to show up and "make sure nothing slips through the cracks." Clearly, it didn't matter if *I* slipped through the cracks.

Take Your Meds: Although I'm usually not a fan of taking medication, I was ecstatic when my psychiatrist prescribed me an antidepressant and meds for my ADHD. Even though they initially gave me extreme headaches, it was still worth it. I finally stopped feeling like I was drowning. If you break a toe, you don't just leave it there and keep walking on it. You buddy tape it to the neighboring toe for support. You rest it so it can heal. Taking the medication felt like buddy taping for my brain. I finally had the support I needed.

Negotiate Your Boundaries: Capacity management was next. Calendar management too. The truth was that I could no longer sit and work for long hours. (Not surprising since I barely had enough energy to walk my dog for 10 minutes at a time.) The max I could last at one sitting was 45 minutes, and I tried to not even do that. Pushing myself to the max is what had got me here in the first place. Though I still had projects to work on, I just did what I could when I could. I refused to push myself.

My primary goal was to rest.

I renegotiated commitments, including with my publisher. I just couldn't do it. There was no way I could write, and definitely not write at speed, in the state I was in. Thankfully they extended my deadline so that I could get some rest. I also put a recurring "Reclaiming My Time" reminder on my calendar for three days a week with no end date. Mondays, Wednesdays, and Fridays were for ME, so for the most part, I stopped booking appointments on those days. I no longer had to wrangle my calendar into submission. No more random, last-minute meeting invites. No more people double-booking me for no reason. Having more mastery over my time was absolute heaven.

Pour Into Yourself: With a bit more space to exhale, I was able to dedicate more of my time to doing all the things that I knew were good for me. I spent quality time with my family. Touched base with my friends. Connected with my TGE community. I meditated, journaled, and dove even more deeply into breathwork, yoga, and Reiki. More walks. More reading. More naps. Lots and lots of naps. Yes.

152 Love Yourself

The freedom of feeling tired and actually being able to rest is a top-tier experience. Top. Tier. I no longer had to fight my way through fatigue to attend meetings that should have been emails. Amazing.

"Nothing" was also a daily line item on my to do list. Swathes of time with zero commitments. Heaven. And I developed a "to *not* do" list as well. Things that were just ... NO. Not gonna happen. I put my boundaries all the way up, and it was life changing.

Step Away From Social Media: I also stopped showing up online as frequently. I reduced my posting to the bare minimum, which often meant not posting at all. Y'all ... the relief. The thing about posting is that if your content performs well, you then have to keep showing up. That is not a bad thing in itself; some might argue that it's a good problem to have. It can be very fulfilling to have meaningful conversations in the comments with the people with whom you are in community. But you must have capacity. Managing parasocial relationships takes time and energy.

Every post you make, every comment you respond to, is a debit from your energy account. I go into this in more detail in Chapter 9, "Curate Your Energy." Since social media was depleting my energy, I reduced my level of participation. I went from creating and posting new content every day, sometimes twice a day, to posting once or twice a week. Then that dwindled to almost zero. I still occasionally did my #StandupSaturday and #SundaySalutation posts, and every now and then I would do an affirmation, but the only series I was relatively consistent with was my #FootwerkFriday posts on LinkedIn. Those brought me and everyone else so much joy. My blogs—my personal one and the TGE blog—were temporarily abandoned. My *Fresh Air* newsletter too. For more than a year the last post on the TGE Instagram account was "Happy New Year." When I felt up to it, and not a moment before, I started posting again.

My TGE family was very understanding. During one of our Collective Breath community check-ins I told them what was going on, and that I needed rest. They were completely supportive. Many of them started posting more frequently in order to take some of that responsibility off of me. Many of my sistas reached out to offer words of support as well as practical assistance. It was lovely to be loved on. This is the beauty of being in community with the right people. Alignment is everything.

Get More Rest: Stress can cause insomnia, and insomnia can in turn increase stress. It's a cruel Catch-22. So, next up was to address my sleep issues. I took melatonin, powdered magnesium, valerian root, and drank quite a bit of chamomile tea. If there's a shortage of any of those, I definitely contributed to it. One of my doctors also prescribed me a sleep aid. In their words: "You can't heal if you don't rest."

Agreed, doc. Agreed.

A Soft Life Is a Rested Life

Curating a gentler life includes making rest a priority. Ideally, we want to avoid experiencing burnout at all by proactively putting measures in place to prevent it.

We need to identify the root causes of why we're so tired, then build habits and life systems to address them. It's a good idea to start by visiting your doctor to have them assess whether there are any medical issues at play.

When we think of rest, physical repose is usually what first comes to mind: Sleeping, napping, lying down for a moment or two. Putting our head down on a pillow, our feet up on a footstool. Placing a cushion at our backs for maximum comfort. That's a part of it, but there's more.

In my research, I came across the work of Saundra Dalton-Smith, MD, author of *Sacred Rest*. If you've ever heard about the various kinds of rest that humans need, it is thanks to Dr. Dalton-Smith, who developed the 7 Types of Rest Framework[18] to help people minimize burnout. In addition to the seven recommended by Dr. Dalton-Smith—physical, mental, emotional, sensory, creative, social, and spiritual—I propose two more: Cellular and communal. So, there are nine kinds of rest, and yes, we need them all.

Here's how you can incorporate every form of rest into your life.

Love Yourself

The Nine Types of Rest

1. Physical Rest

Sleep: There are four kinds of physical rest that the body needs, the most important of which is sleep. Go to your bed, lie down, and drift off to dreamland. Your body and mind need sleep to be able to function optimally. And by function optimally, I don't mean work; I mean exist.

Sleep deficiency can contribute to many chronic health issues, including hypertension, cardiovascular disease, stroke, obesity, and depression. It can also make people more accident-prone, for example in the case of drowsy driving. Been there.

Sleeping well can literally save your life.

Set yourself up for successful sleeping. Make your bedroom a relaxing haven. Get high-quality, grown-up bedding that feels good against your skin. If you're sensitive to light like I am, use blackout curtains to make your room blissfully dark. Create a soothing pre-bedtime ritual. Do some meditation, journaling, or breathing exercises to help you relax. Dim the lights, and turn off all your electronic devices. If possible, go to bed at the same time every night. Building a bedtime routine will train your body and mind to automatically start winding down when you're ready to sleep.

Nap: A brief nap can work wonders. Time it: Aim for between 10 and 30 minutes, and make sure to set an alarm. The best time of day for napping is in the early afternoon around the siesta period, between 1:00 and 4:00 p.m. This will help ensure that you (a) don't oversleep and (b) don't sleep too close to your actual bedtime. The last thing you want to do is take a late, unstructured nap and then end up being awake for the rest of the night.

Rest Your Eyes: "You sleeping Granny?"

"No sweetie, I'm just resting my eyes."

Every West Indian child has had this kind of conversation with one of their elders. Resting one's eyes is a sort of semi-lucid nap. You're what Bajans call "halfway between sleep and wake." You're not sleeping so hard that you start snoring, but you're a couple of levels down from being fully alert. It's deeper than a meditation and lighter than a nap. The great thing is resting your eyes can happen anywhere: In your car during your lunch break, in the quiet room at work, in your comfy chair at home, on a picnic bench in a park—you choose. When I used to work on the Jersey City waterfront, at lunchtime I would find a quiet spot under the shade of a tree and drift for a few minutes. It enabled me to go back to work feeling fresh and focused.

If you don't have time for a full nap, resting your eyes can still help you feel reinvigorated.

Move: Although we often associate physical rest with sleeping and being stationary, it can also include movement. Physical rest can be both active and passive. Active rest can include yoga, tai chi, walking, swimming, and even cycling. Some of these activities might surprise you in that they probably don't sound particularly restful, but it's a matter of intensity. Casual strolling versus high-powered hiking; steady-state bike riding versus Olympic-level speed cycling; slow jogging versus sprinting around a track. Ease and moderation are key. The goal is to enjoy a little low-intensity movement and release some endorphins without exhausting yourself.

2. Mental Rest

Have you ever gone into a room to get something but then you have no idea what? It happens to us all from time to time, but if it starts occurring more frequently, you might need mental rest. Same for if you have difficulty focusing, or if you find yourself repeatedly reading the same paragraph without retaining anything. If you're making lots of mistakes, losing the plot in the middle of meetings, and experiencing brain fog, it might be a sign that your mind is tired.

Take a break. Pushing through is not the answer.

If you tend to sit at your computer for hours, schedule breaks on your calendar—and actually take them. Give your mind a respite from intense concentration.

Let your brain cells relax.

156 Love Yourself

3. Emotional Rest

You can't pour from an empty cup. It's a cliché, but it's true. So many of us find deep meaning in being there for others—but we do it to our detriment. We give and give and give until we're depleted. And while we often share our material resources, a lot of us give even more freely of ourselves: Our time, our attention, our energy. We show up, empathetic and emotionally available, to listen, commiserate, advise, and hold space. We lather, rinse, and repeat this day after day, then have nothing left for ourselves and our loved ones. In our state of depletion, we can find ourselves using unhealthy coping mechanisms to self-soothe, or snapping at those close to us because our nerves are frayed.

We need not only to refresh but also to reframe:

First, our function in life is not solely to pour. The focus should not be on resting *in order to* work or on filling our cups *in order to* pour. Resting simply because we need or want it is enough. Even if no one else benefits from us being rested, it is enough that *we* benefit.

Rest is, first and foremost, for us. Filling our cups simply because we deserve replenishment is enough. Though it is of course nice to share, if we never pour a drop from our proverbial cup, that is also okay. We must prioritize ourselves.

However, if you choose to be there for others, let this be your guide: Don't pour from your cup; serve from your saucer. What's in your cup is yours. Everybody else can have access to some of your overflow. (Again: Not all of your overflow, some of it.)

There are three habits involved in getting emotional rest: Reduce, Regulate, Replenish.

Reduce: *Minimize the amount of emotional energy you expend*

One of the best ways to get emotional rest is to stay away from chaotic people. Avoid drama kings and queens. When energy vampires approach, run the other way. Spend time in the company of folks who are positive, uplifting, and peaceful.

It's also crucial to enforce healthy boundaries. Make yourself less available. Take fewer calls. Answer fewer emails. Do less unseen emotional labor. Set aside a couple of hours (or days) where you don't take any random requests. Stop saying yes to things you don't really want to

Curate Your Capacity: Rest

do. Say no, and say it with your chest. Their emergency is not your emergency. They will figure it out whatever it is. In this Soft Black Woman era, we're letting people handle their own stuff. We ain't saving anybody but ourselves.

Regulate: *Regain emotional balance*

If your emotions are in a heightened state, take a break. Walk away for a moment if you can; take a few deep breaths; have a good cry. All of these can help you to feel calmer. Journaling can also be helpful. Simply freewriting about how you're feeling can get some of that dysregulated energy out of your body so you can return to center.

Replenish: *Refill your emotional energy reserves*

If you're feeling emotionally overwhelmed, it can be helpful to talk to friends if they have the capacity, and for some issues it's even better if you speak to a professional, such as a therapist. Another approach is to simply do something nice for yourself. For me, that often looks like sitting in silence and letting the calm soothe my spirit.

4. Sensory Rest

Sensory deprivation is an effective way to help your mind and body relax.

As I mentioned earlier, back in the day I used to work as a management trainee at an all-inclusive hotel in Barbados. I often pulled double shifts with a short break in between. To decompress, I would go into the sauna where it was dark and quiet, and spend some time completely alone. No people. No noise. No scents. No lights. Just a beautiful cocoon-like nothingness. Absolute heaven. The reduction in stimuli helped me get regulated and release any stored stress. It was like a soft reboot for my system.

Another way to enjoy sensory rest is to reduce your exposure to electronics. Do a digital detox. Most of us have a borderline addiction to screen time: We'll be simultaneously scrolling on our phones, semi-watching TV, and checking out a YouTube video on our tablets. And Alexa might be playing some music in the background as well. It's too much. Are we relaxing, or are we numbing? Whatever the answer is to that question, what is sure is that minimizing all this input can help us wind down, especially just before bedtime.

Our senses are fried. They need rest.

5. Creative Rest

Remember fun? Remember doing things like coloring, crafting, dancing, and singing just because you liked them? Remember riding your bike just because you enjoyed it, rather than feeling obligated to train yourself to elite cyclist level? Remember the days before every hobby had to be monetized? Remember creating and doodling without deadlines attached? We need to bring those days back. We need to give ourselves permission to be creative just for the joy of it. Burnout can also be caused by being "all work and no play."

We need to reconnect with our inner child and reignite our ability to frolic. We must let ourselves do things badly; lovingly laugh at ourselves when our projects go pear-shaped. We must give ourselves permission to daydream: To gaze into the middle distance, thinking of everything and nothing, while the sun shines on our face. To sit by the sea and stare at the waves. To let our minds drift and get lost in time. Our brains need a break from constantly producing and strategizing. Do something different. As my maternal grandfather used to say, a change of occupation is rest.

Creative rest can also include seeking out inspiration. Art. Music. Fashion. Beauty. Travel. Nature. Anything that elevates. Galleries, museums, parks, and Pinterest are your friends.

A change of scene is another form of creative rest. That can be anything from taking a 15-minute walk in nature, to a full-scale vacation. Passports, tickets, flights, hotels, tours, the whole shebang. While a one-week break is not a solution to years of burnout, taking frequent mini-vacations can help prevent you from burning out in the first place. Use your PTO. All of it.

6. Social Rest

As a confirmed introvert, social rest is an absolute necessity for me. Being around too many people for too long drains me, so after socializing I need to recharge my battery.

Alone.

That said, social rest has two sides. It's not just about spending time by yourself, it can also be about spending time with others. The key is to make sure that the people you spend time with elevate your energy. In Chapter 5, "Curate Your Circle," I provide pointers for identifying people you want to have around you and those you don't. With the right people, even though I'm introverted, I will happily enjoy silently sharing space, talking on the phone (gasp), or body doubling.

Body doubling is one of my favorite activities. Essentially, it's sharing space with someone, either in person or virtually, to get silent support while you complete a task. My awesome therapist Candice explained that it is especially useful for people like myself with ADHD. Body doubling promotes co-regulation, supports executive function, and helps increase dopamine levels, all of which make it easier to get things done.[19]

The people I most enjoy body doubling with are my mom, my sister, my niece, and my person. Spend quiet, quality time with people who make your spirit feel at peace.

7. Spiritual Rest

Whether or not you are religious, spiritual rest is needed. An acknowledgement that there is something greater than yourself. A remembrance that you are a necessary part of the Universe. A connection with the Divine. An internal communion. A return to purpose. A grounding in meaning. A belief that you belong. Inspiration. Surrender. Transcendence.

If you're spiritually depleted, you might feel meaningless, unimportant, unmoored. Spiritual rest can bring you back to center.

This will naturally look different for everyone depending on their belief system. As a Reiki master who was raised Christian and is interested in Buddhism, what works for me is a combination of prayer, meditation, Reiki, and contemplation. I keep what works and ignore the rest. What works for others can be reading the Bible, Quran, Torah, or other book connected to their faith. Many folks find comfort in going to church, mosque, temple, or engaging in community service. Find what works for you, and ease your spirit.

8. Cellular Rest

In addition to being bombarded by external stimuli, our bodies also have a lot to process in terms of what we expose them to internally. Yes, I'm talking about food.

The frequency with which we eat, the amounts we eat, and what we eat can overburden our digestive systems. If we're honest, much of what we ingest is not healthy for us. *Psychology Today* explains that:

Cellular / systemic rest is the rest of the whole body system from an internal level. What we put into our bodies matters. Processed foods,

160 Love Yourself

junk foods, or high-fat / high-sugar foods are extremely difficult for our bodies to digest. Much of the energy we produce goes into the digestion of these foods, which leaves us feeling fatigued, tired, or lethargic.[20]

That post-meal drowsiness or ethnic fatigue that many of us experience can very easily start expanding to an almost-constant state of exhaustion. Our digestive systems need rest too.

Resting our system could mean eating healthier foods in moderate amounts, incorporating more vegetables and whole foods, or ingesting fewer mystery ingredients. (If you can't pronounce it, pause and ask yourself whether you really want to eat it.)

Cellular rest could include paying attention to your portion sizes or trying intermittent fasting. For some people, it could mean eating larger, healthier meals more consistently. (We can also stress our cells by *undereating*.) Giving your body a rest from the inside out could also look like eating more slowly and mindfully, rather than scarfing down your food on the fly.

No judgment here because I am *very* well acquainted with my buddies, Ben and Jerry, who have comforted me more times than is healthy. I know what it's like to have the urge to eat your feelings after a stressful day—and give in to that feeling. (Why is their vegan Chocolate Fudge Brownie "ice cream" so good?! Whyyy?!) Having an occasional treat is fine, but indulging every night as a coping mechanism is probably not good.

I've mentioned food, but of course what we drink makes a big difference as well. Soda, alcohol, caffeine, and fluorescent-colored, sugar-laden, science experiment-looking drinks ... none of this is good for us, at least not in excess. Moderate your intake.

My recommendation for us all is that we (to paraphrase calypsonian Patrice Roberts) "drink water and mind our business." Stay hydrated and elevated.

Of course, consult with your doctor or nutritionist before making any major dietary changes, especially if you are on medication.

9. Communal Rest

Since I'm a community builder, it probably comes as no surprise that I believe communal rest to be a valid and necessary form of relaxation. Like navigating life, resting can be more powerful when supported by one's village. There is something deeply healing about resting as a collective. It's co-regulation at scale, and it's a beautiful thing. We must encourage each other to prioritize rest. It's also imperative that we make it safe to rest, and

Curate Your Capacity: Rest 161

remove the shame so many of us feel about embracing a slower pace. We need to give each other permission to relax. The best way to do that is to normalize resting as a society. One of our collective goals must be to create communal spaces and shared experiences that are centered around rest.

A great example of this is the Collective Napping Experience, hosted by Tricia Hersey, that allows people to rest, dream, and heal in a shared space.

In The Great Exhale community, we share tips on relaxation, meditation, and sleep. We also consistently encourage our community members to rest. One of the best testimonials I ever received about the community was from a member who said she felt free and comfortable to relax and do nothing. The world demands so much of us; sis was happy to be able to chill. Doing less and resting more is the goal.

A word to the wise: Don't fall into the trap that so many high-achieving people do and make resting into its own exhausting project.

Yes, I'm looking at you, sis.

Put away that "recovery spreadsheet" you just created. Delete that project plan. Step away from that bulleted checklist. We can't #BlackExcellence our way through our resting time. We can't #BlackGirlMagic our way through our healing. We can't "I'm a strong Black woman" our way to the other side of burnout. There are no gold stars being distributed, so ... relax. Breathe. It's okay to take it slow. The goal is to make our rest something that actually restores us and *gradually* curate a life we don't need to constantly recover from.

Don't burn out trying to heal from burnout.

Rest Is the New Success

Having experienced both a well-rested life and its opposite, when I was planning The Great Exhale, I knew that I wanted to make rest one of the central tenets of the community. We cannot live a soft, serene life if we are not rested, so rest is something we talk about often. We inspire each other to:

Relax

Decompress. Step off the treadmill of constant busyness. The goal is to #DivestAndRest.

Exhale

Do breathing exercises to regulate our bodies and minds.

Soothe

Find healthy ways to comfort ourselves.

Transcend

Transmute our energy from stress to happiness.

"Rest is the New Success" is one of our mantras inside The Great Exhale. And yes, I absolutely made it into a T-shirt. We remind each other to do less and rest more. To start the week slow. We talk about #MinimalMondays where we prompt each other to do the least. We encourage each other to take what my friend Anta Gueye-James calls "unthreatened naps," where you have no obligations waiting for you on the other side of your slumber—so you can rest fully, sleep deeply, and wake up completely refreshed.

Our goal is to step away from grind culture. To #DivestAndRest. I'm not saying that we should not work. But work should not be our be-all and end-all. Equilibrium is needed. The focus should be life-work balance, in that order.

Life comes first.

Our sense of self should not be tied to our jobs or titles. Our function in life is not to mindlessly produce. Our worth is not predicated on how much we do. That we exist is sufficient. We are enough, just by dint of our beingness. Part of our purpose on this earth is to actually enjoy our life. And to fully enjoy it, we must be rested and refreshed.

Rest, sis. Rest.

Elevation: Vibrate Higher

Exhalation: Breathe Easy

4-7-8 Breath

Close your eyes and place the tip of your tongue just behind your upper front teeth. You're going to inhale through your nose for a count of four, hold your breath for a count of seven, and then exhale through your mouth for a count of eight, making a wooshing sound. Let's begin:

(continued)

(continued)

Inhale for 1, 2, 3, 4

Hold for 1, 2, 3, 4, 5, 6, 7

Exhale for 1, 2, 3, 4, 5, 6, 7, 8

And again:

Inhale for 1, 2, 3, 4

Hold for 1, 2, 3, 4, 5, 6, 7

Exhale for 1, 2, 3, 4, 5, 6, 7, 8

Once more:

Inhale for 1, 2, 3, 4

Hold for 1, 2, 3, 4, 5, 6, 7

Exhale for 1, 2, 3, 4, 5, 6, 7, 8

Continue your 4-7-8 breathing for as long as you wish. When you're ready, return your breathing to its normal pace, and open your eyes.

Affirmations: Speak Life

- I am giving myself permission to rest.
- I am surrounded by people who inspire me to relax.
- In the spirit of self-love, I am blessing myself with rest.
- I am choosing to rest and do less. I have already done enough.
- I am willing to release all shame about resting. I am worthy of enjoying rest.

Introspection: Journal & Heal

- When do you feel most relaxed?
- If you had to plan a restful weekend, what would it look like?
- What did your family and wider culture teach you about rest?

(continued)

164   Love Yourself

(*continued*)

- What does the word "lazy" mean to you? Do you equate resting with being lazy?
- Root cause identification: What is making you tired? Why? Who is making you tired? Why? How can you remove the tiredness triggers from your life?

Curation: Do the Work

List the nine types of rest. Under each, write a few ways that you can incorporate that form of rest into your life.

Appreciation: Express Gratitude

What are you grateful for? Count your blessings:

- I am grateful ...
- I am grateful ...
- I am grateful ...

Celebration: Razzle Dazzle

Flex on 'em, sis! What are you proud of? Celebrate yourself:

- I am proud of myself for ...
- I am proud of myself for ...
- I am proud of myself for ...

Meditation: Think Blissfully

Lie down and close your eyes; get nice and comfortable. Breathe gently through your nose, becoming more aware of the sensation of your breath in your nostrils and at the back of your throat. Smile softly.

Gradually start breathing more slowly, making your exhales twice as long as your inhales. Inhale for a count of three and exhale for a count of six.

(*continued*)

(continued)

Let's begin.

Inhale: 1, 2, 3; exhale: 1, 2, 3, 4, 5, 6

Inhale: 1, 2, 3; exhale: 1, 2, 3, 4, 5, 6

Inhale: 1, 2, 3; exhale: 1, 2, 3, 4, 5, 6

Starting with your head, relax your body bit by bit.

Focus on your head, becoming aware of any tension in your scalp, eyelids, forehead, ears, and jaw. Make a conscious effort to relax anywhere you feel tightness. Mentally tell yourself, "Head, relax; head, relax; head, relax."

Bring your attention down to your neck, moving it gently forward and back, then from side to side. Mentally command your neck to relax.

As you continue scanning your body, focus on your shoulders, which so often carry stress and tension. Bring them up to your ears, squeeze them there for a second, and then let them fall gently. Repeat this a few times. Mentally tell yourself, "Shoulders, relax; shoulders, relax; shoulders, relax."

Feel your belly and chest rising and falling with every inhale and exhale. Focus on your chest and solar plexus to see if there is any tension there. Consciously release any tension every time you breathe out. Mentally command your chest to relax.

Continue doing this for the rest of your body. Consciously relax your arms, hands, fingers, back, pelvis, hips, legs, all the way down to your feet. Then mentally tell yourself, "Body, relax; body, relax; body, relax."

Remain in a relaxed state for as long as you like. When you feel ready, return your breathing to its usual pace, gently open your eyes, and sit up slowly.

Asé.

PART III

Be Yourself

7 | Working While Black: Learn

Invocation

Most High,

Please place Your Holy Protection around me
Please cloak me in your light, guarding me from all isms and schisms
Please bless me with
People and environments that are psychologically safe
In my career may I thrive

May I be mentally at ease, physically secure, and creatively fulfilled
May I be strategically savvy
Politically powerful, and professionally promoted
May I be divinely connected, lavishly rewarded, and financially abundant
In my career may I thrive

May You free me from the shackles of corporate redlining
May Working while Black become my secret sauce for success
May everything designed to bury me
Instead serve to help me flourish
In my career may I thrive

May my melanin, genius, and excellence forge pathways for me to prosper
May I be treated not as an imposter, but as a professional who belongs
May Your Benevolence and my Blackness combine to help me shine
In my career may I thrive

May You forge from solid iron the rungs on which I climb
That they might never break; that I might never stumble
May You place angelic guardrails on the glass cliff every time
So I can walk head high; so that I never tumble
May You shatter all glass ceilings so I can rise with pride
No need to hide my light; no need to show up humble
In my career may I thrive
In my career may I thrive
In my career may I thrive

Amen

A Note:

As I explained in the introduction, this chapter is slightly different from the others in that it is more expository than prescriptive in nature. It was originally part of the next chapter: "Curate Your Career," but I realized that the explication of Black people's lived experience of navigating corporate spaces needed to stand on its own. Non-Black folks need to know why so many Black people in corporate spaces feel like we can't breathe. I therefore split the chapter in two. This chapter discusses what I have coined the Working While Black Effect, while the next chapter follows the structure of the other chapters, providing tips on how to make work ... work for you.

~ ~ ~

Caution: Caucacity Ahead

"You can't sit here. You have to sit at the back of the bus."

I looked confusedly at the driver, genuinely wondering if he had lost his mind. He must have, right? There's no way he could be compos mentis. I mean ... what in the Rosa Parks was this?? What century were we even in? How could this be happening?

But happening it was.

Like mine had, the bus dispatcher's jaw dropped. She was also a Black woman. Everyone else on the company shuttle looked exaggeratedly up at the ceiling, down at their phones, or out of the windows, trying to pretend that they had not heard this ridiculousness. None of them intervened, but hey, that's the norm. So much for allyship. Bystanders be bystanding.

I remained seated.

The dispatcher walked over—eyes squinted, lips tight, jaw clenched—to show her support. "You can sit anywhere you want," she said in a tense, staccato monotone, addressing me but keeping her unblinking gaze firmly fixed on the driver. She spoke with just enough bass and emphasis to let him know that when necessary, she was about that life, and he better not try nothin'. Clearly, she was team #FAFO.

As the bus pulled off, she and I exchanged an exhaustion-tinged sista-girl half smile of solidarity and shook our heads slowly, eyes downcast.

This was just a random Tuesday, and I hadn't even arrived at the office yet. Nothing like an early-morning microaggression to get the day started.

Now I had to swallow my annoyance, gather my patience, step foot onto the corporate plantation, and speak with my chipper Chanté Moore–whistle-register voice for the rest of the day. I was expected to smile, appear docile, appease massa, and act as if nothing had happened. Bonus points because I also had to endure being gaslighted by the couple of white colleagues I had told about the incident, and by one who had witnessed it. I should have known better. I had to listen to them defend the driver, and say with *certainty* that I *must* have misunderstood the words "sit in the back of the bus." And if I hadn't misunderstood, they were *100 percent sure* that he didn't mean it *that way* and that he definitely was not racist. Oh, and neither were they. They are some of the "good ones."

Sigh.

172   Be Yourself

This is but one example of the kind of tomfoolery that Black people have to deal with in majority-white companies. Day in, day out. Unceasingly.

Welcome to the Working While Black Effect.

My West Indian upbringing had prepared me for a lot of things, but not this.

- It didn't prepare me for the gaslighting, the glass ceiling, and the microaggressions.
- It didn't prepare me for the deliberate derailments, disrespect, and doubting of my abilities.
- It didn't prepare me for the expressions of surprise when my excellence revealed itself.
- It didn't prepare me for the lack of balance: For the inhumane pace and paucity of time off.
- It didn't prepare me for the presenteeism: For the pressure to show up even if you were extremely ill.
- It didn't prepare me for the expectation that work had to be prioritized above everything else, even your family.

It didn't prepare me.

Working While Black ... in Barbados

I was raised in Barbados. It's an island in the Caribbean with a population that at the time was approximately 98 percent Black, so everywhere I went, there were melanated people peacefully existing and joyfully thriving. Before I even knew the phrase "Black excellence," I saw it embodied all around me:

- Prime Minister—Black
- Artists and creatives—Black
- Bosses and colleagues—Black
- Intellectuals and educators—Black
- Corporate and civic leaders—Black
- Doctors, plumbers, lawyers, politicians—Black
- Tastemakers, cultural icons, local and regional stars—Black

Working While Black: Learn

173

As a Black person, growing up, being educated, and starting one's career in a majority-Black society changes how you move through the world. There is no concept of being a "minority." There is no concept of genuflecting your way through life asking for acceptance, or of trying to squeeze into spaces where you are unwelcome. You naturally stand tall, hold your head high, and shine.

Nature and nurture work in synchrony. You are born into an environment where it is easier for you to thrive; in fact where you are *expected* to. You are encouraged to dream big and aim high. You are not seen as deficient. You are not seen as a failure who *might* make it "in spite of." Success is prophesied for you from the beginning. More importantly, you are given opportunities and support so that you *can* succeed.

In a Black-majority country—at least in mine—you are raised and nurtured in a way that promotes your full becoming. It instills you with so much confidence that it is hard to even understand it when people don't believe in you. I can't speak for everyone, but this was my personal experience.

What growing up in a majority-Black country meant for me was that:

My melanin did not cast me as intellectually inferior. I was expected to be brilliant.

Almost everyone I encountered, from janitors to journalists to justices of the peace, was Black. And smart. For the most part, everybody responsible for my education was Black. At primary school all my teachers were Black. At secondary school most were Black, and at college—the University of the West Indies (UWI)—all my lecturers were Black. In fact my father and many of his peers were UWI lecturers. During my first year on campus, almost daily someone said to me, "Are you Hurley's daughter? I'm expecting big things!"

I remember feeling the weight of having to live up to him, my mother, and my sister, all of whom had graduated from UWI with honors. #NoPressure, right? At the same time, what an absolute blessing it was to know that I could "be it" because in my own family I could "see it." All of them had also gone to France after graduation to teach English as a Second Language (ESL), so I had that on my bucket list too. (Yes, we all studied languages. The DNA is undefeated.) I knew a postgrad trip to

174

Be Yourself

Europe was a possibility, because I had already seen it achieved. And, yes, it ended up happening: My year in the south of France was fab.

In my second year at UWI, when my French Language grades plummeted after I had been physically assaulted in public by someone I was dating (trauma will do that to you), my professor came to me privately and asked what was wrong. I had gotten a C in my final exam. "You're a good student," she said. "I will help you. I might not be able to get your overall grade back up to an A, but I can work with you and get you up to a B." Unlike some of my experiences while studying, and later working, in the US, in Barbados there was no surprise when I excelled. The surprise (and concern) happened when my academic performance *slipped*. The A was expected. The C was not. She knew I had the work ethic, the talent—and the brains. Buoyed by her guidance, empathy, and support, I put in the work. At the end of the term, I got a B, and the recognition for being "Most Improved." Dr. Farquhar, I thank you.

My melanin did not cast me as a common-class criminal. I was assumed to be trustworthy.

Most of the store managers were Black. So one thing I never experienced in Barbados was getting followed around a shop as if I were about to boost some merchandise. I remember more than once going into Bridgetown to buy cloth, thread, or shoes with my mom. One of her mantras as a designer and artist was "Look at your materials in daylight to see their true colors. That way you get an accurate match." She would simply ask the store assistant if we could take the items just outside the store's front door, and they would let us. They knew we weren't about to abscond with an end of fabric, a spool of thread, or one shoe. They knew we could be trusted.

My melanin did not increase my odds of police-inflicted mortality. I was expected to always return home safe.

The police were Black. I don't need to explain what a difference that makes. I was pulled over by the police a grand total of one time—ever— because I had come to a rolling stop at a stop sign. (I mean ... the sign was right outside the police station, so it would have looked bad if he *didn't*

Working While Black: Learn   175

pull me over. I had to humble myself and take the L.) I told the officer a heartfelt mea culpa, and thankfully he let me off with only a warning. The important thing is though, when interacting with him I never once feared for my life.

My melanin did not cast me as incapable, undesirable, or as a "diversity hire," with all the implications thereof. I was a prize candidate. I was a star employee. I was expected to excel. And I did.

My bosses were Black.

- It was a Black boss who told me to look for another job because there were no growth opportunities for me at a certain company. They knew I could soar someplace else, and they wanted that for me.
- It was a Black boss who hired me because of my excellent credentials— *and* my potential.
- It was a Black boss who not only saw the potential in me, but also chose to nurture it.
- It was a Black boss who paid me the salary I deserved from the beginning.
- It was a Black boss who mentored me and taught me the ropes.
- It was a Black boss who coached me when I made a mistake, rather than putting me on a PIP (a performance improvement plan).
- It was a Black boss who made sure I never did non-promotable tasks.
- It was a Black boss who sent high-profile assignments my way so that I could shine.
- It was a Black boss who promoted me in less than a year.

Conversely, one of the most problematic people I worked with in Barbados, who actively tried to undermine me at every turn, was someone I call "Expat Karen." She seemed annoyed that I existed, and made it her business to make my working life as miserable as possible. (Oh and by the way, can we start calling "expats" immigrants? Just saying.) Unfortunately, Expat Karen's cousins are alive and thriving in the United States, and they put a lot of time and effort into roadblocking Black women, all the while smiling in our faces, comparing "tans," and trying to touch our hair.

176   Be Yourself

Elevating with ease is what I was used to in Barbados, so in terms of the intersection between my race and my career, moving to America has been one long, loud record scratch.

In Barbados I knew I was Black, of course (it is where the Slave Codes[1] were developed, and in some ways Barbadian society still reflects that), but I never spent all day every day aware of my blackness. I did not feel the weight of constant caucasian scrutiny. I did not experience continual judgment and condescension from other people of color. And I never felt at a disadvantage. I was proud of myself and confident in my abilities. Life was set up for me to succeed—and I felt like I could.

Working While Black ... in the US

Working while Black in the United States has done its best to reduce that self-confidence. Occasionally, it has succeeded. Naturally, I noticed the Working While Black Effect in my own career, but I also observed it playing out to varying degrees in the careers of other Black and minoritized people with whom I shared cubicle space. The daily push against the systematic diminishment of one's character and career is part of what makes navigating white-majority corporate spaces in melanated skin so exhausting.

Now please do not read what I have not written. This does not imply that my every interaction with Black people in the workplace was positive, nor does it imply the inverse—that every interaction with non-Black people was negative. That is definitely not the case. However, in general my career blossomed more quickly and effortlessly when I was in a majority-Black environment and stalled once I moved to a majority-white one. Do with that information what you will.

Lived experience matters—and so does data. Harvard conducted a study of more than 9,000 early-career employees, called "Intersectional Peer Effects at Work: The Effect of White Coworkers on Black Women's Careers." The study examined the retention and turnover gap between Black and white co-workers. Its findings back up my experiences:

Black women are the only race-gender group whose turnover and promotion is negatively impacted by White coworkers ... Black women who were initially assigned to Whiter teams are subsequently more likely to be labeled as low performers and report fewer billable

Working While Black: Learn 177

hours, both of which are predictors of higher turnover and lower promotion for all employees.[2]

And there you have it. The Working While Black Effect is real.

The Full Definition of the Working While Black Effect

I've mentioned "working while Black" a few times. For those of you who don't know (my non-Black readers, this one's for you), the phrase refers to the cluster of daily diminishments, psychologically harmful behaviors, and emotionally taxing experiences that Black people, especially Black women, encounter in white-majority workplaces. I have identified 12, which I will expand on.

Ask any Black person, whether they are entry level, middle management, or in the C-suite; in corporate, retail, or academia. Whether they're they're full time, part time; in the public or private sector. No matter the variables career-wise, the constant is that they have experienced some or all of the 12 elements that comprise what I have termed the Working While Black Effect (WWBE).

The WWBE is a syndrome composed of an interconnected web of behaviors and occurrences. It includes simultaneously being invisible and hypervisible; overworked and underresourced; last hired, but first fired; over-credentialed but underpromoted; managing, but not viewed as management material; being perceived as excessive yet inadequate. It also includes experiences such as being tone policed, unsponsored, and of course, being called "angry" or "aggressive" just because our faces are at rest.

The Working While Black Effect in Action

Let me give you a few more examples of the WWBE because my impression is that most minimally melanated people have no idea how much of an additional psychological burden Black people bear at work.

And you need to know. And once you know, you need to decide if you care. And if you *do* care, you need to decide if, or how, you will adjust your beliefs and behaviors. You need to determine, "Based on this knowledge, who do I choose to be?"

In the lives of public figures, the WWBE looks like former Vice President Kamala Harris, with her stellar reputation, experience, credentials, eloquence, policies, and (ahem) actual plans, losing the 2024 election to an unqualified felon who should never have been allowed to run in the first place. As political commentator Van Jones said: "He gets to be lawless, and she must be flawless." The Working While Black Effect also looks like:

My forever FLOTUS, Michelle Obama, being criticized about (checks notes) her arms, and my forever POTUS, Barack Obama, being criticized about (checks notes again) wearing a tan suit.

Actress Taraji P. Henson weeping because even though she is so tenured in her acting career she still has to fight for decent roles and equitable pay. Although she has achieved A-list status in Hollywood, on every project she still feels like she's starting over at the bottom.

The iconic Angela Bassett being harshly criticized because she showed disappointment over (once again) not winning an Oscar that she deserved to have won. Honestly, she should already have won quite a few, starting all the way back with *What's Love Got to Do With It*.

Halle Bailey receiving racist backlash because she was cast as Ariel in Disney's *The Little Mermaid*. Apparently, she is considered "too Black" to play the role of a mythological character in a fictional story.

Supreme Court Justice Ketanji Brown Jackson being publicly flayed for days during her SCOTUS confirmation hearing. Remember that one tear? It still breaks my heart. It also looks like her being left, for the most part, to deal with the bullying on her own. From the outside looking in, it seemed as though only a comparatively small number of people stepped forward to *publicly* defend and protect her. (Thank you, Cory Booker.)

Dr. Bonnie Candia-Bailey, a former vice president of student affairs at Lincoln University of Missouri, being bullied and unsupported to such a degree that she ended her own life in order to get some relief. May she rest in peace.

Those of us who are not so visible also have to navigate the treacherous white-majority waters. Just because the daily race-related paper cuts are not occurring in public doesn't mean they're not occurring at all. Trust me, they are.

And now, let's get into the details. The WWBE comprises:

1. Pay Inequity

Let's talk about the coins, y'all. Because of the history of the United States (yes, I'm referring to slavery), Black women have traditionally been forced to work for free. And although slavery ended centuries ago, the idea that our

Working While Black: Learn 179

labor is worth less than that of others is still prevalent. To this day, there is an enormous wage gap between Black women and every other ethnic and identity group.

Our labor is literally undervalued: In the United States, as of 2024, for every dollar earned by cis-het white men, Black women earned a mere 64 cents. A report by the Institute for Women's Policy Research revealed that, at that rate, it would take Black women *two hundred years* to achieve pay equity.[3]

So it's not only that Black women need to work twice as hard to get half as far in terms of career pathing, we also have to work twice as hard while sometimes making less than half as much in terms of remuneration. This has adverse consequences for our quality of life and our ability to build generational wealth. Compared to white men, Black women lose close to a million dollars over the course of their career.[4] No amount of "just buy fewer lattes" and "cancel your Netflix subscription" can compensate for this.

I, and many of the activists, speakers, and authors in my circle, have unfortunately had direct experience of pay inequity. Compared to our white or PoC counterparts our honoraria are smaller, our perks are nonexistent, and our contract terms are not as favorable. We are expected to cover our own expenses: Travel, lodging, meals, marketing—all of it. More than one event organizer (with big-name sponsors listed prominently on their site, mind you) has approached me to "support" their cause but then fallen silent when I ask them about their budget.

Companies want to pick our brains but not pick up our expenses or pay our invoices. We are boldly asked to work for free or even, in some cases, to pay for the "opportunity" to line other people's pockets. I call instances like this a "faux-portunity" or "noportunity" because the "opportunity" is an illusion: It does not exist. And my answer is, therefore, "No." It's wild to me because we are the draw. These companies want to use our names, images, reach, reputations, and IP to attract a paying crowd, and we're supposed to be grateful for "exposure." Well, we're already exposed, or you would not have found us, so … no. Pay us. And you know which two words precede that.

If y'all (corporations and individuals) want to make some real progress with addressing pay inequity, I share what my buddy Steve Jones and I say all the time: "Say it with your checks."

2. The Broken Rung and The Glass Cliff

I remember reading an article once about Nike's CEO Elliott Hill having worked his way from being an intern all the way up to the C-suite. It's a wonderful accomplishment of course, but one that many Black and brown people, and Black women in particular, don't get to experience. The reason? The broken rung. Compared to men, it is exponentially more difficult for Black women to make that first crucial move from entry level to management. Lean In reports that although Black women advocate on their own behalf and ask for promotions, those promotions are often denied. Believe me, I've been there:

> Black women ask for promotions and raises at about the same rates as white women and men—yet the "broken rung" still holds them back at the first critical step up to manager. For every 100 men promoted to manager, only 58 Black women are promoted.[5]

For the comparatively small number of Black women who receive promotions, at some point, their ascension up the career ladder grinds to a halt. They hit the glass ceiling, and are then pushed over the glass cliff:[6]

> Advancing to a senior position is only the first component of the glass cliff phenomenon. Once there, many women find they do not receive the support, power, respect, time, and other resources necessary to succeed in the role, especially in a time of crisis. In other words, they are essentially set up to fail. It's true that in a crisis, many new leaders, regardless of identity, may stumble. But women, and especially women of color, face additional barriers while also managing a culture that might not previously have had a woman, especially a woman of color, in a leadership position. They may experience, for example, a disproportionate share of the blame when things inevitably go wrong, even if their actions are no different from those of a male leader.

3. The Pet To Threat Phenomenon

Dr. Kecia M. Thomas, dean of the University of Alabama at Birmingham, coined the phrase "Pet to Threat"[7] to describe the experience that many professional Black women have of being adored then abhorred. It's related to the glass cliff phenomenon described above.

Working While Black: Learn   181

Here's how it works:

We are initially hired with much fanfare. We are perceived as being an asset, as having high potential, and (this is an important nuance) as being malleable. Some of us are hired to lend credibility and social capital to companies and institutions trying to position themselves as being progressive. Our faces on the company website add diversity clout.

As we advance in our careers; as our power, stature, authority, and tenure increase, the tides turn and we are perceived as being a threat. Once we start flexing our strength as strategic leaders capable of managing people and charting the direction of a department (or, rarely, of a company), as opposed to taking direction from a white colleague to whom we report, things change.

I haven't been able to find data to confirm this—maybe I'll conduct a study in the future—but my experience and observation have been that in general white people have a viscerally negative reaction to reporting to anyone Black. It completely messes with their world view, and they fight it with every breath in their body. There might be some epigenetic reason for this as a result of the history of the transatlantic slave trade. The overseer gene never rests. Black women are expected to serve others, take orders, be grateful for crumbs, be "corporate Mammys," and know our place. And in a white-centric world, the belief is that our place is to follow, not to lead.

Moving from pet to threat frequently results in Black women being put on performance improvement plans (PIPs), often as a precursor to being demoted or fired. Alternatively, some opt to leave corporate or academia altogether and become entrepreneurs instead.

4. The Black Girlboss Paradox

In her article "Claudine Gay and the Black Girlboss Paradox,"[8] Kimberly Bryant, founder of Ascend Ventures and founder of Black Girls CODE, addresses an unfortunate pattern in which Black women are excessively, and often unfairly, criticized:

> We Black women are simultaneously celebrated as resilient, capable leaders and are often hailed as heroes or saviors in times of crisis. Yet we face relentless and disproportionate scrutiny, underestimation, and marginalization.

182 Be Yourself

As Black women continue grappling with this paradox, despite achieving high levels of success and leadership, they continue to grapple with a disproportionate level of criticism, skepticism, and doubt about their capabilities and achievements. It's what I've begun referring to ... as the Black Girlboss Paradox.

5. Being The Only

Many Black people are the only melanated or marginalized person on their team, or sometimes even in the entire company. Being the only can lead to feelings of isolation, a lack of psychological safety, as well as experiences of exclusion, racism, and misogynoir.

A few years back, after another day of trying to chop my way through the corporate jungle with a dull cutlass, I was over it. Frustrated, and needing to vent, I wrote this post:

I just ... I LOATHE being the only Black person on a team. Loathe.
Every day it's some new form of disrespect and gaslighting.
Every. Single. Day.
I loathe it.
Ugh.
The caucacity, combined with full-chested mediocrity, is at an all-time high.
The Beckery. The Karenization. The Chaddishness.
Bombastic side eye to de whole ting.
Bun fiyah pun it.
I just can't.
Sigh.
Signed,
A Tired Black Woman.

In cases where there *is* more than one Black person in a company, what I have personally observed is that they are often assigned to different teams or orgs, so that the possibility of interaction is limited. I'm not quite sure what management expects to happen if a group of us gathers together ... hmmm ... (Stares in marronage.⁹)

6. Being The Representative

Ask the average Black person: We collectively hold our breath whenever drama unfolds on the news, and we send up a prayer about the alleged perpetrator: "Melanated Jesus, please don't let them be Black." Why? Because we know that whatever crime that person has allegedly committed will become part of the "that's how Black people are" stereotype. We are all judged and found wanting, based on the actions of one individual. That approach translates to the workplace as well. Many of us feel immense pressure to perform, knowing that if we slip up (or are perceived to have done so), it makes it harder for any other Black person coming after us. Our achievements come as a surprise and make us "exceptional." Our failures are expected and are generalized to apply to every member of our racial community.

7. Code Switching

Remember when I mentioned my "Chanté Moore-whistle-register voice?" That's an example of me code switching. Sometimes, I might even include some vocal fry and uptalk for a little razzle dazzle. Yes, I do it (or at least I used to), and I ain't ashamed. If you have a "telephone voice" or a "customer-service" you code switch too.

Many Global Majority people, especially those of us like myself with a non-American or non-British accent, modulate our speaking voices when we're in professional spaces. We might even change the way we speak depending on our audience. My family, Bajan friends, American friends, colleagues, and bosses might all get a slightly different version of my voice and lexicon. (I mean, if I say "wuhloss," "cawblimmuh," or "cheeseonbread" to someone who isn't from Barbados, they're just not going to get it.) In some ways, code switching is about having range. I have deliberately never lost my Bajan accent, but I do know how to alter it just enough so that I don't have to repeatedly be told by colleagues that they can't understand what I'm saying.

Britannica.com defines code switching as "[The] process of shifting from one linguistic code (a language or dialect) to another, depending on the social context or conversational setting."[10]

The definition is correct to a degree. However, what it does not fully address is (a) the "why" behind code switching, and (b) that there are other forms of code switching besides linguistic ones.

184 Be Yourself

The intersections of race, class, and social context underpin code switching. At its most benign, it is a sociological tool that helps us communicate that we comprehend relational and situational context. We use it to signal our standing with the people with whom we are interacting. Most of us speak more casually at home or in the company of friends versus at work or among strangers, and that is as it should be.

However, when one layers in sociopolitical factors such as race, the practice is less benevolent. Although all people code switch, some of us do it because we feel obligated to, or because it simply makes life easier.

Once race is involved, code switching becomes a survival technique. It is meant to make people of the Global Majority more "palatable" and less threatening to white people. It's a subtle way of saying, "Don't exclude me; I'm one of you," "Trust me; I'm a professional," or at its most extreme, "Don't kill me; I'm harmless." The goal is to make the hegemonic class more comfortable, with the hope that they will leave us alone to live and work in peace.

Sometimes, code switching occurs organically; at other times, it is very strategic and deliberate. At home, when I pick up a call from an unknown number, the seamless slide from speaking in dialek to conversing in my plummiest customer service English is beautiful—and automatic. At work, Black people code switch in order to minimize exclusion and maximize belonging. We code switch to reduce the frequency with which we're found wanting.

Linguistic Code Switching: As I alluded to earlier, linguistic code switching can involve changing one's accent and / or vocabulary. It's "Hello, Chad" versus "Wah gwan my bredren?" The practice of code switching extends beyond language however. It is linguistic, behavioral, *and* sartorial.

Behavioral Code Switching: One of the best examples of behavioral code switching is seen in corporate corridors across America. My personal experiences and observations are as follows: If I see a white person in the hallway, we will usually exchange what I call "the grimace." It's a blank-eyed, tight-lipped "smile" that serves to acknowledge the presence of another human being, and also to communicate, "Please don't talk to me."

Working While Black: Learn 185

Contrast that with "the nod," which is often exchanged between melanated folk. Our eyes meet, we both raise our heads slightly, and there's a subtle but genuine smile. The subtext is "I see you, my sista. I see you my brotha. We gon' make it."

If these examples aren't clear enough, all I can suggest is that you google Barack Obama greeting people. For a giggle, take a look at the Key and Peele version. Watch that video, and you'll learn everything you need to know about behavioral code switching.[11]

Sartorial Code Switching: I definitely get a different response from people if I dress in a J.Crew-esque, "Ms. Congeniality" manner—white button down, pearl studs, slate gray pants—versus if I show up to work in bright colors, bold patterns, and my signature headwrap. One way I can guarantee to be "randomly selected" for inspection at an airport is to wear one. Works every time. Yes, I'm looking at you, LHR.

Sartorial code switching is, of course, about fashion, but for Black people, it's also about hair. Black women especially code switch our hair to reduce scrutiny and prevent those uncomfortable and intrusive conversations about our latest style. One of the best examples of this is Michelle Obama's "White House hairstyle" versus how she started wearing her hair once Barack's second term came to an end. Michelle wore her hair straightened when she was the FLOTUS to keep white America comfortable. As comedian Paul Mooney once said: "If your hair is relaxed, white people are relaxed. If your hair is nappy, they're not happy."[12]

Once her White House sojourn was over, it seemed like she mentally threw up the deuces and went straight to the salon to get her hair braided. The new look represented Mrs. Obama in her fullness. This was Michelle LaVaughn Robinson Obama of "Who's gonna tell him that the job he's seeking just might be one of those Black jobs" fame. As soon as she stepped out on stage that night with "The Braid," and that "Who gon' check me, boo?" energy, we knew it was about to get saucy. Other people's comfort be damned.

8. Hair Discrimination

Speaking of code switching hair: Imagine being told that your hair is illegal. Imagine being told that your hair, as it naturally grows out of your scalp, is "inappropriate" or "unprofessional." Imagine being sent home from work because you're wearing your hair in a natural or culturally resonant style, such as braids, locs, or an afro. Imagine being worried about whether you'll be able to get a job or promotion, not based on your qualifications but because of your hairstyle. Race-based hair discrimination is another burden that Black people bear. And yes, there is data to support it.

In research jointly commissioned by Dove and LinkedIn, "The NEW CROWN 2023 Workplace Research Study,"[13] it was found that "Black women's hair is "2.5× more likely to be perceived as unprofessional."

The study also revealed that:

Bias against natural hair and protective styles can impact how Black women navigate the hiring process.
- Approximately ⅔ of Black women (66%) change their hair for a job interview. Among them, 41% changed their hair from curly to straight.
- Black women are 54% more likely (or over 1.5× more likely) to feel like they have to wear their hair straight to a job interview to be successful.

Hair discrimination has led Black women to have a negative experience or outcomes within the workplace.
- Black women with coily / textured hair are 2× as likely to experience microaggressions in the workplace [as] than Black women with straighter hair.
- More than 20% of Black women 25–34 have been sent home from work because of their hair.

Young Black professionals are feeling the pressure from hair discrimination the most.
- Nearly half (44%) of Black women under age 34 feel pressured to have a headshot with straight hair.
- 25% of Black women believe they have been denied a job interview because of their hair, which is even higher for women under 34 (⅓).

In addition to outright discrimination, there is also the curiosity factor to deal with: Non-Black people are inordinately interested in Black hair. That curiosity, combined with caucacity, leads them to believe that they have the right to interrogate us about our hair, or worse yet, touch it, often without asking. There are few things as annoying as going in to work and having to dodge unwanted comments, backhanded compliments, and random hands getting frisky with your follicles.

I truly don't get the hair touching thing. Not once in my life, not even for a second, have I ever seen a colleague—far less a complete stranger—and thought, "I wonder what their hair feels like. I'm going to touch it." Transpose that to another part of a person's body: "I wonder what their [body part] feels like. I'm going to touch it." See how weird and creepy that sounds? Do you understand now that uninvited hair touching is assault? Okay, good. Now do better.

I say this on behalf of me and every Black person: You cannot touch our hair.

9. Microaggressions

"You have to sit at the back of the bus" was definitely a microaggression. The term *microaggression* was coined by Dr. Chester M. Pierce, who was a professor emeritus of psychiatry and education at Harvard. He was also a senior psychiatrist at Massachusetts General Hospital. In 1970, Dr. Pierce defined microaggressions as the subtly demeaning insults and nonverbal put-downs often used against minoritized people.

Derald Wing Sue, PhD, author of *Racial Microaggressions in Everyday Life: Race, Gender and Sexual Orientation*,[14] later expanded on the definition as follows:

> Microaggressions are the everyday verbal, nonverbal, and environmental slights, snubs, or insults, whether intentional or unintentional, which communicate hostile, derogatory, or negative messages to target persons based solely upon their marginalized group membership.

Part of what makes microaggressions so toxic and hard to confront is their subtlety. People sometimes have difficulty recognizing—or admitting—that a microaggression has taken place. And it's hard to address what is not confessed.

188   Be Yourself

An important detail is that "micro" refers to the (mis)behaviors occurring in one-to-one situations as opposed to on a "macro" or systemic level. Micro does not mean that the behaviors are miniscule in their impact, because they are not. Being on the receiving end of microaggressions can wreak havoc with one's self esteem and mental health.

In her article titled "Anatomy of a Microaggression,"[15] author and anti-racism educator Sharon Hurley Hall describes how marginalized people often process being microaggressed. As she depicts in Figure 1, the typical sequence of events is as follows:

First, the microaggression takes place and you experience the harm, then you replay the incident over and over in your mind, gaslighting yourself in the process. To make sure that what you experienced actually happened and that you are not overreacting, you might decide to run the scenario past a trusted friend. If they believe and validate you, you might decide to confront the person who committed the harm, and the situation is handled. If your friend doesn't believe you and gaslights you instead, you crawl back into your shell and never mention the incident again. Whichever way the scenario plays out, the pain stays with you, and the trauma keeps replaying itself in your mind. The next time you are microaggressed, you feel the sting even more keenly.

Hurley Hall also describes the effect on Global Majority people of being exposed to microaggressions multiple times over the course of one's career:

Every time there's another microaggression, you are quicker to recognize it, to feel the hurt. Every time you trust your environment a little less. Every time, you die a little inside.

This is just what happens or could happen ONE time. And everyone has their own experience of this.

Now imagine you are a Black or Brown person, a person who faces isms.

Imagine you have been in the workforce for decades. Imagine you've been working 50 weeks a year in the US, or around 46 to 48 in the UK or Europe.

Imagine only ONE microaggression a week (and know that there are likely more).

Working While Black: Learn   189

Do the math.

This is why we are "sensitive," why "we make everything about race," why "we can't take a joke." It isn't effing funny. And it happens way too often.

It's why some people who look like me and people who face isms don't want to rush back to offices. Sure, microaggressions can happen when working remotely, and they sting just as hard, but there are fewer chances and it's much easier to avoid them. Plus nobody looks at you strangely if you cry ... The question for would-be allies is: How can you avoid being the person that causes this harm? And How can you be the person that interrupts others who are causing harm in this way?

The funny thing is: Black people experience microaggressions all the time, but non-Black people seem clueless about their existence. It's similar to how almost every woman has been sexually assaulted by a man or knows someone who was, but no men seem to be acquainted with any of their guy friends who have committed those acts.

Since I'm a fan of clarity, here are some examples of typical microaggressions. Dr. Sue, whom I mentioned earlier, subdivides microaggressions into microassaults, microinsults, and microinvalidations:

Microassaults are intentionally discriminatory behaviors.

Examples:

- Telling racist jokes and saying the "N" word.
- Displaying the confederate flag or other problematic emblems.
- Passively allowing racist behavior to take place unchecked. Inaction is an action.

Microinsults are discriminatory comments or actions that are often though not necessarily unintentional.

Examples:

- Telling people of color that they're "so intelligent," "so articulate," or "not like the others."

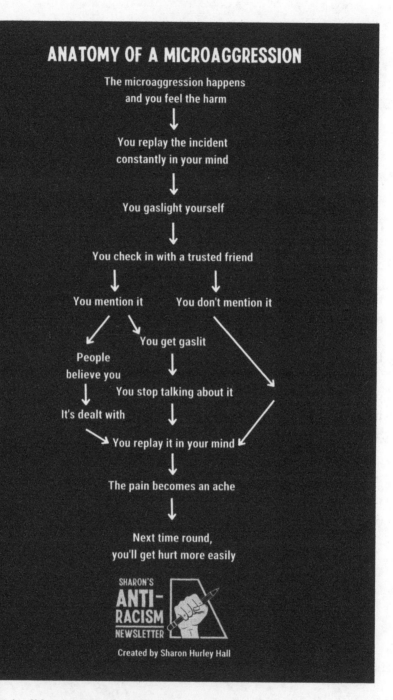

Figure 1 "Anatomy of a Microaggression"
Used with permission. © 2022 Sharon Hurley Hall.

Working While Black: Learn

- Assuming that Black people are "the help" or the most junior people on a team.
- Telling Black people that they were "lucky" to get their job or calling them a "DEI hire." (This one is particularly egregious, since it's the professional way of calling someone the N-word with the hard "-er."

Microinvalidations undermine or negate the experiences of marginalized people.

Examples:

- Mistaking Black team members for one another.
- Denying anyone's lived experiences with racism.
- Gaslighting marginalized people with phrases like "That's reverse racism," "We're in a post-racial society," or "I don't see color."

But Wait, There's More

Underpinning all the other elements of the WWBE are phenomena explored by noted scholars Dr. Moya Bailey, Kimberlé Crenshaw, and Cheryl L. Woods-Giscombé, PhD: Misogynoir, intersectionality, and the Superwoman Schema respectively.

10. Misogynoir

The word *misogynoir* was coined by Dr. Moya Bailey, Associate Professor of Communication Studies at Northwestern University and co-founder of the Black Feminist Health Science Studies Collective. She created the word to explain how the confluence of sexism and racism affects Black women. In her book, *Misogynoir Transformed: Black Women's Digital Resistance*, she explains the origins of the term:

> "Misogynoir" ... is a term I created in 2008 to describe the anti-Black racist misogyny that Black women experience, particularly in US visual and digital culture. Misogynoir is not simply the racism that Black women encounter, nor is it the misogyny Black women negotiate. Misogynoir describes the uniquely co-constitutive racialized and sexist violence that befalls Black women as a result of their simultaneous and interlocking oppression at the intersection of racial and gender marginalization.

192 Be Yourself

The term is a portmanteau of "misogyny," the hatred of women, and "noir," the French word for "black."[16]

11. Intersectionality

Undeniably, people of other races, genders, and identities experience isms, but to put it in layman's terms, Black women get it worse. This is because of how our intersecting identities collide with the structures, systems, and people that oppress us.

Which leads us to *intersectionality*.

Kimberlé Crenshaw, Distinguished Professor of Law at Columbia University and UCLA and co-founder of the African American Policy Forum (AAPF), coined the word to express the unique struggles faced by people with multiple marginalized identities as well as the ways in which racism, discrimination, and gender-based violence inform Black women's lived experiences:

> Because the intersectional experience is greater than the sum of racism and sexism, any analysis that does not take intersectionality into account cannot sufficiently address the particular manner in which Black women are subordinated. Thus, for feminist theory and antiracist policy discourse to embrace the experiences and concerns of Black women, the entire framework that has been used as a basis for translating 'women's experience' or 'the Black experience' into concrete policy demands must be rethought and recast.[17]

12. Superwoman Schema

Known informally as the "Strong Black Woman Syndrome," the **Superwoman Schema** is a framework created by Cheryl L. Woods-Giscombé, PhD, senior associate dean of the PhD division at the University of North Carolina at Chapel Hill School of Nursing.[18]

In her seminal study, "Superwoman Schema: African American Women's Views on Stress, Strength, and Health," Dr. Woods-Giscombé exposes what so many Black women know experientially: We are expected to be strong and stoic no matter what. According to Woods-Giscombé, Black women who exemplify the Superwoman Schema exhibit five characteristics:

1. Obligation to manifest strength
2. Obligation to suppress emotions

Working While Black: Learn 193

3. Resistance to being vulnerable or dependent
4. Determination to succeed despite limited resources
5. Obligation to help others

On corporate plantations, the Superwoman Schema plays out in numerous ways. Take another read of everything I outlined as being a part of the WWBE. Now imagine experiencing some or all of that daily for years or even decades but not having the freedom to express how it makes you feel, or to take a hiatus in order to recover. It would be enough to break even the strongest among us.

The expectation is that Black women are supposed to be overworked, underpaid (or not paid at all), bullied, microaggressed, excluded, and everything else we are subjected to in professional spaces and just ... take it on the chin. We're expected to be resilient in the face of inhumane treatment and unholy levels of stress. Nobody cares whether we thrive. People barely care whether we survive.

It can feel like we're in a *Hunger Games*-style competition, which is designed so that no matter what, we can't "win." If we smile, we are classified as "lacking gravitas." If we keep our faces at rest, we're accused of being "the angry Black woman." If we show any so-called "weakness" (such as crying), we are criticized for being "unprofessional." If we excel, we're "doing too much." If we don't, we're "not ready for a promotion."

We're expected to keep proving ourselves again and again, while others slide by based on potential. We're expected to prioritize the comfort of those who torment us daily. We're expected to take hit after hit after hit and keep bouncing back. I mean, who wouldn't need some space to exhale after dealing with all that?

The stereotype is so embedded in the culture that non-Black people seem to truly struggle with viewing us in any other way. It's almost impossible for them to acknowledge our multidimensionality.

A few years ago, I experienced a white woman parroting the "you're so strong" messaging directly to me. I was truly curious as to how somebody who had never met me had come up with this analysis of who I am. It made such an impression that I posted about it:

I remember participating in an online class a while back, and we were each asked to describe one other participant. The resident Karen told

194   Be Yourself

me and the group that I "remind her of a huge redwood tree" because I am "so resilient, unmoving, and incredibly strong."

Then, as now, I was irritated by that harmful, micro-aggressive comment disguised as a compliment.

I challenge you to find other adjectives for describing Black women. You are not restricted to "strong," "exotic," or "angry."

We are more than that. We are human. We are not beasts of burden. We have value beyond our ability to survive adverse circumstances, bounce back from struggle, and take on more than our fair share of labor.

So don't call me a "strong Black woman." And don't call me "resilient." See me in my fullness.

I am—we are—many things.

White women aren't the only ones who are allowed to cry, to show vulnerability, to be worthy of grace, and help, and tenderness.

Call me soft, and sweet, and delicate. Call me happy, and quirky, and carefree ... I dream of gentleness, of ease, of support. I dream of being able to lean on others.

I am not your strong Black woman.

When I encourage Black women in The Great Exhale to take their cape off and breathe—and when I encourage you to do the same—it's the superwoman cape that I'm referring to.

It's time for us to rip that cape off, throw it on the ground, and burn it to a cinder.

Burn the cape, sis.

Freedom awaits.

Asé.

So, What Now?

WHEW!

That's a lot, right? Picture yourself enduring these soul-crushing experiences day after day, year after year, without respite. Do you understand now why Black women are tired? Why we don't feel psychologically safe? Why we don't trust corporate spaces? Why we don't feel free to "bring our full selves to work?"

Our full selves are not accepted. Our full selves are under attack. Our full selves deserve better.

This is why so many of us are selecting self-employment over the daily professional struggle. The constant corporate-sanctioned career-focused hazing simply doesn't seem worth it. So instead, we are choosing US.

For My Non-Black Readers

I've shared all this to help educate you about what most of your Black colleagues are going through, with the hope that your empathy and ethics will stir you to do better. Be the person that you imagine or proclaim yourself to be.

If you had time to post a black square and write a performative caption during the racial reckoning of 2020, then you have time to interrupt bias when you see it. You have time to advocate and speak out publicly. You have time to be actively anti-racist. Your silence is complicity.

The system exists, but the system is composed of individuals. We need structural and systemic change as well as individual and behavioral change. You might not be able to change the system, but you can change yourself. Do what you can to help your Black colleagues breathe a little easier.

There are so many small but impactful actions you can take as an individual:

- If you have privilege, use it for good.
- If you see something, say something. Interrupt bias and microaggressions in the moment. Publicly. Skulking around in the hallway to commiserate after the fact doesn't count.
- Hiring managers: Fight for pay equity for the Black and Global Majority people on your team. Let us end this horrific habit of paying people the lowest amount possible (or nothing at all) just because you can. Let us end the trend of Black people being the highest qualified and lowest paid. Use your power and influence to bring about change.

196   Be Yourself

- Pronounce people's names correctly. This is the bare minimum. If you can pronounce Tchaikovsky, onomatopoeia, or schadenfreude, you can pronounce our names. Google them beforehand and listen to the pronunciation guide. Better yet, ask the person (a) what name they prefer to be addressed by and (b) how it is pronounced. (Bizarrely enough, people have found ways to mispronounce my name, which truly takes effort.)
- Look at the microaggressions examples and try not to do any of them. No "You're so articulate." No "Where are you *really* from?" No hair touching.
- Be a good human. Do we really need more anti-bias training? Most of us know what it feels like to be bullied. We know what it feels like when someone is mean to us. So let's not bully others. Let's not be mean. Let the Golden Rule obtain. If you don't want it for yourself, don't inflict it on others.

For Organizations

This education is for you as well. Knowledge is one of the catalysts of change. If you're listed as one of the "Best Places to Work," my question is, Best for whom? If you claim that your company is inclusive, my question is, Inclusive for whom? If you purport to have created a psychologically safe culture, my question is: Safe for whom? Because despite your proclamations, Black people, particularly Black women, do not feel safe at work.

As a corporate entity, you have the power and means to make positive changes at scale. Don't look at what other companies are doing. *You* lead the way. Act. Let's move past the "listening and learning" and advance to the "addressing and progressing." I'm a fan of verbs. What are you *actually doing* beyond posting performative statements and stock photos of Global Majority people on your website? I don't have all the answers, but I do have some suggestions for how you can provide space to exhale for your Black and Global Majority employees.

Working While Black: Learn 197

Prioritize and Fund DEI: A rollback on DEI initiatives is anti-Blackness at scale. We can tell what you prioritize based on how budgets are allocated.

- Make a focus on diversity, equity, and inclusion one of the central tenets of your organization.
- Fund, hire, and remunerate appropriately. Give your DEI directors more than a title. To implement meaningful, lasting changes they need power, influence, budget—and backing from the C-suite.

P.S. As soon as you start talking about "diversity of thought" and "the business case for diversity," we know you're being performative.

P.P.S. If in doubt, take a page out of Costco's playbook.

Prioritize Psychological Safety: Firstly, the goal is to establish a culture that your employees don't need to be protected from and that they don't feel the need to escape from.

- Create a culture from the top down that encourages life-work balance, taking time off, taking breaks, and having flexibility. For example, there are a few organizations that have twice-yearly company-wide shutdowns, usually a week in summer, and a week over the Christmas season. This is in addition to any PTO that employees have accrued. Initiatives like this place employees' well-being front and center and make it easy for people to take guilt-free time off so they can completely decompress.
- Provide resources and accommodations such as remote work options, mental health support, quiet rooms, self-care benefits, and gym memberships. Again, these benefits should be a bonus, not triage against a harmful organizational culture.
- Diversify your C-suite and management team. There should be no monochromatic teams of pallor.
- Hire and train good people. Don't fall victim to the "evil hero" stereotype: The thinking that it's okay to keep "superstar" employees around even when they are demonstrably toxic and harmful to others. You can find superstar employees who know how to treat people humanely.

Be Yourself

- Let employees know that they are psychologically safe by having a zero-tolerance policy on bullying, racism, and microaggressions, and by also having a no-retaliation policy for victims who report.
- Tie managers' performance and bonuses to psychological safety metrics.

Prioritize Community and Safe Spaces

- Create and fund Employee Resource Groups (ERGs) for your Black and Global Majority employees. If that is not possible, then provide them with access to spaces like Therapy for Black Girls or The Great Exhale as part of your benefits package or employee assistance program. In particular, Black employees who are "the only" need additional support.

Prioritize Good Hiring Practices

- No more tokenism. Make your teams more diverse.
- No more cronyism. Hire outside your social circle.
- No more nepotism. Your cousin might actually not be the best person for the job.
- Establish transparent and equitable pay for all employees.
- Banish the phrases "DEI hire" and "diversity hire" from your corporate vocabulary.

Deprioritize Performativity: When your Black and Global Majority employees express that they're being harmed and you respond by providing pool tables and free pizza, it's a slap in the face. Less pizza, more pay equity. Blue bracelet-style performativity is a no.

For My Black Readers

I've shared all this to let you know that you are not alone, and what you're going through is not a figment of your imagination. The system, alas, is operating as designed. I've also shared this to hopefully inspire some self-reflection. Given that this is how things are, how do you choose to proceed with your career? What do you want for yourself? How are you going to curate your career to minimize harm and maximize health? How will you create space to exhale in your work life? You don't need to answer these questions now, but at least start thinking about them. In the next chapter, "Curate Your Career," we'll explore them more deeply.

And now, let's breathe and meditate, because after this chapter of all chapters, we definitely need to woosah.

Elevation: Vibrate Higher

Exhalation: Breathe Easy

Sighing Breath

Sit with your feet on the floor, about hip width apart, or in a comfortable cross-legged position.

Close your eyes softly, breathe normally, and bring your attention to your body. See if you can feel tension anywhere: your forehead, your jaw, your neck, your shoulders. Tune in to your stomach, back, hips, and thighs. Breathe normally for a minute or two, and consciously relax any tense areas.

Now that you're a bit more relaxed, let's start our sighing breaths. You'll be inhaling through your nose for a count of three, and exhaling through your mouth for a count of six.

Let's begin:

Inhale for 1, 2, 3
Exhale and sigh for 1, 2, 3, 4, 5, 6

Inhale for 1, 2, 3
Exhale and sigh for 1, 2, 3, 4, 5, 6

Inhale for 1, 2, 3
Exhale and sigh for 1, 2, 3, 4, 5, 6

(continued)

(continued)

With every exhale, with every sigh, visualize all stress leaving your body.

Inhale: 1, 2, 3

Exhale: 1, 2, 3, 4, 5, 6

Inhale: 1, 2, 3

Exhale: 1, 2, 3, 4, 5, 6

Inhale: 1, 2, 3

Exhale: 1, 2, 3, 4, 5, 6

Continue your sighing breaths for as long as you wish, until you feel more regulated.

When you're ready, return your breathing to its normal cadence and open your eyes.

Affirmations: Speak Life

- I am smart, savvy, and strategic.
- I am giving myself permission to be paid what I'm worth.
- I am navigating corporate spaces with ease, safety, and success.
- I am guided to spaces, people, and companies that are safe and supportive of me.
- I am always Divinely protected: The weapons may form, but they will never prosper.

Introspection: Journal & Heal

- Can colleagues be genuine friends?
- Do you ever feel like you have to work "twice as hard"?
- What is the most harmful experience you ever had at a job?
- What is your experience of working in white-majority companies?
- Have you experienced the Working While Black Effect? In what ways? How did it make you feel?

(continued)

(continued)

Curation: Do the Work

Dear Non-Black Readers,

This is your moment. Ally is a verb. Action is required. If being a true ally is something you aspire to, these are some things you can do. While you cannot crown yourself with an ally title, actions like these will move you closer to having marginalized communities view you as one:

1. Reread this chapter.
2. Throw away that blue bracelet.
3. Identify one concrete action that you will take to address—and reduce—the Working While Black Effect. Here are some suggestions:

   - If you witness Black people being microaggressed or harmed in any way, speak up and defend them in public.
   - Leverage your privilege to help close the equity gap.
   - Put genuine diversity into practice: Increase the numbers of Black women you employ.
   - Mentor, sponsor, promote, and protect Black women.
   - If you are a hiring manager, or someone with influence over compensation, ensure that Black women are remunerated equitably.
   - Resist the urge to act punitively toward Black women.
   - Believe Black women.

Appreciation: Express Gratitude

What are you grateful for? Count your blessings:

- I am grateful …
- I am grateful …
- I am grateful …

(continued)

(continued)

Celebration: Razzle Dazzle

Flex on 'em, sis! What are you proud of? Celebrate yourself:

- I am proud of myself for ...
- I am proud of myself for ...
- I am proud of myself for ...

Meditation: Think Blissfully

Metta Meditation: Loving-Kindness

Sit comfortably, with your back straight and your eyes closed. Smile gently.

Focus on your breath, inhaling and exhaling slowly through your nose for a count of five.

Inhale: 1, 2, 3, 4, 5
Exhale: 5, 4, 3, 2, 1

Inhale: 1, 2, 3, 4, 5
Exhale: 5, 4, 3, 2, 1

Inhale: 1, 2, 3, 4, 5
Exhale: 5, 4, 3, 2, 1

Keep breathing softly and slowly. Now visualize an image of yourself in your mind. Place your hands on your heart, and say these words to yourself, either mentally or out loud:

May I be safe, happy, and healthy
May I be peaceful, blessed, and at ease
May I be abundant, compassionate, and grateful
May I be free from all pain
May I be filled with loving-kindness

(continued)

(continued)

Next, bring to mind someone you love very much. Say to them:

> May you be safe, happy, and healthy
> May you be peaceful, blessed, and at ease
> May you be abundant, compassionate, and grateful
> May you be free from all pain
> May you be filled with loving-kindness

Now, imagine someone you feel neutral about, and say those words to them as well:

> May you be safe, happy, and healthy
> May you be peaceful, blessed, and at ease
> May you be abundant, compassionate, and grateful
> May you be free from all pain
> May you be filled with loving-kindness

Next, think about someone that you experience as difficult. Say to them:

> May you be safe, happy, and healthy
> May you be peaceful, blessed, and at ease
> May you be abundant, compassionate, and grateful
> May you be free from all pain
> May you be filled with loving-kindness

If challenging feelings come up, like anger, sadness, or regret, that's okay. Do your best to observe and experience them fully. If tears start to fall, that's okay too. Let it all out.

Now think about the planet; about as many people as you can. Say these words:

> May all beings be safe, happy, and healthy
> May all beings be peaceful, blessed, and at ease

(continued)

204   Be Yourself

(*continued*)

　　May all beings be abundant, compassionate, and grateful
　　May all beings be free from all pain
　　May all beings be filled with loving-kindness

Finally, focus on yourself again, wishing yourself these things:

　　May I be safe, happy, and healthy
　　May I be peaceful, blessed, and at ease
　　May I be abundant, compassionate, and grateful
　　May I be free from all pain
　　May I be filled with loving-kindness

　　Bask in the positive energy for as long as you wish, and when you're ready, open your eyes.

　　Asé.

8

Curate Your Career: Strategize

Invocation

Most High,

Today and every day I pray for alignment:
May my values and vocation be in perfect concordance
May my work serve to make the world a better place
May my calling seamlessly combine purpose, passion, and profit
May my career be blessed

Today and every day I pray for enjoyment:
May I absolutely love the work that I do
May I daily operate in my zone of excellence
May I earn my living honestly, and easily find fulfillment
May my career be blessed

Today and every day I pray for abundance:
May I be rewarded and remunerated equitably
May the benefits truly benefit me
May all the bags be fully secured
May my career be blessed

206 Be Yourself

Today and every day I pray for ascension:
May I rise unfettered to my Divinely selected level
May I embrace collaboration over competition
May I always remember to lift as I climb
May my career be blessed

Today and every day I pray for safety:
May I always be protected by Your Holy Light
May I daily be shielded from harm
May any weapons that form all fail to prosper
May my career be blessed

Today and every day I pray for equilibrium:
May I enjoy life-work balance, in that order
May my work pour into me rather than depleting me
May it bring me elevation and ease in equal measure
May my career be blessed

Amen

~ ~ ~

Corporate Shenanigans

"What kind of pole was it?"

One of my caucasian colleagues asked me this during a "getting to know the new girl" session, and I was truly confused. I looked around at the whole group: A bunch of white women snickering and exchanging "inside joke" glances. This was her second time asking, so I attempted to get clarification:

"I'm sorry," I said, "I honestly don't understand. What do you mean?"

"Well you said you used to be a dancer, so which direction was the pole?"

My brain kept refusing to comprehend the question. In retrospect, I realize that it had been trying to save me from tomfoolery.

"Horizontal or vertical?" she continued. "I bet it was vertical."

Underneath my melanin, I blushed bright red. Light finally dawned.

Karen thought I was a former stripper.

Now ... nothing against strippers: Work is work. However, we had been discussing what hobbies and interests we had when we were growing up. As in *during childhood*. My response had been that I used to dance. Or maybe I had said that I used to be a dancer. But c'mon. They knew good and darned well that I had not been out there working a pole and making it rain during my formative years. But they just couldn't resist being messy, especially to the only Black woman in the group. They knew that nobody would stop them and that nobody would protect me.

"It was horizontal, as in a ballet barre," I finally responded. "I studied ballet, jazz, modern, African, Caribbean folk, and even a bit of ballroom and tap."

I felt embarrassed, and also infuriated, that their first instinct was to think that the only kind of dance I was capable of doing was pole dancing.

This is but one example of the kinds of hurtful and harmful interactions Black people are often subjected to at work. For us, white-majority spaces are simply not safe.

And don't think that white people don't know that. They do. They know exactly what they're doing and exactly how it feels, which is why whenever you ask any of them if they would change places with a Black person, they fall silent. They don't want to because they know how they treat us, and they would never choose that for themselves. They know how uncomfortable we are trying to navigate through the landmines they place in our paths daily, but they don't have to care, so they don't. Unearned privilege and unacknowledged racism have them in an absolute chokehold.

They absolutely know how uncomfortable it feels to be constantly surrounded by people who don't look like you. I found this out personally when I invited a non-melanated colleague of mine to a highly melanated gathering. (Not a cookout though. As a core element of my self-care, I don't extend cookout invitations to colonizer descendants.) Anyhoo, I thought we were going to have a bonding moment and enjoy a few hours together soaking up some healing and culture. However, she texted me shortly before the event to say that she was bringing along a (white) friend because having another white person there would make her feel more comfortable. She knew she was going to be "in the minority" for like four hours, and even that was too long. She didn't want to feel uncomfortable being in the company of people who did not look like her. So: She got it. They get it.

208 Be Yourself

This is why no amount of blue bracelets, pink hats, or black squares make a difference to most Black women. The main color that needs to be contended with is white. Let's start by dealing with that. Let's begin by dismantling the white supremacy industrial complex. And here's a hint: Wearing accessories ain't gonna do it.

It was alarming, though not surprising, that after the results of the 2024 election, the first instinct of a certain subgroup of white women was to identify themselves as "safe" just because they had a few minutes of being judged by the color of their skin rather than the content of their character. To whom it may concern: The fact that your first response was to center yourself and engage in performativity indicated that you are still extremely unsafe for the Black people in your circle. And as I often say on social media: "If it don't apply, scroll on by." Please don't start mentally responding with "Not all white women." I never said that it was. If it doesn't apply to you, you shouldn't be feeling defensive.

How to Curate Your Career

This book is about making choices: It's about curating your life so that it operates to your benefit and frees you to enjoy greater ease. The curation process is one of examination, interrogation, selection, and implementation, so you end up with an "exhibit"— your life—that is pleasing to your spirit, supportive to your mind, and healthy for your body.

Because adulting is a scam and capitalism is a hater, our professions play an enormous role in our existence on this earth. So much so that we can't truly redesign our lives without considering what kind of career we want, and how to approach it so that we succeed—in whatever way we define success. For that matter, we need to decide if we want a career at all. Because it's perfectly okay to be happy with a job.

There are entire books written on this subject, targeted specifically to Black women and women of color. *The Memo* by Minda Harts is an excellent one.[1] Harts makes the undisputable point that *if* a traditional career is what you truly want, then you must play the game according to the rules that have been established because patriarchy and white supremacy aren't going anywhere anytime soon. Until changes are made at a systemic level, it is what it is. She's 100 percent right.

Curate Your Career: Strategize

209

For some of us (including me at one point), that is the path we desire. We enjoy the daily joust; the thrust and parry; the schemes and strategies. We enjoy proving the naysayers wrong and proving our cheerleaders right. We want to ascend the corporate ladder and eventually sit pretty in the C-suite. And that is perfectly okay. We are allowed to want what we want. We are allowed to seek success in whatever ways are meaningful to us.

We are also allowed to change our minds about how we define success.

Space To Exhale is about exactly that: Pausing to reflect, taking a breath, and choosing a different path. As the years have passed, my definition of success has evolved. To paraphrase James Baldwin, "I do not dream of labor."

For me, *rest* is the new success.

My career is a *part* of who I am, but it is far from being my everything. My job is not my identity. My title is not tied to my sense of self-worth. And my self-worth does not increase based on how busy I am.

#BookedAndBusy has its place, but so does #BlessedAndRested.

And although I am not *yet* at the stage where I'm relaxing in my summer mansion in Monaco, wearing stilettos, a FeNoel robe, a crystal crown, and a gold bikini while being fed chilled grapes as I lounge poolside, I have taken, and am continuing to take, steps to incorporate more rest into my professional life. I'm redefining my working life to suit ME.

This is not laziness. This is not a cop-out. This is not quiet quitting. This is me choosing me. It is a conscious and strategic reallocation of my time, energy, focus, creativity, and resources. I must be the primary beneficiary thereof. And in your life, you must be the person who benefits most from those things as well.

Over the years, I've experienced every aspect of the Working While Black Effect, which I outlined in the previous chapter, and it's exhausting. It wears you down. Weathers you like water on stone. To be honest, I want better for myself. I want better for us all. I have no problem with putting in the work and doing what needs to be done to help a project succeed, but the daily "myth of Sisyphus" experience is for the birds.

Once I realized the full scope of the WWBE and the immense pressure it can exert on one mentally, physically, and financially, I decided that this was not the way for me. I am declining to struggle, and am instead choosing the path of least resistance. At some point, if you keep hitting

210 Be Yourself

your head against a wall, you have to realize that there must be another way: A way that does not harm you. If you can't go through, go around. Choose differently.

Recognize When The Reckoning Happens

Over the course of my career, there have been so many times when I have thought "Is this all there is?" So many times when I have felt like I can barely breathe from the crushing anxiety, from the tightness in my chest, from the constant stress. Countless times when I have crumbled under the weight of being continuously overworked. Innumerable times when I've cried in the ladies room after another full day of isms, disrespect, and microaggressions. So many times that I've felt like I don't fit in and never will.

One of those times when I experienced that sense of "I don't belong here," I was (per usual) the only Black person in yet another meeting that should have been an email, surrounded by a group of people who were enthusiastically discussing—wait for it—laundry detergent. And I mean, they were genuinely beside themselves with excitement. High pitched and super animated. Vocal fry on mosquito frequency, buzzing like fuzzy tinnitus. Mentally, I was like ... are these people okay?! I was truly confused and concerned. I understand bringing a measure of enthusiasm to what one is working on, but the level of excitement seemed incongruent with the nature of the project. They had "I won the lottery" energy for an "I found a penny on the sidewalk" event.

I worked for a retailer that specialized in consumer packaged goods and household cleaning supplies, and we were kicking off yet another soap powder promo. Scintillating. I mean ... we all knew that we were heading toward another "25% Off Detergent" headline, with "Save on [insert list of brands]" for the subhead. Did we need a one-hour, 10-person meeting for that? Did we need a meeting that felt like a ticker tape parade? Did we need another "Whoever speaks the loudest wins" moment? Couldn't we just do the work and keep it moving? Could we not keep the brief ... brief? Did we have to behave as if that detergent and wet wipes made our souls sparkle like fresh-washed crockery? It was so weird to me. Especially since their excitement seemed genuine.

Curate Your Career: Strategize 211

So, as I slo-mo looked around the room wondering how I had ended up here (thank goodness for my sunglasses, 'cause my face has zero filter and always speaks in her outside voice), I thought to myself, "These people can't be for real," followed by, "There has got to be more to life. God did not create me to write about detergent."

Admit Your Truth

After detergent-gate, something clicked inside me. From that moment on, I started gradually approaching my career more realistically. I accepted that:

- I do not fit in—and I am okay with that. I never have, and to be honest I do not want to. The detergent dynamos are not my people.
- I do not want to be a people manager, at least not in the traditional sense. Some folks love it, but I am not one of them. And that is okay.
- I do not want to spend my days putting in face time, playing politics, and currying favor with people who do not care about me. Waste of time.
- I prefer to be an individual contributor, or better yet, be my own boss. I love collaborating with the right people, but for the most part the ongoing group project of corporate life is hell.
- I work best on my own. And at my own pace. The creativity cannot be rushed. The muse needs room to breathe.
- I love having mastery over my time. I don't want to work late or put in overtime. I don't want to have to deal with corporate Chads and Karens clocking my every minute. Been there, done that, over it. I will provide excellent work, as contracted, during the agreed hours, and that is it.
- I do not want to attend the "unhappy hours." I rebuke them with my entire spirit. The so-called happy hours are not happy for me. I'm an introvert, a teetotaler, and a highly sensitive person. Those after-work gatherings in smelly bars mean being around too many people, too much alcohol, and too much noise. No. I want to clock out, go home, bond with my family, and play with my puppy.
- I'm a fan of rest, of calm, of a gentler pace. I have no desire to spend my days in a state of constant tension, panic, and dysregulation. I love being able to take breaks and settle my spirit. When I spent a year in Nice, in the south of France, I absolutely loved my school's approach

212   Be Yourself

to the workday. We took a break at about noon, and most of the teachers walked away from their classrooms and gathered to break bread (and drink wine!) at the communal lunch table. That went on until about 2:00 p.m. There was no grabbing a hurried bite at one's desk. There was no guilt for taking a moment to eat and reset. There was no rush. It was blissful. And the work still got done.

These were some of the realizations that bloomed in my mind. That is what works best for me. But we are all different. This is a judgment-free zone, so I hold space and understanding for my sisters who are still seeking corporate glory. I get it. I truly want us all to thrive, shine, and succeed in whatever ways serve us best.

Pivot, Prioritize, and Protect Yourself

If you're a Corporate Queen of Color who is still pursuing the dream, I have some advice for you:

Get Informed
First things first, secure yourself a copy of *The Memo*, and take Minda Harts's advice. She's gone through it so you don't have to, and she's laid out a framework for you to follow.

Do It for the Joy
Combine what you love with your career. Several years ago, I made the conscious decision that I would build my career around writing since it is one of the loves of my life. For most of my professional life I have therefore been a copywriter in one form or another. My thinking was if I have to work every single solitary day, I might as well do something I love. That way, in the midst of bad bosses, tight deadlines, crazy hours, cameras-on calls, unreasonable expectations, and meetings that should have been emails, I would still be able to squeeze some joy from my workdays.

Do It for the Purpose
If you can, seek employment with a company that focuses on mission-driven work and whose values align with yours. Knowing that there is a greater cause to which you are contributing makes up for a lot. If that is not possible, then

find an organization that supports (or at least does not impede) your personal, purpose-led initiatives. Find an employer that does not hate on your side hustle. Pursue companies that are aligned with your values and that have positive employee reviews on Glassdoor. You can also check out Inside Voices,[2] a Black-owned firm founded by Ekow Sanni-Thomas that makes it easy for employees to anonymously review their companies, particularly in terms of how they perform in the areas of inclusion, equity, diversity, and anti-racism.

Do It for the Culture—and the Coins

In other words, prioritize being paid, and being paid equitably. Joy and purpose have their place, as does being down for the culture. But practicalities exist. As I often say: Exposure doesn't pay the bills. The time for providing free labor is over. Money isn't *everything*, but it has a huge impact on many things, including your lifestyle, health, and levels of freedom. Financial security can also help support your mental wellness. So do your best to make sure that you are properly paid. There are billions of dollars floating around out there, and at least a few million are earmarked just for you. Claim them.

On the flip side, not all money is good money. Seek out the good money. Better yet, get your energy vibrating at a level where good money always finds you.

Take Your Time Off

Take every solitary second of your PTO. You earned it. It is part of the compensation package you negotiated so fiercely, so take what's yours. If you feel any guilt about taking time away from work, release it, sis. In 99 percent of cases, you are a number and a line item to these organizations. It's in the name: "Human **Resources**." If and when you leave, whatever the circumstances, you will be replaced in a heartbeat. So yes, you work for the job, but the job must also work for you. That includes taking time away to regroup. Life first. Job second.

Seek Support

Your career, like so many things in life, is both an individual and a group project. You can go it alone, but it is so much easier if you get some support along the way. Look for mentors, sponsors, and advisors who can help you navigate your career strategically, who can act as sounding boards, and who can counsel you when things go pear shaped. Actively build relationships and deposit into people so that when you need to make a withdrawal, they don't feel used.

214 Be Yourself

In addition, seek community. It's so important to your mental and emotional well-being. If your organization has an ERG for Black employees, join it. If they don't, then join a community of like-minded people. I happen to know of a great one, lol! Think of The Great Exhale, and communities like it, as an external ERG. And don't let anybody shame you if the community you join is racially homogeneous. People seem to support these—unless the community is Black. But as we've established, working while Black on majority-white teams is bad for your health—and your career. So go and be among your people, IRL or virtually. Prioritize your health, get the support you need, and join the sisterhood.

A Note on White Women's Tears

More Black lives have been taken and more Black bodies incarcerated than we probably even know of as a result of white women's tears (WWT). I am willing to bet that if a study was done on the effect of WWT on Black folks' professional lives, there would be a correlation between Black people in career-ending situations and white women playing the tearful damsel card. As I mentioned in the "*Working While Black*" chapter, I personally have experienced being fired after a white woman cried when she was held accountable for having been racist toward me.

The thing is, white women cry because it works, and they know it. They are raised and taught to do this. I remember a trend on TikTok a while back called the #TurnItOff challenge (aka the #WhiteWomenFakeTears challenge).[3] Thousands upon thousands of videos of women of Caucasus bawling their eyes out, and then suddenly just stopping, and giving a little smile and wink for the camera. Truly disturbing.

I say fight fire with fire. Or rather, water with water.

We must give ourselves permission to cry.

Cry like a white girl, sis.

Cry early.

Cry often.

Cry.

How I Find Space to Exhale in My Career

This is ongoing, not a one-and-done event. Here is the process that I follow to ensure that I am prioritizing me, and getting enough room to breathe in my career. I give myself permission to:

Examine the Evidence

After the breakdown I experienced in 2024, I knew that I needed to make serious life changes. There had to be a better way. I spent a lot of time pondering questions like: What is working for me? What is not? How do I want to feel? What do I want my days to be like? What brings me comfort? What brings me joy? What do I want more of? Less of? Who and what do I love? Who and what loves me back? What depletes or elevates my energy? Is the work ... working? I completely reevaluated my vision for my life—especially my career.

Get Grounded in My Values

I also reevaluated my values. As we gain life experience, what is important to us changes. I asked myself: Is my life aligning with my values right now? So, how about you? Are you in integrity with yourself? If so, great. If not, it's time to get in alignment. I wrote a whole chapter about curating your values because they are your north star in life. When you're living in congruence with your value system you walk tall. You sleep good. You breathe easy. You are able to fully exhale. I want that for me and for us all.

Take another look at the "Curate Your Values" chapter. As you do the work of identifying (or redefining) your values, be prepared to dig a little deeper. For example, if you list "success" as one of your values, what does success mean to you? Answer honestly. So many of us are subscribing to success metrics that were never designed with us in mind. It's as if we hop on one of those automatic walkways at an airport, moving—but not making progress. Because guess what? We got on the wrong one, and we're being carried toward a gate that is not ours. We're going in the entirely wrong direction, and now we have to hop off and start pelting all the way across the terminal, huffing and puffing, dragging our carry-on, hoping to make our flight. (Sorry; had a moment there. Traumatic Miami airport memories, lol. Yes, I made the flight. Last person on.)

But seriously: What does success mean to you? And is it even one of your values? It might not be, and that is okay. Your definition of success might be different from the "norm," and that is also okay. You're allowed to prioritize family, relaxation, creativity, health, and enjoyment over climbing the corporate ladder.

I remember once living in the country in Pennsylvania and working in midtown Manhattan. On the best day, that's a four-hour round-trip commute.

216   Be Yourself

Most days, it took longer. Having mastery over my time has always been a value of mine, so I took steps to remedy the situation. I found a job that was 10 minutes from my house. I would even sometimes drive home and have lunch. Most days, I was home by 5:15 p.m. It was heavenly.

I didn't include these in my values list, but for me: Rest is a value. Comfort is a value. Family is a value. Creativity is a value. Being a time millionaire is a value. I need to have agency over my time so I can express my creativity, connect with my loved ones, and spend as many delightful hours as possible snuggled in a blankie, resting on my couch.

That means that I respect and perform any job I'm paid to do, but it is not my be-all and end-all. My job is not my identity. It is a contractual agreement that benefits both parties, and that is all.

Dem people don't own me.

Stop Code Switching

As I've mentioned before, code switching does not only take place linguistically and behaviorally, but also sartorially.

Both my parents are pretty sharp dressers, and I inherited those genes from them. My closet is truly a wonderland. I used to love getting dressed up for work in my coordinated suits, accessories, and heels. Always heels. Full face of makeup. Hair *done-done*. It was part of my daily armor. If I left home without earrings and I had enough time, I would go back home and get some. (Don't judge me, y'all.) I used to work at a company at which women were required to wear skirts and pantyhose. This is sartorial code switching, and it has its place. There's nothing wrong with dressing for work like it's an occasion.

But after a few years, I just didn't want to be bothered anymore. I prefer to dress up if I want to—not because I am obligated to. I want to be comfortable. The work is still going to get done no matter how I'm dressed or how I wear my hair. That has meant choosing to work with companies that don't require formal business attire.

Now I'm not suggesting that you show up for work unwashed and unkempt (you know who you are; yes we can tell), but I *am* suggesting that you prioritize comfort. These days, I don't code switch my look anymore. I wear sneakers and jeans to work. No makeup; only sunscreen. I have also stopped code switching my hair. No more relaxers. (No judgment at all to

Curate Your Career: Strategize 217

those of you who choose to embrace the creamy crack. I've been there.) I already know I'm not going to fit in, so I do me. I wear my hair in braids, a huge afro, or most frequently in a head wrap. I go to work comfy.

Accommodate Myself

Like many of us, I have spent hours in those office buildings with the huge banks of windows. I love the views and the natural light, but my photophobia won't let me be great. So I wear my sunglasses at work, and I sit in the darkest possible space by myself, as opposed to with everyone else at the row of desks. That lets me avoid the glare from the sun as well as the harsh fluorescent overhead lights.

Prioritize Me

This takes practice, especially for Black women, since we are socialized to put everyone else first. Over my career I've gotten better at honoring my introversion and neurodivergence. Even though it did not do me any favors in the popularity Olympics, I spent as much time as possible on my own.

Now that working remotely is an option, I work from home as often as possible. If I *must* go into an office, I find quiet, dimly lit areas where I can focus. To be clear, earlier in my career, I had a different approach, and it was the right one for that period of my life. I was never the life of the party, but I would definitely participate in whatever themed office events or group activities were in play. And, yes, I would even attend the "unhappy hours."

These days, I decline to participate in group activities and those bizarre team-building exercises. How am I gonna trust fall into the arms of people who stab me in the back daily? Nope. Also, I absolutely do not want to go out for drinks. I mean I don't even drink. This might not be the correct decision for everyone, but it is right for me. I minimize interaction as a means of minimizing harm. There's nobody asking me, "What direction is the pole?" anymore.

Work to Rule

Remember when the "quiet quitting" trend was making the rounds? First of all, quiet quitting is not a thing. It's called working to rule. You do what you're paid to do and no more. I can't do long days and double shifts anymore. And even if I could, I don't want to. What are we working for? This is the real question. If you're "working for the good of your

218　　　　　　　　　　　　　Be Yourself

family," but you are so busy that you never see them, or so bad-tempered that you can't get along with them, then (and I say this with love) you're lying to yourself about your true motivation.

I remember the days of coming back home after work and wall-sliding to the floor in tears and exhaustion. I want better for myself. I want better for us all. We should not exchange our ancestors' plantations for servitude of another kind. Do what you're paid to do, and save your magic for yourself and your loved ones.

Choose Differently

At some point, I had to decide what kind of professional life I wanted. Did I want a career or a job? Did I want to be an employee or an entrepreneur? Or both? Did I want to "hit the ground running" and "move at a fast pace," or get gently grounded and then proceed at a measured, sustainable walk? The answer might not lie in the binary, but rather somewhere along the continuum. However, the important thing is to interrogate the decisions that have gotten you to this point. There are no wrong answers. You have to know what's right for *you*.

For me, the answer is somewhere in the middle, because bills. Few things relieve stress like direct deposit. That said, I am in the process of curating my life so that I am no longer dependent on direct deposit. My goal is ultimately to be my own boss, to be a full-time professional author, community builder, and creative, in ways that are meaningful to me. That life is loading, and its becoming is beautiful to see.

The importance of community, family, money, and a support system cannot be overstated. Choice is often circumscribed by one's level of privilege. Take all the tech bros who start their origin stories with "I launched my company from my parents' garage." Or the ones who share that they took a year off to ideate, and while they were imagining the future they lived in their folks' basement or survived on their inheritance. Not everybody has parents with an empty room, basement, or garage where they are welcome to stay while they build. Everyone does not have inheritance money or savings that they can draw on. What about the people who quit their jobs and never looked back? (I actually did this once. I tell you all about it in Chapter 10.) The point is, in order to be able to walk away from your job, you must have some kind of support system in place. You must have a level of privilege. You will need the wherewithal to survive. Plan carefully.

Curate Your Career: Strategize   219

My goal is also to avoid stress, so I have chosen not to go scorched earth and "fire de wuk"* with no plan or backup income. I'm using the displacement method, so that the transition from full-time employment to full-time entrepreneurship is easier on me.

Put Life First

Most of us go through a period where we become cathected with our career; bonded to our job. We conflate our title with our identity. I've never gone quite that far, but there have definitely been instances in my career when I overidentified with work and put it first in my life. However, that led to imbalance, exhaustion, and burnout. As I now say, the goal is life-work balance in that order. Life comes first. I make a clear demarcation between my professional and personal lives. I choose to divest and rest.

Set Boundar-ease

That's not a typo. Boundaries bring ease to your life. These are some of the professional boundaries that I have established:

- Where possible, I insist on agendas for meetings.
- I say no to unreasonable requests and timelines.
- If the meeting is unfolding in an unstructured manner, I propose a reschedule.
- I no longer give colleagues my personal phone number. We can communicate via email, Teams, Slack, Zoom, Monday, Notion ... whatever. That's more than enough. My private number is just that: Private.
- I no longer connect with colleagues on social media. In some cases, if they slipped in before I established that rule, I block them.
- When I'm off, I'm off. At the end of the workday, I set my status to away and silence all notifications. When I'm on holiday, I'm on holiday. I don't take my work laptop or work phone with me. We can chat when I get back.
- I have my lunch hour blocked on my calendar. If I'm in office, I eat lunch solo as often as possible. I have my end-of-workday blocked as well. That time is mine.

---

*"Fire de wuk" is a Bajan expression that translates to "fire the work;" in other words: Quit your job.

220 Be Yourself

Seek Sanctuary in Community

As I described in the previous chapter, the Working While Black Effect can have far-reaching consequences not only on Black women's careers, but also on our mental health. We cannot fully heal in isolation, so I built The Great Exhale for myself and Black women like me who are tired of being strong and putting ourselves last on our priority list.

It's a new day, and we're saying "No."

- We're saying no to putting work first in our lives.
- We're saying no to being the "Strong Black Woman."
- We're saying no to prioritizing other people's comfort.
- We're saying no to being active participants in our own demise.
- We're saying no to merely surviving.

We're also saying "Yes."

- We're saying yes to putting life first and work second.
- We're saying yes to being a Soft Black Woman and embracing our gentler side.
- We're saying yes to putting ourselves, our lives, our health, and our comfort first.
- We're saying yes to being the architects of our own beautiful becoming.
- We're saying yes to fully thriving.

P.S. One more time with feeling: Life-work balance, in that order.

Elevation: Vibrate Higher

Exhalation: Breathe Easy

Five-Finger Breath

Sit comfortably, and close your eyes.

Bend whichever arm is comfortable for you and turn your palm toward your face.

(continued)

Curate Your Career: Strategize

(continued)

Spread your fingers apart slightly, and then using the index finger of the other hand, lightly trace the outside of your hand starting at the base of your thumb.

Let's begin:

For this breathing exercise you're going to be breathing through your nose, and tracing the outline of the fingers of one hand with your other hand.

As you trace up from the base of your thumb, inhale for 1, 2, 3. As you trace down to the other side of your thumb, exhale for 1, 2, 3.

Inhale for 1, 2, 3 as you trace to the top of your index finger, and exhale for 1, 2, 3 as you trace down to the other side of it.

Trace to the top of your middle finger, inhaling for 1, 2, 3; then exhale for 1, 2, 3 as you trace to the bottom of it.

Inhale for 1, 2, 3 and trace to the top of your ring finger. Exhale for 1, 2, 3 as you trace to the bottom of it.

Trace to the top of your little finger, inhaling for 1, 2, 3; then exhale for 1, 2, 3, 4, 5, 6, tracing the outside of your little finger, going all the way down to the outside of your wrist.

Continue this for as long as you are comfortable, either changing directions on the same hand, or alternating hands.

When you're ready, lower your hands and open your eyes.

Affirmations: Speak Life

- I am fulfilling my Divine Assignment.
- I am successful in ways that are meaningful to me.
- I am divinely supported in achieving life-work balance.
- I am working less and earning more, under grace, and in perfect ways.
- I am so happy and grateful that my income is always increasing in blessed and miraculous ways.

(continued)

(continued)

Introspection: Journal & Heal

- Describe your dream job, ideal career, or perfect workday.
- Do you feel psychologically safe at work? If yes, why? If no, why not?
- If money were no object, what would you do for work just because you love it?
- What aspect of your job do you enjoy the most? What do you enjoy the least?
- What does life-work balance mean to you? What are ways that you can accomplish it?

Curation: Do the Work

What is important to you in terms of your career? What are your main motivators? Why? Here are some thought-starters:

- Flexibility (e.g., remote / hybrid / in office)
- Company (e.g., FAANG)
- Clear career pathing
- Responsibilities
- Commute
- Location
- Prestige
- Money
- Title

Appreciation: Express Gratitude

What are you grateful for? Count your blessings:

- I am grateful …
- I am grateful …
- I am grateful …

(continued)

(continued)

Celebration: *Razzle Dazzle*

Flex on 'em, sis! What are you proud of? Celebrate yourself:

- I am proud of myself for ...
- I am proud of myself for ...
- I am proud of myself for ...

Meditation: *Think Blissfully*

Sit or lie down comfortably. Take a few moments and focus on your breath. Feel the cool air enter your nostrils and pass by the back of your throat. Let your abdomen rise gently as you inhale, and fall gently as you exhale.

When you're ready, softly close your eyes.

Gradually slow down your breathing so you're inhaling and exhaling through your nose for equal counts of five. With every inhale, welcome a sense of peace and ease. With every exhale, release all stress from your body.

Let's begin.

Inhale: 1, 2, 3, 4, 5; exhale: 5, 4, 3, 2, 1

Inhale: 1, 2, 3, 4, 5; exhale: 5, 4, 3, 2, 1

Inhale: 1, 2, 3, 4, 5; exhale: 5, 4, 3, 2, 1

Keep breathing like this for a few cycles until you feel more relaxed.

Keeping your eyes closed, imagine that the inside of your eyelids is a movie screen. On this screen, project an image of a place where you feel happy, healthy, and at peace. It could be a beach, a forest, a garden, even a city. It could be your home, or your favorite hotel. You get to choose. Now imagine that you get to work in your happy place, in exactly the way you like.

(continued)

(continued)

You get to choose how your workspace is set up.

You get to choose how many or how few days you work.

You get to choose who you work with, and how, and when.

You get to choose what a perfect work day feels like for you.

You get to do work that you love, and make millions doing it.

You're doing what you've always dreamed of doing, and it feels great.

Take a few minutes and let your vision become clearer.

The more you think about how much you love working in your perfect environment, doing exactly what you want, how you want, with whom you want, and earning a generous income, the bigger your smile gets. You feel happier and happier because your career dreams are coming true.

What a beautiful, beautiful feeling.

Stay there for a while, basking in the glow of contentment. Feel the fulfillment. Feel the abundance. Feel the bliss. Feel the gratitude.

When you're ready, let your breath resume its normal cadence. Slowly open your eyes, and return your attention to the room you're in. Give yourself a few moments to absorb the positive vibes.

If you like, write in your journal about the meditation experience, and make a note of how you felt, what you thought, and what your goals are for your career.

Embrace every possibility for you to thrive.

Asé.

9

Curate Your Energy: Elevate

Invocation

Most High,

I come to You today in gratitude for our connection

Thank You for being my Source
For keeping me filled with Your Love, Your Light, Your Energy

How you make my heart feel glad

Today and every day, may I vibrate at the highest possible frequency
Uplifting my Self
Uplifting my folks
Uplifting the world

May I make it a daily practice to elevate my energy
Through blissful moments of sacred serenity
Through gatherings with my chosen community
Through curating who stays near to me
Through meeting you in prayer

When I'm nestled in those prayerful moments
May I choose to listen to that still, small voice
Guiding me lovingly along the path of elevation
And may I walk that path willingly, with constant delight in my spirit

From my core to my aura
In every muscle, system, and chakra
May I embody, emit, and attract good energy

May I vibrate high, and be one with The Light
May I vibrate high, and be one with The Light
May I vibrate high, and be one with The Light

Forever and ever,

Amen.

~ ~ ~

Good Vibrations

"@HappyHappyPhoenix is a pretty unique IG handle. I'm sure there's a story behind it. Does it have a special meaning?"

I've been asked this question in quite a few interviews, and the short answer is yes, it does. I came up with it after going through some serious issues in my personal life several years ago. Now I'm not sharing the details, because as Tabitha Brown (aka our beloved Auntie Tab) says, "that's my business," but suffice it to say it was one of those "I am never going through that again" moments in life. And I haven't.

I believe that, as far as is possible, everything in your life should be an affirmation of who you are and what you desire—even your social media handles. @HappyHappyPhoenix was that for me.* I wanted a high-vibrational handle. I desired a double-dose of happiness for myself, so I affirmed it.

It was meant to be a constant reminder to seek light and stay positive; to pursue happiness. It was a call to elevation. A harbinger of joy. A reminder

---

*I have since changed my IG handle to @TheLisaHurley for branding purposes, but @HappyHappyPhoenix is a part of who I am, and will always have a special place in my heart.

to vibrate higher. Inspiration to be the energy you seek. It acknowledged that issues in life will happen, but they can be transcended.

Joy cometh in the morning. Success is guaranteed. After the storm, the calm.

There will be ashes, but you will rise.

Amen? Amen.

Assess Your Energy

Has your check engine light ever been on? Do you drive with your tank below "E"? I don't mean in your car, I mean in your body and in your life. In the "Rest" chapter, it's clear that I had gotten to the point where the lights and alarms on my dashboard were all flashing frantically at the same time, and there was no gas left in the tank. The fuel in my life—my energy—was completely drained.

Energy Is Currency

I subscribe to the theory of the energy bank account—there is a system of debits and credits—and at that time my balance was below zero. (Yes, this is a brand new analogy, but bear with me.) I had gone into overdraft; I had let all my resources be depleted. While I did what I needed to do to get my energy account back into good standing, the goal is to avoid draining it in the first place.

You can't live a soft life in a state of energetic depletion. To keep your vibration and vitality at optimal levels you must make recurring deposits.

How to Curate Your Energy

As I mentioned, like a regular bank account, your energy account operates based on debits and credits. When curating your energy, the first step is to identify what (and who) makes energetic withdrawals from your life as well as the things, behaviors, and people that pour into you and make deposits.

What Drains Your Energy?

Let's start with the withdrawals. Begin by identifying who and what makes you feel drained, so that you can address the deficits. Some of the things that can deplete your energy are:

228   Be Yourself

Overdrive

Working ourselves to tatters. Feeling exhausted, but pushing through. Staying in a constant state of busyness. Doing too much and not giving ourselves any rest. All this is living in overdrive. Consistently pushing ourselves beyond our capacity is a fast track to burnout. I rebuke hustle culture. It is quickly ending us all.

Lack of Boundaries

As a still-recovering people pleaser, this is a big one. I have often gotten involved in projects to a level that is way above my capacity because I didn't want to say no and disappoint someone. Thankfully, I have become much better at saying no, enforcing my boundaries, and prioritizing my peace.

Neglecting Self-Care

Nothing depletes your energy like not handling your basic needs, and that includes self-care. When you ask most people about self-care, they usually mention spa dates and massages. Those matter, but caring for yourself goes deeper than that. Are there ways in which you are neglecting yourself in your day-to-day life? There are no gold stars for trudging through life parched and exhausted. Some examples of self-neglect are:[1]

- Not drinking enough water
- Not eating nourishing foods
- Not getting adequate sleep or rest
- Not attending to your daily hygiene
- Not taking your prescribed medications
- Not getting enough exercise or movement
- Not getting medical care when you need it
- Not allowing yourself to enjoy fun activities
- Not eating on time, thereby letting yourself get too hungry
- Not cleaning your space or home (to the extent that it is *consistently* filthy, smelly, unsanitary, or hoarded out)
- Not caring about your appearance (to the extent that you *consistently* wear clothing that is visibly unkempt and in need of laundering)

According to *Psychology Today*,[2] self-neglect can also include prioritizing the needs of others, having an overly busy schedule, and not using your talents.

If any (or all) of these apply to you, no judgment here. For some of us, this might just serve as a wake-up call: We might not even have realized that this is what was happening in our lives, and we can now start to do better.

For others of us, the behaviors on the above list could be symptoms of deeper mental and physical issues for which one might need support from one's family, community, or state. For more information on how to identify and deal with self-neglect, the National Adult Protective Services Association (NAPSA) provides resources and action plans.[3] Another useful resource is selfneglect.org.

Sleeplessness

This one is a basic, but it's so important. If you're not getting enough sleep you will often feel like you're dragging your body around behind you. You'll feel like you have post-meal fatigue—but all the time. Chronically exhausted. Over time, this puts you into a state where you're not fully functional.

Food

Not all food obviously, but food that is full of mystery ingredients just doesn't work with my system. For the most part, I can't eat anything canned because my body rejects it. I experience migraines and extreme fatigue. I grew up eating fresh, home-cooked food basically every day (thanks, Mama Bear), and that's what my system likes. That's not to say that I cook three square meals for myself daily (I much prefer the eating side of the food prep equation), but if I'm ordering in, I get foods that are identifiable, and that give me energy. Alcohol depletes my energy and makes me feel ill, so I avoid that as well.

Clutter

Few things bring one's energy level down like a cluttered space. This is sometimes a struggle for me because my OCD tendencies, ADHD, and depression are in an ongoing battle. I'm sharing this because we need to end the stigma around it. Like I've said before, I am not here positioning myself as any paragon of virtue. We're all on this journey together.

When it comes to clutter, I have alternated between two extremes. On one end of the spectrum is my house giving show-home vibes: Staged to the nines like she's ready for her HGTV début. Visitors to my home, even good friends, have often asked me if I'm hosting a party because when my house is done, it's *done-done*, down to the dining table being set with linen napkins and my "good crockery." On the other end is what Marla Cilley, aka FlyLady, calls C.H.A.O.S. (Can't Have Anyone Over Syndrome). I think you get the picture: I'm talking tornado-adjacent. When my mental health is in a good space, my home reflects that, and vice versa.

What I know for sure is that every item in your home has an energy signature, and clutter means stuckness. The piles and disorder drain our energy. This is one of the reasons why I rebuke the concept of a junk drawer. Why do we need to create a special space for junk within our home? If it's junk, you probably don't need it.

Speaking of which, holding on to things we don't need can also bring our vibration down. Get rid of that stuff from your ex. Donate clothing that reminds you of a time in your life you would rather forget. Release it with gratitude for the time it has served you, and a blessing for whoever will receive it next. I recently donated a coffee table that I had been holding on to for years. It was a gift from a friend, so I appreciated it for that reason, but it just never fit right. It was too large for my space, and since I no longer entertain like I used to, it served no purpose. Every time I walked around it, I felt annoyed. I gave myself permission to let it go. I said a prayer of thanksgiving over it and sent it on to bless the space of someone else. As soon as the donation company carted it away, I felt an immediate wave of relief. It created a sense of expansiveness in my home. I felt lighter. I exhaled.

Complaining

An occasional venting session can be cathartic, but constant complaining is draining. Similarly, spending time around people who are constantly critical of others also depletes your energy. Them dumping all their pessimism onto you, their resistance to finding a solution, their refusal to see good in anyone else makes you feel like you're swimming in an ocean of negativity. If you are the complainer in question, please know that you're not only adversely affecting people around you, but as *Harvard Business Review* explains,[4] you're harming yourself as well.

Noise

Being exposed to too many noises at too loud a volume for too long shuts down my system to the point where I can barely function. I once accompanied some "nieces" of mine to the big Toys "R" Us in Manhattan back in the day. It was a few days before Christmas. Thankfully, there were other adults in our party because as soon as I stepped foot in the door, I had to step right back out. The cacophony. The lights. The (understandably) unhinged energy of excited, Santa's-in-town, sugar-laden children. It all hit me like a physical force, and I got nauseous. I rejoined the group after a while, but it took me a good three days to fully recover.

Talking on the phone to people while they're doing a million (loud) things is also draining. I. Can't. Hear. You. All I can hear is the clanging of whatever is going on in the background. It takes so much mental effort to try and keep track of the conversation that I feel depleted and overwhelmed by the end. I don't say anything because I know I'll come across as cranky, but … whew. It's difficult to deal with.

Social Media

De innanets can be a whole dumpster fire, and constantly doomscrolling on social media is a surefire way to bring your energy down. Tune in to how you feel after you've spent a few hours scrolling on the interwebs, minding people's business, comparing yourself to strangers' curated lives, and jumping into people's comments section to tussle. It's like leaving your small appliances plugged in all the time. You might not see that they're pulling energy, but trust me, they are. Just check your bill.

In addition to minimizing your scroll time, I have two other pieces of social media advice for you:

1. **Block the people who only tag you into a fight like you're a wrestler.**

Your role in life is not to be people's online bouncer. Now I have publicly defended friends of mine who were being attacked, and some of my

232   Be Yourself

friends have done the same for me. But strangers on the internet? The random rage baiters? Block dem. Also block the people who are angry ALL THE TIME. The Venn diagram of these people and the ones who constantly complain is a circle. Some folks only have one setting, and it's exhausting. Disengage. Your peace is priceless.

The ones who only communicate with you when they want to siphon your connections and engagement? Block dem too. There are a few people on LinkedIn who never interact with or amplify my content—not a like, not a comment, not a share—but somehow find the time to repeatedly ask me to amplify theirs. They truly seem to believe that it's my job. Most times they don't even bother prefacing it with a salutation; they just rudely toss the link into my DMs. Once I notice the pattern, they get blockt.

2. Block the people whose content makes you feel bad about yourself.

I was once connected on social media to a woman whom I admired. She was a supersmart thought leader and an outspoken activist. She didn't have a large following, but that's not what it's about for me. I am interested in whether someone's content resonates no matter how many followers they have. If you have five followers but your posts make sense, I will support.

Initially, I didn't notice it, but over time I realized that if she engaged in my comments at all, it was to criticize me and my initiatives. She was especially critical of my work around creating soft, safe spaces for Black women and would write unhinged screeds under my posts (or sometimes under other people's) trashing me and what I was trying to achieve. She claimed that what I was doing was not "real activism." That by focusing on Black women's healing, relaxation and psychological safety, I was not "doing the *real* work."

I truly did not understand it, because I had never spoken or written a critical word about this person. In fact, I had supported, reposted, and amplified their work on multiple occasions. It seemed as though the more she perceived that I was glowing up, the angrier she became. Every time it happened, it disturbed my spirit. It felt horrible. But then I realized that there was absolutely no need for me to be in community with her. Why was I doing that to myself? I released the need to be liked. Under her last passive-aggressive comment about me and TGE, I simply commented with the prayer hands, disconnected, and exhaled. I immediately felt better once that toxic, monitoring-spirit energy was no longer in my life or on my feed.

A few of my friends later informed me that she had launched an initiative similar to TGE. Bonus points because she plagiarized my copy. All I could do was laugh. If only more people knew the full phrase: "Imitation is the sincerest form of flattery *that mediocrity can pay to greatness*."[5]

Socializing

This is a personal thing that definitely doesn't apply to everyone. As an introvert (proud INFJ here), being around too many people for too long saps my energy. When necessary, I can socialize with strangers, and I definitely enjoy hanging out with "my people," but after a while, no matter who you are or how much I love you, I just need to sit quietly by myself, stare at a wall, and get back to center. It's nothing personal (my true friends know this); it's just how I am. Everybody is different, so for extroverts "people" might be in their "energy amplifiers" column. Speaking of which:

What Increases Your Energy?

Now for the deposits into your energy account. Identify what makes you feel vibrant, then do more of that. Pour into yourself. This is one of the best ways to reduce, or better yet eliminate, burnout and chronic stress. Some of the things that can increase one's energy are:

Rest

I wrote an entire chapter about rest because it is one of the areas in which so many Black women struggle the most. We tend to lead with our inner caretaker, critic, or perfectionist. We often offer what we ourselves would like to receive—nurturance, protection, support—then end up giving and doing too much. As a result, we feel fried and fatigued. One of the most effective ways to increase your physical and etheric energy is to get enough rest. It's easy, and best of all it's free.99!

Routines and Rituals

When I have my daily routines in place, they act as a strong foundation from which I can thrive. I can't do confusion and last-minuteness: That makes me feel scattered. Sticking to my routines puts me in a state of feeling calm, regulated, and energized.

234 Be Yourself

One of my favorite routines is my nightly skincare extravaganza. It's a lot, and I love every moment of it. Glass skin, here we come. I double-cleanse my face and décolleté, do some massage or gua sha, and apply a variety of different serums. In between times, while each layer dries, I do a little bit of yoga. It's an absolutely lovely way to end the day. It elevates my energy because it is an act of self-love. It's a reminder that I am worth being treated with care.

Don't let the "rituals" word throw you off: I'm not talking about waving a wand and turning in a circle. (Though if that's your thing, do you.) What I'm referring to is bringing a sense of ceremony to the mundane. For example, when my sister visits me, we set aside time every morning to select a card from my angel card deck. It helps us start the day on a meditative, mindful footing. There is always a message, and we use it to guide us throughout the day.

When my mom visits, we have a tea and coffee ceremony every morning to get the day off to a gentle start. (I'm the tea drinker, and she's the coffee drinker.) We sit comfortably, sip slowly, and enjoy the moment. It's a very different feeling from gulping down your coffee or breakfast in the car on the way to work. Mummy and I also have a nightly snack ceremony. It's not so much about scarfing down the calories; it's more about intentionally sharing a (literally) sweet moment of connection. We toast each other with our cookies or cupcakes, giggle at the silliness of doing that, then settle in to enjoy snackies and movies. After a while, I turn all my lights to the color purple (it's her favorite) and let the relaxing hue start lulling us to sleep before it's time to actually turn in and go to bed.

Ingesting the Right Things

This is about food, but it's not only about food. What you ingest includes media, music, books, and more. Nourish yourself, sis. You are worthy. Nourish your body, mind, spirit, and senses. As much as you can, ingest nutrition, information, and entertainment that make you feel uplifted. Almost daily, I make it a point to read something positive. It doesn't have to be anything long. Most mornings I read a few paragraphs from *A Course in Miracles*.

Every so often I go to *LoveForYall.carrd.co*, aka *Love Notes for Black Women in Academia*,[6] which was created by one of my awesome TGE members Chantell Frazier, PhD.[7] Even though I'm not an academic, I still go and read them from time to time. They're incredibly uplifting. Do yourself a favor and check them out. You'll feel better immediately, I promise.

Positive People

One of the things I love most about my life partner is he is one of the most positive, uplifting people I've ever met. No matter what is happening in life, he can find the bright side. He lives in the energy of sunshine, good vibes, and the silver lining. He's hilarious too, and who doesn't love a good laugh?

Most of the people I'm really close to have similar qualities. I feel better, brighter, happier, after interacting with them. Hopefully, the feeling is mutual. The company you keep has a huge effect on your daily energy levels. Seek out high-vibrational people.

Alone Time

I feel kind of bad for saying this, but when the shelter in place edicts were issued during the pandemic, nothing much changed for me. I was already home. Since I've always been a fan of inside, and since alone time is like oxygen for me, from that perspective I was good. As an introvert, silence, stillness, and alone time feed my soul and help me vibrate higher.

Saying No

"Your 'No' is legendary."

A good friend of mine once told me this, and it made me giggle. It made me sound fearsome, and I kind of liked it. It also made me feel proud of myself because, as I mentioned in the "Lack of Boundaries" section, I'm a recovering people pleaser. That my 'No' has become a force to be reckoned with makes me happy.

The goal is to curate lives filled with ease, grace, and abundance. And believe it or not, that often starts by saying no. The thing is, agreeing to do things that you don't really want to do never works out well. Neither for the recipient of your efforts, nor for you. Ask me how I know. Not only does it siphon your physical and intellectual capacity, it also depletes your energy. Guilt, anger, resentment, and self-recrimination are not high-vibrational states.

If I ever start to feel guilty about saying no to someone, I remind myself that "no" is a powerful curatorial tool. It scalpels away all the unwanted stuff so you can focus on what you really care about and have capacity for. It also liberates the asker to find someone more available and aligned.

236   Be Yourself

No matter how bad I feel for saying no, it's nowhere near as horrible as I feel for saying yes to something I don't have the capacity to do. I remember that every no to someone else is a yes to myself. If the time or the vibe do not align—say no. Say it with your chest. And revel in the additional space you've created for yourself.

There are times when the person you have to say no to is yourself. Our inner teenagers sometimes have us in a chokehold. Saying yes to things you want to do, but you know are a bad idea, does not serve your highest good.

Shortly after I returned to work from my six-month short-term disability leave, there was a huge conference for the culture I really wanted to attend, and I tried every which way to convince myself that I could make it. But the truth was, I couldn't, for multiple reasons.

First, there was no way that I could rationally ask my employer for a week off to attend a non-work-related conference having just returned from being off for six months. Like ... no.

Second, even though I was in a much better physical and mental state than I had been at the beginning of my sabbatical, I still was not back to 100 percent. Far from it. Recovery is continuous. It would have been a setup for a setback if I had insisted on participating in a full week of outsideness, peopleing, and networking. That would have been a classic case of dropping myself into overdrive and doing too much. So I put my inner teenager in time-out, and my inner adult told her no. FOMO or no FOMO, it was absolutely the right decision.

So: Honor your own boundaries and protect your energy, sis.

Say no.

P.S. See also: "Nah."

P.P.S. "No" is a full sentence.

Social Media—Done Right

Make your feed uplifting.

Uncle Algo will serve you what you indicate an interest in. So, train the algorithm. I have zero interest in trauma porn, and I don't watch videos of Black people being murdered, so it's rare that content of that kind comes across my feed.

I'm not suggesting that you completely block out "reality," but you can find a balance.

Case in point, I follow a lot of activist accounts, and a few that focus on politics. But I also engage with a lot of "cute pets" accounts. Adorable puppies are instant mood boosters. There's a Black woman on IG who spoils her pittie with spa sessions, steak dinners, and soft living. I absolutely love it. I also follow accounts about meditation, fashion, makeup, hair, and beauty. And I never met a meme account I didn't like. They make my heart happy. Life can be heavy; it's okay to lighten it up.

Underdrive

Overdrive is overrated. It often leaves one stressed, overwhelmed, and exhausted.

There is a better way: **Under**drive

Toward the close of *The Year That Almost Ended Me*, aka *The Unraveling*, I came to the decision that I would be pulling all the way back from the too-muchness of it all. I would not be trying to ramp up and "close the year strong." Shoot ... I was just trying to make it to the end of the year, period. Strong where? Strong how? Strong why? My goal was to wind down, ease back, and close the year soft. Per usual, I posted about how I was feeling:

As for me and my house, today and for the rest of the year, I'm not going into overdrive, I'm going into UNDERdrive. The goal is to do less. Because "less" is probably still quite a lot. And I am—we all are—deserving of rest.

I invite you to take a look at your calendar and to-do list, and see how many things you can just ... not do.

- What seems important but really isn't?
- What can you completely decline?
- What can you outsource?

What do you want the rest of your year to feel like? Hectic and frenetic, or happy and peaceful?

How do YOU want to feel? Stressed and dysregulated, or relaxed and rested?

What do you want to experience? Breath held from anxiety and shoulders tight with tension? Or relaxed muscles and easy breathing?

238   Be Yourself

Take a moment today and ponder these questions. Turn your attention inward and see what your mind and body are telling you. Then decide whether or not you're going to listen. We should not be wearing our shoulders as earrings. We deserve to relax and exhale.

Asé

Embracing underdrive is one of the most effective ways I know to bring your energy back to center.

Energy Practices

I believe that energy is everything, and as a Reiki master, it would be remiss of me to not include energy practices that can help to raise your vibration. I also believe that, similarly to taking a daily shower to cleanse one's body, we should also do a daily cleanse of our energy. Sometimes our aura is dusty, and it shows.

As usual, there's no judgment.

When our homes get dusty (as they do simply because they exist), we just set aside some time and dust them. When our windows get dirty, we take out the Windex and start cleaning. We don't judge and berate them because the dust accumulated. We just remove it.

Similarly, when our etheric bodies get a little dull (as they do simply because they exist), there's no need for us to shame ourselves. We just have to notice it—and then do what we need to in order to get them sparkling again.

As with most things in life, consistency makes a difference. Doing a little bit every day will likely have a greater impact than trying to do all the things in a short space of time. In the battle between pure talent and consistent practice, 9 times out of 10 consistency will win. That's why I structured the book so that in every chapter there are myriad opportunities for you to pause, breathe, and elevate your energy. Read a little bit. Pray. Meditate. Journal. Say an affirmation or two. Consistently incorporating some of these practices into your daily routine will have a positive impact and help you feel more high-vibrational.

Prayer: "Ask, and it shall be given you; seek, and ye shall find; knock, and it shall be opened unto you." Matthew 7:7 summarizes the spirit and purpose of prayer. It is a recognition that we are connected to God / Spirit / the Universe; a reminder that the Most High is ready to intercede on our behalf. When I pray, I feel connected, aligned, and uplifted. I feel united with The Oneness. If my prayer is one where I am asking for help, I feel heard, comforted, and unburdened. There is such relief in knowing that although you might not yet know the details, a divine solution is in the works.

Prayers of gratitude are also important: Acknowledging out loud all the blessings you already have. It is easier to stay uplifted when you're focused on what you have, versus what you lack.

Meditation: While prayer is more externally focused—a communication outward with that which is bigger than yourself—meditation is more internally focused. It is a looking within; a deliberate connection with your innermost being; a conversation with your Higher Self. Even just a few minutes of mindfulness a day can calm your spirit, raise your vibration, and get you into Divine Flow.

Affirmations: "In the beginning was the word." John, 1:1. Words are immensely powerful. How you speak to yourself matters. Consciously choosing to address yourself with love is an act of self-care. To paraphrase the saying: Be careful how you speak to yourself because your Self is listening. Much of our internal self-talk is quite harmful and unloving. Saying affirmations and speaking positively to and about ourselves can be life-changing. We should talk to ourselves with gentleness, care, encouragement, and love.

Journaling: Getting the "gunk" out of your mind by writing it down is so healing. It lightens the mind and clears the way for positive vibes.

Breathwork: Breath is life. This is why one of the most important checks made on newborn babies is to ensure that they are breathing properly. Breathwork is the act of consciously controlling your breathing to help reduce stress, increase calm, remove toxins, increase energy, and promote balance. So many of us are socialized to think that being in a constant state of fight or flight energy means we're more successful. We conflate adrenaline with achievement. The real flex is being calm. Breathe.

240   Be Yourself

Aura Combing: Literally pretend that your fingers are combs and untangle the energy field around your body. Bend your fingers slightly and move them through the air around your body. The easiest way to do this is to stand up straight, and starting at your crown, "comb" the energy downward. Do the front of your body first. Comb from your crown to your waist, then bend slightly and comb from your waist to your feet. Do the same at the back of your body. Do this twice daily for about a week and then once daily thereafter. If that's not your thing, try dry brushing. It has a similar effect, plus you get the bonus of lightly exfoliating your skin.

Smudging: Smudge your aura with sage, palo santo, or incense. Nag Champa incense is a popular one. While you're at it, smudge your space as well, focusing on the corners and hard-to-reach places where "energy dust bunnies" can congregate. If you can't deal with smoke, you can use smudge sprays instead.

Nature Bathing: Seek the sun, the ocean, the forest—Mother Nature is incredibly healing. Just a few minutes of sunshine can boost your mood and raise your vibration. Of course, make sure to wear sunscreen.

Reiki: One of the healing / energy modalities of which I'm a big fan is Reiki. According to the Barbados Reiki Association:[8]

- Reiki is an ancient science of energy and healing art from the East. It is a precise tool for balancing your whole physical, mental, emotional and spiritual dynamic
- Reiki reduces stress and revitalizes you to help maintain good health, a positive attitude to life and inner peace
- Reiki energy promotes a powerful and beautiful personal transformation
- Reiki has helped the sick by relieving pain and symptoms and can restore wholeness and health
- Reiki is cross-cultural, is not a religion and does not require faith in it to be effective

My mom (the person who introduced me to Reiki) starts every day by giving herself a Reiki treatment. Though I'm not as consistent as she is in terms of getting a full self-treatment in, I definitely give myself a little Reiki every day. It's extremely relaxing. Reiki has become very widely known and more accessible, so if you're not a Reiki practitioner, it's easy for you to find one and get a Reiki treatment.

Elevation: Vibrate Higher

Exhalation: Breathe Easy

Box Breathing

Sit or lie down comfortably, and close your eyes. Breathe through your nose, becoming very aware of the breath gently entering and leaving your body with every inhale and exhale. Feel your abdomen rise as you inhale, and fall as you exhale.

As you get more comfortable, imagine that there is a square projected on a screen in front of you. Just for fun, try to see the square in your favorite color: A healing green, a soothing blue, a radiant red ... whatever color you like.

You're going to start breathing in counts of four. Imagine that as you inhale, you're tracing the four sides of your beautifully colored square. Inhale for four as you go up the left side of the square from bottom to top. Hold your breath for four as you go across from left to right. As you trace down the right side of your square, exhale gently for a count of four, then hold again for four as you trace the bottom of the square. Let's do a few rounds of box breathing together:

Inhale: 1, 2, 3, 4
Hold: 1, 2, 3, 4
Exhale: 1, 2, 3, 4
Hold: 1, 2, 3, 4

Inhale: 1, 2, 3, 4
Hold: 1, 2, 3, 4
Exhale: 1, 2, 3, 4
Hold: 1, 2, 3, 4

(continued)

242　　Be Yourself

(continued)

    Inhale: 1, 2, 3, 4
    Hold: 1, 2, 3, 4
    Exhale: 1, 2, 3, 4
    Hold: 1, 2, 3, 4

Repeat this a few more times until you feel more relaxed.

Affirmations: Speak Life

- I am choosing to vibrate higher.
- I am vibrating at the frequency of love.
- I am giving myself permission to thrive.
- I am giving myself permission to curate a life I love.
- I am grateful that my daily routine uplifts my mind, body, and spirit.

Introspection: Journal & Heal

- What inspires and energizes you?
- What do you love most about yourself?
- What makes you feel calm and grounded?
- What does the term "vibrate higher" mean to you?
- What are three ways you can raise your vibration today?

Curation: Do the Work

Do an audit of your energy account. Over the next seven days:

- Identify what (and who) is draining your energy balance.
- Identify what (and who) is increasing your energy balance.

Appreciation: Express Gratitude

What are you grateful for? Count your blessings:

- I am grateful …
- I am grateful …
- I am grateful …

(continued)

(continued)

Celebration: Razzle Dazzle

Flex on 'em, sis! What are you proud of? Celebrate yourself:

- I am proud of myself for …
- I am proud of myself for …
- I am proud of myself for …

Meditation: Think Blissfully

Sit comfortably. Place your hands in your lap, with your left hand resting in your right hand. Inhale gently but deeply through your nose, imagining healing, cleansing energy moving into your body. Exhale through your mouth, releasing all tension. Inhale the healing, exhale the stress.

Inhale, and as you exhale, feel your eyebrows relax.

Inhale, and as you exhale, feel your top lip relax.

Inhale, and as you exhale, feel your jaw relax.

Unclench your teeth, feel your neck relaxing, and drop your shoulders.

Now that you're more relaxed, focus fully on your breath, paying attention to how it feels entering your nose and exiting your mouth.

On your next inhale, mentally say, "I am vibrating higher," and as you exhale say, "Amen."

Inhale: I am vibrating higher.

Exhale: Amen.

Inhale: I am vibrating higher.

Exhale: Amen.

Inhale: I am vibrating higher.

Exhale: Amen.

(continued)

244   Be Yourself

(continued)

Continue repeating this mentally for a few minutes; as long as you are comfortable.

When you're ready, release the affirmation and just let your breath flow naturally. Gently open your eyes, and bring your attention fully back into the room.

Stay seated for a while and absorb the good vibes.

Asé.

10

Curate Your Soft Life: Exhale

Invocation

Most High, I pray you:

Grant me the grace to live a life more easeful:
Soft
Centered
Serene

May I daily practice the pause:
Rest
Recline
Renew

Grant me the grace to treat myself like a gem:
Unique
Worthy
Priceless

246 Be Yourself

May I daily practice self-care:
Love
Comfort
Nurturance

Grant me the grace to embrace my soft side:
Sweet
Joyful
Delicate

May I daily find true balance:
Living
Loving
Creating

Grant me the grace to live a life more aligned:
Abundant
Authentic
Amazing

May I daily stay in the flow:
Thoughts
Words
Actions

Most High, I pray you:

Grant me the grace and the space to exhale
Grant me the grace and the space to exhale
Grant me the grace and the space to exhale

Amen.

~ ~ ~

Soft Life Vibes

"Kimonos open!"

This is how my good sis Alexis and I end many of our calls. We shout it to each other and then collapse into giggles. It's our little inside joke, or at least it used to be, lol. Now you all know about it, but we're family so

Curate Your Soft Life: Exhale   247

that's okay. "Kimonos open" is a vibe, a reminder, a rallying cry. It doesn't have to be literal, although it can be.

If you're into robes and kimonos* like we are, just think how absolutely comfortable you feel when you're wearing one, especially at home. It's housedress energy, but elevated:

Soft
Silky
Sumptuous

No tight sleeves
No scratchy fabrics
No constricting collars

We're not belting it either. We're wearing it open. We're letting our waistlines breathe.

For us, "Kimonos open" expresses the energy of ease.

We say it to remind each other to relax. To turn down the Type A, always-on, overachiever energy. To prioritize our restoration. To do less. To be more. To live a soft life.

We're retiring the "Strong Black Woman" stereotype. We refuse to be anybody's superhero. We're burning our superwoman capes.

It's time for the rise of the Soft Black Woman.

Capes off. Kimonos on.

Blankets at the ready.

We are in our soft life era.

What Is Soft Living?

Unsurprisingly, Black people coined the term. We always create the coolness—and the hotness. The phrase originated within the Nigerian social media influencer culture. Despite the prevalent images of the African continent displayed by mainstream media, there is another side. Luxury, limos, lavishness.

---

*As a member of a community whose culture is often appropriated, I want to make it clear that I am not referring to the traditional kimono, which is the national dress of Japan. I have never worn an authentic Japanese kimono because it is not my culture. It is not a garment to be donned as a form of cosplay. I admire from a respectful distance.

248   Be Yourself

For some, therefore, soft living comprises elements of enjoying the spoils of wealth: Opulent mansions, designer clothes, high-end cars, upscale restaurants, five-star hotels, first-class flights. Better yet, make it a private jet moment. I am not among that number, but I believe that people have the agency to define things for themselves.

It's always interesting to me to watch Nollywood movies because that's the lifestyle that is usually portrayed. It's unabashedly upscale, and I'm not mad at it. I say yes to showing range and pushing back against the dominant narrative. Housekeepers, chauffeurs, chefs, groundskeepers: I say yes to it all. To be honest, for a lot of people on the African continent, that's just regular life; it's not even considered a luxury. This is why telling one's own stories is so important. Colonizers will never portray us as conquerors.

While I have no issue with it, I am 100 percent here for #BlackGirlLuxury—there is more to living a soft life than a focus on conspicuous consumption and material acquisitions.[†] In fact, it doesn't have to include them at all. Comfort and ease don't have to be expensive.

In my view, soft living is primarily about leading with self-love, treating yourself gently, prioritizing your peace, and embracing rest, all of which can be done no matter the size of your budget.

Of course, while soft living has its proponents (clearly I am one of them), it also has its detractors. There's a faction out there that gets big mad at the mere idea of people, especially Black women, wanting to live easier, more luxurious lives. Or actually doing so.

I remember back in 2020 at the height of the panorama, one of my favorite influencers, Paula Sutton of Hill House Vintage fame, was attacked by a woman of pallor who angrily announced that she was leaving the app formerly known as Twitter. Why? Because Ms. Sutton had had the temerity to post an impeccably styled photo of herself (let me check my notes here) having a picnic *in her own back garden*. She was minding her business, wearing her broad-brimmed sun hat, bothering no one.

Apparently "Auntie Paula," as she is sometimes affectionately called, unmistakably melanated, fabulously outfitted, elegantly seated on *her* lawn behind *her* Georgian home in the British countryside—had "offended" this person so much that she felt she had to get off the internet.

[†]That said, I'm always ready to be #FlewedOut and indulge in some retail therapy. I'm not about to turn down a trip and some new clothes. #AllExpensesPaid please and thank you.

Curate Your Soft Life: Exhale 249

I mean … good riddance.

But also: It's wild to me how much some groups are angered by Black women existing, or "worse yet," living well.

They're okay if we're showing up as the proverbial "Strong Black Woman." If we're constantly laboring. If we are struggling. If we're living lives that they perceive to be inferior to theirs. If our worldly goods are believed to be nonexistent or of poor quality. If we are going to work to clean their homes, raise their children, or report to them at an office.

But heaven forbid that we live a life elevated.

What really drove that white woman mad was that she did not feel that Paula, or any Black woman, should be owning that kind of home, wearing those kinds of clothes, living that kind of life. It's as if her internal dialog was "Why is this woman sitting on the picnic blanket, instead of standing next to it, serving me??" Epigenetics are a hell of a drug.

But Paula Sutton *is* living that kind of life. Many of us are. Many of us have. We exist beyond the stereotypes.

The number of conversations I've been a part of where the other party has used what I term *The Microaggressive You* is truly troubling. What's *The Microaggressive You*, you ask? It's when a Black person is having a regular conversation about regular things with a non-Black person, who then proceeds to express disrespectful surprise that we have been anywhere or done anything:

YOU own a car?
YOU own a home?
YOU went to Paris?
YOU have a Masters?

Yes, these are all questions I have been asked.

In Paula Sutton's case, had she been in actual conversation with the Karen in question, she might have been asked, "YOU own this house?" So annoying.

In addition to the people who believe that Black women are undeserving of living well, there are those who think that soft living reeks of entitlement and laziness. To which I say: Nope.

And I also say: If it *were* based on entitlement, so what? Black women *are* entitled to rest and live gently. We are deserving. We are worthy. If there is one group that can never be accused of being lazy, it's us. We *been*

250   Be Yourself

working. Our mothers been working. Our grandmothers been working. Our great grandmothers. In fields, factories, and offices. Overtime. Multiple jobs. Side hustles. Family, church, and community care. Making space for others who turn around and squeeze us to the edges. Advocating and voting for rights to benefit humanity only to be abandoned at the polls.

Many of us currently work inhumane hours for mere pennies, so if we want to sit on a couch and relax, we're gonna need y'all to leave us be. We are not being lazy. It's not in our DNA. It's just time for us to rest. Plus, our ancestors worked for free. Our rest counts as part of reparations.[‡]

No matter what they try to make us believe, I'm here to tell you that we, Black women, can have it all, on our terms. We might not be able to have it all *all at the same time*, but we can definitely make our dreams a reality. We *can* live soft, secure, well-supported lives. I believe this strongly, and so does Liku Amadi, founder and business attorney of Anasa Law Firm, and the host of the *Black Women Can Have It All* private podcast:

> For far too long society has dictated what Black women can do, who we can be, and what we can have in life, but Black women can have it all. And it is Black women who get to decide what having it all means.
>
> We can move from desire to design by curating our ideal life. We can be healed, healthy, and exhale not out of exhaustion, but relief. Black women have more power than we think. It's a God-given power. And once we wake up in that power we can learn to live our version of having it all.

Agreed, sis. Agreed.

My Introduction to Soft Living

I was thinking back to when I first encountered soft living before it became a social media trend that grew into a movement.

In some ways, I was introduced to it when my family was living in Trinidad.

[‡] Run us our coins too, though.

Curate Your Soft Life: Exhale   251

It's a very multicultural island, and how it seemed through my childlike eyes (I lived there from ages one to eight) was that everybody got along and celebrated each other's holidays. The island's population includes people of Black / African descent, Indian / South Asian descent, Chinese / East Asian descent, and more. At the time, however, I didn't even fully understand what race was. (It took me years to figure out that one of my mom's closest friends was Chinese. To me, she was just Auntie Wilma.) The main religions are Christianity, mostly Roman Catholic, and Hinduism.

Many of you know that Trinidad is the home of Calypso, steel pan, and Carnival. How all this played out (bear in mind I was very young, so I'm sure there's quite a bit of nuance that I missed) is that there was always a holiday, a fête, a celebration. For example, it seemed as though everybody celebrated Diwali. Everybody participated in Carnival. There were holidays all year round, religious and otherwise, and pretty much if one racial or religious group had a day off, the whole country had a day off. Easter holidays were a thing. There was music everywhere all the time. You could just drop by people's homes unannounced and you would be warmly welcomed, hugged, loved up, fed. And, of course, when they showed up at your house, you would reciprocate. Any impromptu gathering could easily become a lime.[5] Random parties would break out just because. Any average day could become an occasion.

Trinidad is a whole vibe.

In terms of how we lived as a family, I already told you about my mom and her sacrosanct Sunday nap time. So I saw her prioritize rest. But of course she worked too. Both my parents did; however, I never felt like I had to bargain with them to choose me over work. There was balance. So yes, they worked, but they also traveled, partied, hung out with their friends, and enjoyed creative and intellectual pursuits. We had a semi-live-in house-keeper, so my mom was never overwhelmed with the daily minutiae. I never saw her tattered by the too-muchness of it all. She modeled how life could be.

To be clear, it's not that there were no problems. There absolutely were, but she handled them with grace. Apart from anything else, she was

---

[5] In Trinidadian parlance, "liming" means informally hanging out with family and friends, doing literally nothing.

252   **Be Yourself**

surrounded by friends and family, an entire community, who supported her when times were hard.

Speaking of family, my sister Sharon and I often spent Easter holidays with Granny and Gramps, our maternal grandparents. It gave my folks a break, and we got to be with two of our favorite people. They lived in Arima in a sweet two-bedroom house with a huge kitchen that had one of those Dutch doors at the back. I was fascinated that the top half and bottom half could open and close separately. I loved being there. It was clear that they adored us.

Gramps was an insurance agent by day and a lay preacher in his free time. Granny used to work outside of the home, but by the time we came along, her focus was to keep the home running and looking beautiful. There was a division of labor that worked. One thing I always noticed is that after dinner, they would stand at the sink and do the dishes together. She washed. He dried. They looked sweet but comical because he was 6' 4" and she was 5' 2" on her best day. With Gramps being a preacher, of course we spent a lot of time at church, but we also spent long, lovely hours just hanging out, gardening, flying our kites in the park, or telling jokes (Gramps was a real comedian). Balance.

Back at our home in Orange Grove, Tacarigua, we had a backyard in which we grew sorrel, peas, and other goodies. At the right season, my mom, my sister, and I would pick them off the trees and then sit around the kitchen table shelling them, hoping against hope to not encounter a pea pod with a worm in it. (To this day, I don't eat guavas because I once had an unfortunate encounter with a worm when I bit into one. Yuck.) Sidenote: Mummy used to make a nectar-adjacent sorrel liqueur that I'm sure I was not supposed to know about, but I found a way to sneak a sip once. Divine. Five stars.

I am from an era when one would sometimes pick rice.** Not pick it straight from a field; I mean that one could purchase it by the pound, but it was completely unprocessed. So, before cooking it, we would have to remove the grains that were not up to par. You would spread the rice out on a table or in a tray and, one by one, pick out the bad grains, impurities, and unwanted hulls. A culinary curation.

** This is the part where your elders tell you how they used to walk 20 miles to school in the blazing sun, over hills (both ways, mind you) through mud, then come back home and "mind de shop" or "work de lan'."

Curate Your Soft Life: Exhale

Point being though: These are slow, nurturing activities. And if you're lucky like we were, they are communal activities. Growing some of your food. Harvesting it. Prepping it. Cooking it. Then enjoying it together as a family.

Another place that taught me about soft or maybe luxurious living was Martinique, one of the French Caribbean islands. My mom took my sister and me there when we were pretty young, maybe 7 and 11 respectively, to visit her friends Georges and Josianne. The day after our arrival when we woke up for breakfast I could hardly believe it.

Y'all, they served us literal bars of GOODT French chocolate in fresh-baked baguettes. Like … my mouth is watering right now as I remember. It was so freaking delicious and absolutely indulgent. I was like … this is the life!! I missed Barbados, but I also kind of wanted to stay in Martinique. On another random Wednesday, I smelled divinity wafting in through the window. Georges was out on the grill cooking up some steaks. And not any scrawny, chewy ones either—this was top tier, y'all. Top. Tier. Eating well is part of living well.

All of this taught me by example some of the fundamental tenets of what is now called soft living. I learned that:

- You don't have to do everything yourself.
- Living slowly, gently, and fully is a beautiful art.
- There is no shame in self-indulgence and having fun.
- Putting life before work is one of the secrets to happiness.
- Life is to be celebrated; joy can be found if you look for it.
- Nourishing yourself well, in every sense of the word, is vital.
- Family, community, and having a support system are necessary for good health.

A Soft-Life Scenario

A lifetime ago, I was going through some stuff at work and decided that I needed to take some extended time off. And by extended I mean that I quit my job. I then flew to a tropical location to recuperate and gather myself. Although I was not monetarily rich by any means, I was comfortable. And I was wealthy in many other ways:

Soft Starts

I woke up with the sunrise. No screeching alarms. No adrenaline-fueled, fight-or-flight jolts to wakefulness. My body woke gently when she felt ready. It makes a huge difference to start one's day slowly and ease into reality.

Soft Schedule

I didn't know anyone and I was not working, so my schedule was always clear. That meant that I had complete agency over my time. Bliss.

Soft Routine

I blessed myself with an easeful routine: Yoga for an hour. Healthy home-made breakfast by 8:00. Then I wrote all day, mostly songs and poems. Another hour of yoga in the afternoon. Some trash TV for balance, then a walk in nature. Dinner by 8:00, and later, a peaceful sleep.

Soft Pace

All of the above fed into a slower, more sustainable pace. With a less frenetic approach there is time to pause, time to breathe, time to savor every moment. Time to hear yourself think. That's how I was able to write hundreds of songs and poems in a comparatively short space of time. With my mind and body balanced, with no need to rush anywhere, with hours upon hours of silence, I could finally hear my muse.

Soft Weather

There's a reason why in period novels they send the delicate heroine to warmer climes to recuperate. The sun is healing. And it's free. As an island gyal, being in the warmth always makes me feel better.

Soft Beauty

I focused on caring for my skin and not so much on wearing makeup. It was immensely freeing. As a former pageant girl, I'm always going to like a fabulous full-face glam job and some giraffe lashes, but it was great to embrace a simpler approach for a while. To be honest, I just used regular soap and water (gasp), and my skin was glowing.

Soft Clothing

The other great thing about warm weather (and not going into an office) is that there is no need for hard pants and restrictive clothing. Definite housedress, muumuu, kimono vibes. I used to wear suits to work every day, so it was great to enjoy a more comfortable style.

This is what I needed to get myself back to center.

I can hear some of you saying: "Now, Lis, this is not realistic. I can't just quit my job and move to the tropics for a few months." I get it, and you're right.

But …

Take another look at the items on the list. It is possible to implement some of them exactly where you are right now, no flights or financing required. Like I mentioned before, soft living does not have to be expensive. It is accessible.

You can't convince me that it's not possible for you to wear more comfy clothing *today*. That is eminently doable. Again, I'm not suggesting that you go out and purchase a brand-new wardrobe, but surely you can exchange hard pants for sweats like so many of us did once we started working remotely.

You might not be able to have a clear calendar all day every day, but surely you can carve out moments of freedom. An hour here, 30 minutes there. Some people do #NoWorkWednesdays or they do "summer Fridays" all year round. One of my Uber drivers told me that he used to work in finance on Wall Street, but one day he realized that he hated it, especially since he never saw his family. He quit that job, and now he gets to set his own schedule. He earns less but lives more. And he spends lots of quality time with his grandchildren. Point being: You have options.

You might not be able to do yoga for an hour twice a day, but surely you can find 10–15 free minutes a few times a week to move your body in a way that works for you.

You might not be able to spend most of your day following your creative muse, but you can likely set aside some time to enjoy a hobby or do something you love. And over the long term, if your hobby or talent is what you want to do full time, you can make plans for how to achieve it.

There are ways to do this if you really want to.

Soft living is not necessarily about vacations and escape—although those clearly have their place. (Sometimes you need to come to a complete halt, get away, and recalibrate your system. A soft reboot, if you will.) It's more a question of how you can weave moments of softness into your daily routine.

After my hiatus, at some point I returned to reality, but I brought some of my new habits back with me and made them part of my regular, non-vacation life.

#SoftLifeVibes is about curating a life you don't feel the need to escape from.

What Soft Living *Is Not*

Soft Living Is Not Lazy

Living a soft life doesn't mean never working although if someone wants to not work and they can afford it, then leave them in peace to enjoy their life. As my friend Alexis says: "Keep your eyes on your own paper." You do you. Let them do them. Soft living is about achieving a happy medium, and putting life first. As I always say, it's about life-work balance, in that order.

I actually love working—on my own stuff. I love the creative process. I love putting something meaningful out into the world. I just don't want work to be *all* that I do. It can be a part of my life, but not the entire thing. My mom taught me the secret to enjoying a balanced existence—live, work, play, rest—and my goal is to manifest that for myself like she has.

Soft Living Is Not Materialistic

Look, I'm never going to say that money doesn't matter because it does. And it matters a lot. It absolutely makes life smoother. I've lived with it and without it, and I unabashedly prefer the former. Like … who is *willingly* going to choose a life where they have to constantly worry about bills and basic survival needs? Not me. Struggle energy is hard, not soft. That's why "Do it for the culture—and the coins" is one of my mantras. Money facilitates ease.

That being said, there's a world of difference between ordering from UberEats every now and then, or sending your laundry out to be done, and racking up debt trying to portray a lifestyle you can't afford. If you never own a pair of Louboutins, a Birkin, or anything by Chanel, you can still live a soft life. You can still enjoy little luxuries. *You* get to define what soft living looks like for you, and it does not have to take your whole paycheck. Soft living is not about obtaining things, it's about enjoying experiences.

Soft Living Is Not Perfectionistic

Soft living is not a rubric. There is no "ideal" performance or perfect score. Soft living is not an aesthetic. It is not something you do for other people to see. Soft living is not a contest. It's not a self-optimization project on which you'll be judged. Curating a soft life is not meant to become another obsession, compulsion, or source of shame. Soft living is not a beard for self-criticism.

Soft Living Is Not Avoidant

Well … not exactly. It's not about "checking out," neglecting your responsibilities, and avoiding hard things. Trust me, the hard things are coming, but we can reduce the number of hard things we foist *upon ourselves*. On the flip side, it *is* about avoiding some of the traps that modern life thrusts upon us, like hustle culture, burnout, and overwhelm.

Soft Living Is Not Male-Centering

The #HardWigSoftLife hashtag that was trending for a while still makes me giggle, but living a soft life, at least for me, is not about "being feminine," being submissive, or being any version of a trad wife. Soft living is not about marrying up or appealing to the male gaze. And it's definitely not about trying to make myself palatable to someone who in all likelihood is unworthy of me. I have my own table, thank you very much. What are *you* bringing, bro?

What Soft Living *Is*

Before you book that spa appointment, get on that flight, or post that #SoftLife selfie, let's take a step back and start with the fundamentals. Because if you have not addressed these, then your soft life is performative at best and self-sabotaging at worst. "As within, so without" takes intentionality, maturity, and focus.

Self-Acknowledgement

Your soft life journey starts with knowing who you are, what you value, and what makes you happy. You must acknowledge the truth about yourself and what you want out of life. This becomes the basis for curating the life that you desire. This is your compass. So, gift yourself with time and space to sit quietly and look within. And it's okay to want something different from the norm. Not everybody wants a high-powered, super-demanding career, and that's okay. It's also okay if you do. Whatever works.

Self-Prioritization

So many Black women struggle with this, but putting yourself first is an absolute must. No matter how many people try to convince you otherwise, it is not a selfish act. It is an act of enormous self-love. The reason why we're advised to put our mask on first when we're flying on a plane is because we're no good to anyone, not even ourselves, if we don't take care of that basic need. We must give ourselves permission to put ourselves at the top of our priority lists. We must show up with main character energy in our lives. We can't secure the bag if we don't first secure ourselves. Release the guilt, sis. Love yourself. Put yourself first.

Self-Maintenance

This is about the basics, bearing in mind that "basic" is slightly different for everyone. Self-maintenance refers to taking care of one's daily ablutions: Bathing your skin, brushing your teeth, washing and combing your hair. Love yourself enough to look and smell good. Take care of your hygiene. Get clean.

It also includes eating, sleeping, exercising regularly, taking your supplements and medications, and where relevant (for example, with people who have diabetes or hypertension), monitoring your levels. Going for your annual checkups, and handling your other medical needs in a timely fashion count as self-maintenance too.

For most of us, even introverts like myself, some form of social connection is also a part of how we keep ourselves on an even keel. Community connection is self-care. We've become hyperindividualistic, but humans function best as a collective.

Next up: Managing your finances, doing your chores, and paying your bills. In other words—being an adult. So, if you thought that soft living was about shirking responsibilities, newsflash: It's not. You gotta take care of your stuff. That said, there are people who need or want support with some of these activities, and there is nothing at all wrong with getting help.

Curate Your Soft Life: Exhale   259

Outsourcing and automating what you can is definitely a soft life strategy. This is the foundation upon which everything else is built. Hire people. Use services. My mom modeled for me the importance of having household help, so whenever I have been able to, I have hired a housekeeper. When I lived in Barbados, my housekeeper would come every Friday. She would clean the house, naturally, but she also took care of the laundry. Heaven. She would also do a big batch cook to last me a few days. There are few experiences sweeter than coming home on a Friday afternoon and having absolutely *nothing* to do. House sparkling. Clothes clean. Meals cooked. I had a gardener too, so the lawn was gorgeous and my plants were thriving. Make the mundanities of life as frictionless as possible. Embrace the joy of ease.

Self-Care

This is probably where you had expected me to start, but I'm always going to be real with you. And being real means me telling you that you must crawl before you can walk. And that there is an order of things. Take care of the basics and *then* branch out. That's not to say that you must deny yourself all joy in the interim, not at all, but I have to tell you that for me, joyful activities feel sooo much better when I don't have a list of unhandled responsibilities tugging at my mind. I'm able to relax and enjoy myself fully.

The next level up from daily grooming and adulting includes activities like getting your hair done, going to the nail salon, and taking care of your skin. (Everybody's life is different, so some people categorize these as basics. The categories are fluid.) I'm an eyebrow girlie, so brows are always at the top of my list. When my brows are done nobody can't tell me nuffin. I've started dermaplaning my face as well: Menopause is a hater. At one point in my life, I used to get acupuncture and massages several times a week. It was absolute heaven, and helped keep me balanced. One of my non-negotiables is my nightly skin care routine. It puts me in a great mood at the end of every day. And the skin is skinning!!

Back in the day, I would be at the nail salon and barber every two weeks. Yes, I said barber. Ya girl used to rock a buzz cut. I wore my nails super long for balance because I got tired of being called "Sir." Nowadays, self-care looks like *not* getting my nails done. I can no longer stand the odor of all the chemicals, and I'm not going to pay anybody to sit there and feel uncomfortable. If I have a photoshoot to prepare for, then I'll do what I have to do. Other than that, it ain't happening.

For many people, self-care involves water in one form or another. Water is so healing. Staying hydrated is at the top of the list, of course, but there's also taking bubble baths or long showers. (And washing our legs!!) One activity I include in my daily self-care regimen is giving myself a mini pedicure while I'm in the shower. Feet are like but'uh: Soft and smooth.

When I was on short-term disability recovering from burnout, self-care also looked like me taking Ubers everywhere I had to go. (By "everywhere" I mean to CVS to pick up my meds, lol. Other than that I barely left the house. My other main outings were to the podiatrist. How life humbles you.) I tried a bus once, and my body was like "Nah." So I spent a little more money and went to my destinations in comfort.

I also ordered in probably more than I ever have in my life. I just didn't have the energy for cooking. A personal chef is definitely on my vision board. I like to eat, not to cook. I'm grateful that my mom taught me how to whip up a delicious meal, but left to my own devices, all I want to hear is "Dinner is served." Better yet, I love room service energy. Intercontinental me, please.

Something else I did was change my office chair. I had been using one of my dining chairs: Beautiful, but with a slatted wooden back that was not designed for eight-hour days. My spine was constantly aching, and it even started affecting my breathing. Since one thing I don't lack is furniture, I shopped my home. I had a perfectly good office chair in another room. Smooth leather with some beautiful nailhead trim. I wheeled it out, and voilà. Problem solved. It's so comfy.

Counterintuitively, one of the things I *stopped* doing was my hair. Before y'all come for me, I don't mean I stopped washing or combing it: My weekly wash day is part of my self-care routine. I just didn't do box braids for a long time. I let my scalp and follicles breathe. I put my hair in flat twists and threw on a headwrap. I didn't want to be bothered. So I didn't bother.

I share these little examples to reiterate the point that self-care and soft living do not have to be complicated or expensive. We each get to decide what self-care looks like for us, whatever that might be. Dr. Chantell Frazier, a medical sociologist and CEO and founder of Anansi Research, advises that the most important thing is to make self-care a continuous part of our lives, rather than a sporadic effort:

Curate Your Soft Life: Exhale 261

From a sociological and public health perspective, I need you to understand that caring for yourself, physically and mentally, is absolutely crucial. As Black women we are often the most burdened but the least supported members of society. So we need to be engaged in *ongoing* self-care practices—and that includes rest.

Build in time for "little exhales," *and* big ones. Yes: Vacation and PTO are important, but so are regular walks outside. So is five minutes of journaling. So are affirmations, positive music, and joyful movement. So is time pouring back into ourselves, with people who love and truly support us.

We put endless amounts of pressure on ourselves to succeed, knowing that our success is absolutely crucial, but missing that our *being around* is even more crucial. We hold up the sky. There is nothing without us, but that doesn't mean keep pushing through. That means rest, rejuvenate, and relax for the good of your long-term ability to survive and thrive. That means center what you need, not what others need. And give yourself time and space to exhale, as much and as often as you can.

Self-Indulgence

There's a hedonistic energy to self-indulgence. If self-care is an apple, self-indulgence might be a cookie. Nothing is wrong with either: Each serves a function. This is where deep pampering comes in. All-day spa moments. Luxurious facials. A little retail therapy. Spoiling yourself. There is nothing wrong with indulging in life's pleasures; it feels absolutely wonderful! But it's a matter of frequency, intention, and consequences. The main question to ask yourself here is "Is this a bandaid or a benefit?" No judgment either way. Just be clear.

To go back to the top of this chapter, self-indulgence might look like booking that trip to Bali, or that Sedona retreat you've always dreamed of. But if that trip is going to numb you out or put you in debt, then you're actually not caring for yourself at all.

Self-Compassion

Soft living is steeped in self-compassion. Showing ourselves grace. Offering ourselves forgiveness. Speaking to ourselves kindly. Soothing ourselves when we need it. Freeing ourselves from burdens that are not ours to carry.

262   Be Yourself

Walking away from harmful people, places, and systems. We must be willing to release whatever is not serving our highest good. Self-compassion is also about being willing to request and receive assistance. We must invite support from our community and family, whether blood-related or chosen. In short, treat yourself tenderly and let people help you, sis!

Self-Love

This is the big one. This is what soft living is all about. Looking at everything we've covered in the previous chapters, they all point to self-love as the foundation of a soft life. So I invite you to:

Love Yourself Enough to Be True to Yourself: It's okay to know who you are, be who you are, love who you are, want what you want, and when relevant, make it do what it do. Once you're not harming anyone else, do you. Nothing creates soft life vibes like being internally at peace.

Love Yourself Enough to Focus on Your Strengths: This is not to be confused with "being strong." We're rebuking the "Strong Black Woman Syndrome" in its entirety. Rather, it's about recognizing your positives and celebrating your wins. For Black women especially, who are often criticized simply for existing, focusing on our talents and innate good qualities provides much-needed counter-programming to the negative messaging we receive from the outside world.

Love Yourself Enough to Think Highly of Yourself: The easiest way to manifest your soft life is to start by knowing that you are worthy of living it. You. Are. Worthy. You don't need to scale another hurdle, get another degree, or prove one more thing to anyone. Get in the habit of thinking good thoughts about yourself; of talking yourself up rather than putting yourself down. You are amazing.

Love Yourself Enough to Entertain Healthy Relationships: Surround yourself with people who uplift, inspire, and support you. Get in community with kinfolk and skinfolk who speak life into you and over you. Connect with folks who see you as a full and wonderful human being, rather than as a resource or someone merely to be used. Place yourself in the company of good humans around whom you are safe and happy.

Curate Your Soft Life: Exhale 263

Love Yourself Enough to Embrace Life-Work Balance: Choose life. Choose love. Choose family. Choose a career. Then place them in the correct hierarchy—the one that benefits **you.**

Love Yourself Enough to Elevate Your Energy: Pour into yourself. Be a good steward of all your blessings. Even as the world burns around us like an apocalyptic dumpster fire, there is still the possibility of vibrating higher. You don't need to attend every argument you're invited to, or weigh in on every issue. Rise above the fray. Get in alignment. It's time to focus on YOU.

Love Yourself Enough to Want Better for Yourself: If you know your life isn't working the way you'd like, love yourself enough to be willing to change it. For me, "hard living" and hustle culture do not work, so I have chosen an alternative path.

Love Yourself Enough to Take Care of Your Mental Health: Meditate. Get therapy. Where appropriate, take your meds. And don't forget the role that some of the basics play in maintaining mental wellness. Good nutrition, regular exercise, sound sleep, cleanliness, and community connection all help support your mental equilibrium.

Love Yourself Enough to Let Yourself Have Fun: Laugh. Frolic. Embrace the joy of play. Dance badly. Sing loudly. Hang out with your people. Life doesn't have to be so serious all the time. You're allowed to live light.

Love Yourself Enough to Set Boundaries: I keep repeating this in various forms because it's so important. Honestly, this will take care of a good 70–80 percent of any problems you encounter. Free yourself of burdensome obligations, especially those that strangers attempt to impose on you. Say no to them, and yes to yourself.

Love Yourself Enough to Rest: Even before the results of the 2024 election, but definitely since then, rest became a focus. If you know, you know. Put those heavy bags down, sis. Otherwise, like Cousin Badu says, "you gon' hurt yo' back." Drop whatever is not yours to carry. Let dem

264   **Be Yourself**

people take care of themselves. Release that which is not serving your highest good—and rest. Nurture yourself. It is time.

Love Yourself Enough to Be a Soft Black Woman: It takes considerable resolve to push against a dominant narrative, but we can do it. So: Exhale, sis. Relax your jaw. Lower your shoulders. Unclench your fists. Soften that knot in your solar plexus. Breathe. You are allowed to choose a better path for yourself, one that is soft, centered, and serene. You are allowed to be a Soft Black Woman.

Love Yourself Enough to Make Space to Exhale: Slow down. Wind down. Lay your burdens down. Do less, rest more, and make your life stress-free. Release overdrive and embrace *under*drive. The key phrase is "simple and frictionless." Get yourself to the point where you can say "woosah" and mean it. Divest. Rest. Exhale.

Conclusion

A change is brewing in the ether; a change I'm happy to see. More and more Black women are saying "Enough!" We are training the algorithm of our lives to serve us well and act in our favor. We are choosing to prioritize our mental and physical well-being. We are rejecting the expectations of others; freeing ourselves of that weight. We are lightening our load. We are choosing to rest, to heal, to thrive. I absolutely love it.

Probably the best example of this is the G.O.A.T., Simone Biles.

During the Tokyo Olympics, she started experiencing the twisties, which is what happens when gymnasts lose their mind-body connection midair, and are unable to tell where they are, or how they will land. Understandably, this could potentially end in catastrophic injuries, so Biles did the smart thing and pulled out of most of her events. Ultimately, the U.S. gymnastics team took home a silver medal, and Biles took home a bronze in balance beam.

But y'all ...

The hate, judgment, and vitriol that was directed her way was truly heartbreaking to witness. People were sitting on their couches, knee-deep in Doritos, having never won a solitary thing, lambasting her for stepping away.

Thing is she was *already* the G.O.A.T. She might have *wanted* Tokyo, but she did not need it. Also, despite what so many folks had to say, silver and bronze Olympic medals are not a "loss." I mean, they just aren't. Only a fraction of a fraction of a fraction of humankind ever gets to even qualify for the Olympics, far less win a medal—no matter the hue. All medals matter.

Simone stood her ground, ignored the critics, and spent the intervening years between Tokyo and Paris taking care of her mental and physical health. She put herself first and prioritized self-care. A big part of her recovery protocol was going to therapy every week. She got tips and tools for supporting her mental health and getting back to center. She also treated herself with compassion (and common sense) by *gradually* building back up to her usual level of difficulty in her gymnastics skills.

As God so often shows us, a delay is not a denial.

Biles showed up and showed out at the Paris Olympics: She earned four medals, three gold and one silver.

Black women are out here living softly and winning.

We love to see it.

~ ~ ~

June: Too soon
July: Stand by
August: Come it must
September: Remember
October: All over

Growing up in the Caribbean, this is a poem every school child is taught in the English-speaking islands. It's a mnemonic to help us remember when hurricane season happens.

It is interesting to know and experience this truth even from very young: The storms of life are unavoidable.

Barbados is very lucky in terms of where she's positioned on the island chain. She's over there furthest to the east, standing to one side like a bougie auntie in her heels and church hat, quietly minding her business, clutching her pearls, and trying to stay out of trouble. Most years, she succeeds. Most years hurricanes pass her by, making minimal impact.

But there are always those times when a hurricane gets the island squarely in its sights and wreaks utter havoc.

No matter how lucky you are, or how sheltered, at some point you're going to feel Nature's fury. You will be lashed by rain.

The storms are coming.

The weather is gonna weather.

Conclusion 267

And life is gonna life.
That is the reality.

But:

Life is not one continuous storm. There are ebbs and flows. There are periods of calm. Deal with the storms when they come, but allow yourself moments of respite. In fact, take it a step further: Build respite into your daily life. You don't have to live in permanent, adrenaline-fueled fight-or-flight energy.

Give yourself permission to rest.
Give yourself permission to relax.
Give yourself permission to exhale.
Give yourself permission to live a soft life.

Woosah.

Elevation: Vibrate Higher

Exhalation: Breathe Easy

Belly Breathing

Sit or lie down comfortably with your eyes closed.

Gently rest your hands on your abdomen.

Breathe through your nose.

With every inhale, your belly rises, and with every exhale, your belly falls:

Inhale: Belly rises

Exhale: Belly falls

Inhale: Belly rises

Exhale: Belly falls

(continued)

(continued)

Now begin to control the length of your exhales, making them slightly longer than your inhales. Inhale for a count of four, and exhale for a count of six.

Let's begin:

Inhale: 1, 2, 3, 4

Exhale: 1, 2, 3, 4, 5, 6

Inhale: 1, 2, 3, 4

Exhale: 1, 2, 3, 4, 5, 6

Inhale: 1, 2, 3, 4

Exhale: 1, 2, 3, 4, 5, 6

Breathe deep into your belly, making sure it is still rising with every inhale and falling with every exhale.

Continue breathing like this for as long as you wish.

When you're ready, return your breath to its normal cadence and gently open your eyes.

Affirmations: Speak Life

- I love myself enough to put myself first.
- I am in my soft girl era and I love it here.
- I am loving my soft, centered, serene life.
- I am ready and willing to be a Soft Black Woman.
- I am blessed to live a soft life that supports my highest good.

Introspection: Journal & Heal

- What does living a soft life mean to you?
- What can you do to achieve life-work balance?
- What does having space to exhale mean to you?

(continued)

(continued)

- What makes you feel stressed and overwhelmed? How can you reduce or eliminate those triggers?
- How do you react when you see or hear the term "soft life"? How do you feel in your body? Relaxed? Tense? Angry? Grateful? Happy?

Curation: Do the Work

Think about your morning and evening home routines.

- List three things you can easily do to make them simpler and more enjoyable.

Think about your career and your daily work routine.

- List three things you would change about your job if you could.
- List three things you would change about your work routine if you could.

Appreciation: Express Gratitude

What are you grateful for? Count your blessings:

- I am grateful ...
- I am grateful ...
- I am grateful ...

Celebration: Razzle Dazzle

Flex on 'em, sis! What are you proud of? Celebrate yourself:

- I am proud of myself for ...
- I am proud of myself for ...
- I am proud of myself for ...

(continued)

(continued)

Meditation: Think Blissfully

Get into a comfortable position, either sitting or lying down. If it works for you, put a comfy cushion at your back or under your knees. Relax fully into it. Close your eyes, and let's begin.

Keeping your inhales and exhales even, inhale and exhale slowly and gently through your nose for a count of five:

Inhale: 1, 2, 3, 4, 5; exhale: 5, 4, 3, 2, 1

Inhale: 1, 2, 3, 4, 5; exhale: 5, 4, 3, 2, 1

Inhale: 1, 2, 3, 4, 5; exhale: 5, 4, 3, 2, 1

Bring your attention to your heart chakra in the middle of your chest. Place both hands there gently.

Repeat after me, silently or out loud:

- I am giving myself permission to live a soft, serene life.
- I am giving myself permission to live a soft, serene life.
- I am giving myself permission to live a soft, serene life.

Continue inhaling and exhaling for five, relaxing even more.

Repeat after me, silently or out loud:

- I am giving myself permission to exhale.
- I am giving myself permission to exhale.
- I am giving myself permission to exhale.

When you're ready, return your breathing to its regular pace, and open your eyes.

Asé.

Epilogue

Why I Breathe

To understand the Infinite
To catch a whiff, a hint of It
To manifest my soul's desires
To rise like phoenix through the fire
To amplify my depth of love
Express it, both here and above
To magnify my radiant heart
To share my beauty and my art
To hear God when He speaks to me:
These are the reasons why I breathe

To feel my soul expand and stay
Wide open as I sit and pray
For grace and hope; for love and faith
For gratitude in midst of pain
To feel the freedom of release
To live true joy and be true peace
To know that I am one with Him
And I am blessed by seraphim
Who keep me strong when courage leaves:
These are the reasons why I breathe

Epilogue

A softer life awaits
On this side of the veil
A pace more slow
An inner glow
A co-created grail

Yes

A softer life awaits
On this side of the veil
A sense of ease
A gentle breeze
That brings space to exhale

To build connection with my tribe
To feel more balanced and alive
To elevate my energy
To cultivate serenity
To be obedient to my Guide
Make my ancestors smile with pride
To daily give the best of me
Receive all that is meant for me
To know in me He is well pleased:
These are the reasons why I breathe

To understand the Infinite
To catch a whiff, a hint of It
To manifest my soul's desires
To rise like phoenix through the fire
To amplify my depth of love
Express it, both here and above
To magnify my radiant heart
To share my beauty and my art
To hear God when He speaks to me:
These are the reasons why I breathe

© Lisa Hurley

Resources

Mental Health Support and Self Help
- If you or someone you know is struggling, reach out to a mental health professional for help, call the suicide and crisis hotline at 988, go to the closest ER, or call 911.
- African American Behavioral Health Center of Excellence
- Black Emotional & Mental Health Collective
- Hinds Family Care
- LBee Health
- The Empathy Scorecard
- Therapy For Black Girls

Supportive Communities for Black Women
- *Healthy Scholars,* founded by Chantell Frazier
- *The Great Exhale*, founded by Lisa Hurley
- *Transparent & Black*, founded by Yasmine Jameelah
- *Queens & Crowns Network*, founded by LaTonya Davis
- *Win With Black Women*, founded by Jotaka Eaddy

Books
- *Black Girl In Love (With Herself)*, by Trey Anthony
- *Black Liturgies*, by Cole Arthur Riley
- *Black People Breathe*, by Zee Clarke

274   Resources

- *Rest Is Resistance*, by Tricia Hersey
- *The Memo*, by Minda Harts

Podcasts

- *Black Women Can Have It All*, hosted by Liku Amadi
- *Professional Troublemaker*, hosted by Luvvie Ajayi Jones
- *Space To Exhale*, hosted by Lisa Hurley
- *Therapy For Black Girls*, hosted by Dr. Joy Harden Bradford
- *Triggered AF*, hosted by Alechia Reese and Dani Bourdeau

Glossary of Culturally Rooted Terms and Digital Vernacular

Words carry history, movement, and meaning. This glossary honors the ingenuity, adaptability, and vibrancy of Black, African American, and Caribbean linguistic traditions. Whether rooted in ancestral tongues, digital culture, or everyday brilliance, these words reflect our reality, shape our stories, express our vibrancy, and affirm our existence, while also celebrating the dynamism of Black dialects across the diaspora.

B

Big up yuhself *(phrase, Caribbean English, informal)* – A Jamaican Patois expression meaning "give yourself credit" or "celebrate yourself." Often used to encourage confidence, self-pride, and recognition of one's achievements.

Bim *(noun, Barbadian English)* – An alternative name for Barbados, typically used only by locals. See also: **Bimshire**

Bimshire *(noun, Barbadian English)* – An alternative name for Barbados, typically used only by locals. See also: **Bim**

Glossary of Culturally Rooted Terms

Blessed And Rested (#BlessedAndRested) *(phrase)* – A state of deep gratitude and relaxation, often achieved after prioritizing rest, self-care, and spiritual well-being.

Booked And Busy (#BookedAndBusy) *(phrase)* – A declaration of success and productivity, indicating a packed schedule filled with fulfilling work and commitments.

Broughtupsy *(noun, Caribbean English)* – Good manners, etiquette, and proper upbringing, as instilled by elders or guardians.

Bus' *(verb, Caribbean English, informal)* – To burst, break open, or be released suddenly.

But'uh *(phrase, British regional slang)* – A pronunciation of the word "butter" with a hard glottal stop.

C

Cawblimmuh *(exclamation, Barbadian English, informal)* – An expression of shock, surprise, or exasperation, often used when witnessing something outrageous or unbelievable.

Cheeseonbread *(exclamation, Barbadian English, informal)* – A euphemistic phrase used to express surprise, frustration, or disbelief, similar to "Oh my goodness!"

D

Dialek *(noun, Caribbean English)* – A nonstandard or regionally distinct form of a language, often used to refer to the rich linguistic traditions of Caribbean Creole languages and African American Vernacular English (AAVE). Translates to "Dialect."

De innanets *(noun, AAVE / Caribbean English, informal)* – The internet, often used humorously or sarcastically to reference online spaces and digital culture.

Dem *(pronoun, AAVE / Caribbean English, informal)* – Translates to "Them" or sometimes to "Those."

Divest And Rest (#DivestAndRest) *(phrase)* – A call to disengage from oppressive systems, toxic environments, or exploitative labor in favor of rest, healing, and sustainable well-being. Coined by Lisa Hurley.

F

#FAFO *(acronym, informal)* – Short for "F*** Around and Find Out," a phrase warning against reckless behavior that will lead to inevitable consequences.

Glossary of Culturally Rooted Terms

Faux-portunity *(noun, Caribbean English, informal, humorous)* – A portmanteau of "faux" and "opportunity," referring to a situation that is presented as an opportunity but is, in reality, not beneficial or worth pursuing. Often used to call out exploitative offers disguised as golden chances. See also: **Noportunity.**

Fentys *(noun, informal; plural)* – A colloquial reference to Rihanna's luxury fashion and beauty brand, Fenty.

Fire de wuk *(phrase, Caribbean English, informal)* – A term meaning to quit a job, resign, or leave a situation, often used with a sense of empowerment or defiance. It can also imply dismissing someone from their position.

FlewedOut (#FlewedOut) *(verb, AAVE, informal)* – To be flown to a destination (often for leisure or romantic purposes) at someone else's expense, popularized in social media and hip-hop culture.

Footwerk Friday (#FootwerkFriday) *(phrase, AAVE)* – A virtual celebration of dance showcased by sharing dance videos, on LinkedIn and other social media platforms, at the end of the work week. It's a mood booster that marks the end of the work week and the beginning of the weekend. #FootwerkFriday posts typically begin with: "It's #FootwerkFriday and we're dancing into the weekend!" A hashtag and movement created by Lisa Hurley in the early 2020s.

Free.99 *(adjective, AAVE, informal)* – A playful way of saying something is completely free of charge.

Frenemigos *(noun, Spanglish/AAVE, informal)* – A blend of "frenemies" and "enemigos" (Spanish for enemies), describing someone who pretends to be a friend but harbors negative intentions.

G

Goodt *(adjective, AAVE, informal)* – An emphatic form of "good," used to describe something excellent or exceptionally satisfying.

Gyal *(noun, Caribbean English, informal)* – A term for "girl" or "young woman," commonly used in Jamaican Patois and other Caribbean dialects. It can be affectionate, descriptive, or playful, depending on the context.

H

Hard Wig Soft Life (#HardWigSoftLife) *(phrase, AAVE, humorous)* – A witty commentary on maintaining a glamorous or "soft life" (a lifestyle centered on ease and luxury) while not looking glamorous at all, for example by wearing a "hard" or super-obvious wig.

Glossary of Culturally Rooted Terms

I

I'z *(verb, Caribbean English, archaic/informal)* – A contraction of "I is," reflecting African-influenced grammatical structures common in Caribbean Creoles. It translates to "I am."

K

Kiki *(verb / noun, AAVE, LGBTQ+ slang)* – **To laugh, joke, and engage in lively, playful conversation, often used within Black queer and ballroom communities.**

L

Lewk (Look) *(noun, AAVE, informal)* – A distinctive, stylish, or memorable appearance, particularly in fashion and beauty contexts.
Likkle *(adjective, Caribbean English)* – A diminutive form of "little," commonly used in Jamaican Patois and other Caribbean dialects.

M

Movementations *(noun, AAVE, informal)* – A playful way of describing plans, activities, or progress being made, whether socially, personally, professionally, or romantically. Can also describe the joyful way someone moves through the world.

N

Noportunity *(noun, Caribbean English, informal, humorous)* – A blend of "no" and "opportunity," referring to a situation that is presented as an opportunity but is, in reality, not beneficial or worth pursuing. Often used to call out exploitative offers disguised as golden chances. Coined by Lisa Hurley. See also: **Fauxportunity.**
Nuffin *(noun, AAVE / Caribbean English, informal)* – A phonetic spelling of "nothing," often used for emphasis or as part of casual speech.

O

Outchea *(adverb, AAVE / Caribbean English, informal)* – A term meaning "out here," often used to express being present, active, or thriving in a particular space or situation.

Glossary of Culturally Rooted Terms

P

Panini *(noun, AAVE, humorous)* – A slang term for "pandemic," often used to lighten conversations about the global crisis by replacing the word with similar-sounding alternatives. See also: **Panorama**.

Panorama *(noun, AAVE, humorous)* – A slang term for "pandemic," often used to lighten conversations about the global crisis by replacing the word with similar-sounding alternatives. See also: **Panini**.

Periodt *(interjection, AAVE, emphatic)* – An exaggerated form of "period," used to emphasize a statement as final and indisputable.

PoC *(noun)* – Person of Color or People of Color.

R

Raggedyness *(noun, AAVE, informal)* – A state of messiness, dysfunction, or chaos, often used humorously or critically.

Respek *(noun, AAVE / Caribbean English, informal)* – A phonetic spelling of "respect," emphasizing deference, acknowledgment, or regard for someone.

T

Tiredt *(adjective, AAVE, exaggerated)* – A dramatic, elongated form of "tired," used to express extreme exhaustion or frustration.

W

Wah gwan my bredrin *(phrase, Caribbean English, informal)* – A greeting meaning "What's going on, my brother?" or "How are you, my friend?" Commonly used in Jamaican Patois and Caribbean communities as a warm, familiar way to check in with someone.

Wuhloss *(exclamation, Barbadian English)* – An expression of shock, grief, or intense reaction, similar to "Oh my goodness!" or "Wow!" in English.

Acknowledgments

Big tings a gwan!! I can hardly believe that I actually wrote a whole book, but it's real because you're reading it right now. Just … WOW. God is good. So first and foremost, thank YOU for reading my words; for making space in your life to receive them. That is huge, and I deeply appreciate you for that.

Not gonna lie, I also have some Snoop Dogg "I wanna thank me" energy in my spirit, because I received, understood, and executed the assignment. I stayed the course, even when it was tough. I did it, and I am proud of myself.

Writing is a solitary endeavor, but writing a book is definitely a group project. If I were to list everyone I want to thank, it would be the length of another book. I'm blessed to have a whole community of people in my corner. You all know who you are, and I am eternally grateful to you. If I accidentally forgot to name any of you, blame it on ADHD, lol. In my heart, I'm thanking you a million times. My circle is small, so many of you belong in more than one category: Friend, supporter, contributor, early reader, etc. Generally, I've placed you in one category below, but don't think for a moment that I don't know that you poured into me in multiple ways. I deeply appreciate you all. For the most part, I have confined the acknowledgements to those who have directly contributed to *Space To Exhale* in some way, or who helped me get to the point where I could write it.

Acknowledgments

To The One

Thanks and praises to The Most High: Thank you for trusting me with this assignment and for providing everything I needed to complete it, in the perfect way at the perfect time. Thank you for blessing me abundantly. You have ordered my steps, and I am grateful.

To My Family

Mummy, Sharon, Taryn, Daddy, and Anne: Thanks for believing in me. Thank you all for your support, encouragement, feedback, and great advice. Thanks for celebrating every milestone along the way, no matter how big or small. I love you all.

To My Love

Patrick: You're an amazing person, and I feel so lucky that we're in each other's lives. Thank you for being my rock and my safe space; for selflessly gifting me with time to write, and for encouraging me to press on even when I thought I couldn't. Thanks for always cheering for me, praying for me, and speaking life over me. Most of all, thank you for helping me to believe in love again. I love you.

To My Friends

Annie Matthew: GIRL!!! It really happened!! Thanks for being the best bestie ever. I always say that everybody should have an Annie in their life, and I'm so happy you're in mine. Thank you for "choosing me" all those years ago, lol. And thanks also for patiently telling me year after year "Lis, I think you need to write." I finally listened. Luv ya!

Rachael Marshall: One thing you and I know is if you just keep putting one foot in front of the other, you eventually reach your destination. That mini-trek we once took together helped prepare me for this bigger one. Writing this book was a journey, and your support helped me make it to the end. I truly treasure you: Your generosity, sense of humor, thoughtfulness, and sparkly personality. Thank you for being you.

Alexis Mobley: Edge-snatcher and truth-teller extraordinaire: You are one of a kind and I'm blessed to know you. You have such a good heart, sharp mind, and bright spirit. You are "do no harm, take no ish" in human form

Acknowledgments 283

and I appreciate that. You embody the spirit of genuine reciprocity: #BiDirectional. Thank you for lifting me when I was at my lowest, helping me focus, and encouraging me to keep going. #KimonosOpen!

Tammy Triolo: My smart, stylish, empathetic sis with the big brain and even bigger heart: You are the real deal, and I'm grateful that we're in each other's lives. I'm so happy you reached out to me on LinkedIn all those years ago and said, "We need to be friends." (Heaven knows my introverted behind would never have done that, lol.) You were right. Thank you for consistently checking in on me even at times when you needed lifting yourself. Hugs and more hugs.

To My Publisher and My Editorial Team

Wiley: None of this would have happened without you, so thank you! I will forever be thrilled that the same publisher whose name was on my textbooks in high school has now published my book. It's a beautiful full-circle moment that I will always cherish.

Victoria Savanh, my wonderful Acquisitions Editor: I can't thank you enough for seeing me and taking a chance on me. You changed my life and helped make one of my childhood dreams come true. Thank you.

To Jeanenne Ray, Associate Publisher; Purvi Patel, Managing Editor; Trinity Compton, Editorial Assistant; the Wiley Editorial, Design, and Production teams, and everyone who helped bring *Space To Exhale* to the world: I appreciate you more than I can say. Thanks for putting so much time, care, and attention into "my baby," and getting her fully ready for the world.

Adaobi Obi Tulton, my amazing Developmental Editor and newfound cousin: Thanks for getting me. Thanks for protecting my words, respecting my voice, and helping my stories to shine. Thank you for advocating on my behalf. You are the absolute best. #SimSimma

To My Book Coach
Luvvie Ajayi Jones
Luvvie: What can I even say? When I was writing these acknowledgements, I wanted to include a section titled "People Without Whom This

Book Would Not Have Happened" and put you and *The Book Academy* at the top of the list. Because the truth is that it would probably still be buried in my "Maybe Someday" folder were it not for you. When I went all the way back in my drafts, I realized that I had actually had the idea for *Space To Exhale* several years ago, but I somehow could not make any progress with it—until you and TBA showed up.

Thank you for being a catalyst.

Thank you for stepping more fully into your purpose and thereby empowering me to step more fully into mine. Without The Book Academy and The Book Proposal Power Program, I would not have been able to move ahead with Wiley when they reached out to me. Thank you for getting me ready, and for keeping me focused. Thank you for embodying excellence. Thanks for pushing me, when necessary, to aim higher; for the times when you dragged me—with love—into being the best version of my creative self.

To you, Macy Robison, the entire TBA team and community, and my sisters in The Bestselling Book Academy: Thank you all from the bottom of my heart.

To My Cover Designer

Rose Reynolds

Rose: You did it!! Thank you for stepping up and giving it your all as usual. Thanks for blessing me with your creativity. Your brain is a beautiful place, and your work ethic is second to none. I absolutely love my cover. It truly looks like a breath of fresh air. Can't wait to collaborate on more creative projects in the future.

To My Legal Counsel

Liku Amadi

Liku: Where do I even start? I didn't even know which category to include you in. You have shown up as so much more than a lawyer. You have helped to keep my companies in good standing and my emotions on an even keel. Thank you for all your excellent advice, but also for being a staunch supporter and loyal friend. Thank you for offering to help—and *actually helping*—when you could see I needed it. Thank you for keeping me encouraged. You are an absolute gem. See you in Monaco.

Acknowledgments 285

To My Contributors

To all of you who blessed the book with quotes, thanks so much for taking the time and for supporting the mission. And, of course, to all my advance readers, early reviewers, and everyone who so generously wrote a blurb: Thanks a million!! Every time I look though the book and see your names it warms my heart. I appreciate you all.

To Those Who Kept Me Lifted, Then and Now

Special mention goes to: Lola Bakare, Janelle Benjamin, Evan Birkhead, Dana Brownlee, Kimberly Bryant, LaTonya Davis, Brianna Doe, Greg Duncan, Yinka Ewuola, Kelly Fuller, Anta Gueye-James, Tom Hadnot, Lauren Howard, Steve Jones, Elaine Lin Hering, Mita Mallick, Isvari Maranwe, Michael Rudder, Dr. Kathryn Tapper, David & Madeline McQueen, Val Powell, Elona Washington, the Barbados Reiki Association, and my entire Reiki family around the world. Thanks also to my pocstock family, and my medical dream team.

To My TGE Community

My sistas, I love you. Thank you for supporting The Great Exhale and helping to make it a soft, safe, uplifting space for us all. Look how far we've come!! We live and breathe this work together, and it's a beautiful thing to experience. Thank you for believing in me, and keeping me lifted. Thank you for showing me grace, and not giving up on me. Most of all, thank you for being patient while I gave myself some much-needed space to exhale. Ya girl is back. Let us all continue exhaling together.

To My Fur Baby, King

Thank you for rescuing me. You're a good, good boy.

About the Author

Lisa Hurley is an Anthem Award-winning activist, writer, and community builder. She is the Founder of The Great Exhale, a soft virtual space where Black women can relax, heal, and thrive. Her work operates at the nexus of self care, community care, joy, and rest.

Hurley is an Executive Member of the International Academy of Digital Arts and Sciences, a board member of Yuvoice, and a Juror for the Anthem Awards. A Founding Member of The Book Academy, she is also a graduate of the University of the West Indies, and of New York University.

A respected figure, Ms. Hurley has been honored as one of the Top 20 Entrepreneurs to follow on LinkedIn, voted as one of LinkedIn's Top 50 Black Creators, and recognized as a Top 10 Anti-Discrimination Activist worldwide. Her words have been quoted in Forbes, Essence, Entrepreneur, and Adweek.

Lisa is a Reiki Master who is known for her good vibrations and inspiring affirmations. In her free time she enjoys hanging out with her pup, bonding with her family, reading a good book, and expressing her creativity through fashion. Of Caribbean heritage, Lisa is a world traveler with an understandable preference for warmer climes. Her love languages are sunshine, laughter, and naps.

Notes

Author's Note

1. Chisolm, A. (2024b, December 16). *How the 92 Percent of Black Women Are Interpreting the Election Results | Black Girl Nerds*. Black Girl Nerds. https://blackgirlnerds.com/how-the-92-percent-of-black-women-are-interpreting-the-election-results/.

Introduction

1. x.com. (2012). *X (Formerly Twitter)*. https://x.com/THEKIDMERO/status/935550320154996736.
2. Every Level Leadership. (2024, September 18). *Black Women Thriving Report - Every level leadership*. https://everylevelleads.com/bwt/.
3. National Partnership for Women & Families. (2024, September 10). For the First Time in 20 Years, Gender Wage Gap Widened, with Women Paid Just 75 Cents to a Man's Dollar. https://nationalpartnership.org/news_post/first-time-20-years-gender-wage-gap-widened-women-workers-paid-just-75-cents-to-mans-dollar/.

Chapter 1

1. Black Women Photographers. (n.d.). About Black Women Photographers, a free global community and directory of 1000+ Black photographers. Black Women Photographers. https://blackwomenphotographers.com/about.

290 Notes

2. Simeon, A., & Irungu, P. B. P. (2019, August 26). The Most Eye-Catching Beauty Moments From Afropunk. Refinery29. https://www.refinery29.com/en-us/2019/08/241451/afropunk-festival-hair-makeup-beauty-looks-2019.

3. Nasdaq. (2020). Amplifying Black Voices: August | This month, https://www.facebook.com/watch/?v=362467548085709.

4. Alfaro, L. (2020, August 21). Amplify Black Voices: Polly Irungu. Nasdaq. https://www.nasdaq.com/articles/amplify-black-voices%3A-polly-irungu-2020-08-21.

5. Co-Chair of the SDG Advocates—Mia Mottley. (2022, April). UN Office for Partnerships. https://unpartnerships.un.org/prime-minister-barbados-mia-mottley.

6. World Health Organization: WHO. (2022, September 22). The Global Leaders Group host side event at UN General Assembly on Antimicrobial Resistance (AMR). World Health Organization. https://www.who.int/news/item/22-09-2022-the-global-leaders-group-host-side-event-at-un-general-assembly-on-antimicrobial-resistance-(amr)#:~:text=%E2%80%9CAs%20we%20continue%20together%20towards,Mottley%2C%20Prime%20Minister%20of%20Barbados.

7. Used with permission. © Terry Arthur, 2013.

Chapter 3

1. THE NIFCA STORY – National Cultural Foundation, Barbados. (n.d.). https://ncf.bb/the-story-of-nifca/.

2. *Landship Experience—The Barbados Landship Unique Culture & Youth Programs.* (n.d.). https://landshipexperience.org/.

3. Csikszentmihalyi, M. C. (2008). *Flow: The Psychology of Optimal Experience.* Harper Perennial Modern Classics.

4. Ikigai: The Japanese Secret to a Joyful Life. (2024, February 29). *The Government of Japan—JapanGov.* https://www.japan.go.jp/kizuna/2022/03/ikigai_japanese_secret_to_a_joyful_life.html.

Chapter 4

1. (T-2.VI.9:18) All quotes are from *A Course in Miracles,* copyright ©1992, 1999, 2007 by the Foundation for Inner Peace, 448 Ignacio Blvd., #306, Novato, CA 94949, www.acim.org, used with permission.

Notes 291

2. Jones, L. A. (2021). *Professional Troublemaker: The Fear-Fighter Manual.* Penguin.

3. https://www.verywellmind.com/top-reasons-to-smile-every-day-2223755.

Chapter 5

1. Fraga, J. (2022, November 25). *The Opposite of Schadenfreude Is Freudenfreude. Here's How to Cultivate It: The joy we derive from others' success comes with many benefits. The New York Times.* https://www.nytimes.com/2022/11/25/well/mind/schadenfreude-freudenfreude.html#:~:text=The%20term%20is%20inspired%20by,is%20not%20a%20German%20word.

2. Chapman, G. (2014). *The 5 Love Languages: The Secret to Love that Lasts.* Moody Publishers.

Chapter 6

1. Hersey, T. (2022). *Rest Is Resistance: THE INSTANT NEW YORK TIMES BESTSELLER.* Hachette UK.

2. The Nap Ministry. (2024, November 9). *The Nap Ministry.* https://thenapministry.wordpress.com/.

3. Lorde, A. (2017). *A Burst of Light: And Other Essays.* Courier Dover Publications.

4. DOL Blog. (2021, August 3). *5 Facts About Black Women in the Labor Force.* https://blog.dol.gov/2021/08/03/5-facts-about-black-women-in-the-labor-force.

5. All Things Equitable Inc. (n.d.). *All Things Equitable Inc. | Workplace DEI consulting firm in Toronto.* https://www.allthingsequitable.ca/.

6. https://www.youtube.com/@AllThingsEquitable.

7. Wagner, E. (2023, February 13). *Ellen Wagner on LinkedIn: BLACK HISTORY MONTH |* https://www.linkedin.com/posts/ellen-wagner_black-history-month-activity-7030960871744929792-QCeN/.

8. The American Institute of Stress. (2024, November 8). *WORKPLACE STRESS - The American Institute of Stress.* https://www.stress.org/workplace-stress/.

9. 88% of Black women sometimes have, often, or always experienced burnout. Every Level Leadership. (2024b, September 18). *Black Women Thriving Report - Every Level Leadership.* https://everylevelleads.com/bwt/.
10. World Health Organization: WHO. (2019, May 28). *Burn-out an "occupational phenomenon": International Classification of Diseases.* World Health Organization. https://www.who.int/news/item/28-05-2019-burn-out-an-occupational-phenomenon-international-classification-of-diseases.
11. Calm Editorial Team. (2024, March 18). *What is burnout? 22 signs you're facing it (and how to recover)—Calm Blog.* Calm Blog. https://www.calm.com/blog/beat-burnout?undefined&utm_medium=organic&utm_source=blog&utm_campaign=how-to-recover-from-burnout.
12. https://www.indeed.com/career-advice/career-development/causes-of-burnout.
13. *Burnout.* (2024, June 27). *Psychology Today.* https://www.psychologytoday.com/us/basics/burnout.
14. Lmsw, M. W. (2023, February 26). *Am I burned out? How to recognize the 12 stages of burnout.* Forbes. https://www.forbes.com/sites/melodywilding/2023/02/21/am-i-burned-out-how-to-recognize-the-12-stages-of-burnout/.
15. Bernier, D. (1998). A study of coping: Successful recovery from severe burnout and other reactions to severe work-related stress. Work & Stress, 12(1), 50–65. https://doi.org/10.1080/02678379808256848.
16. Mayo Clinic. (n.d.). *COVID-19: How to manage your mental health during the pandemic.* https://www.mayoclinic.org/diseases-conditions/coronavirus/in-depth/mental-health-covid-19/art-20482731.
17. World Health Organization: WHO. (2022a, March 2). *COVID-19 pandemic triggers 25% increase in prevalence of anxiety and depression worldwide* [Press release]. https://www.who.int/news/item/02-03-2022-covid-19-pandemic-triggers-25-increase-in-prevalence-of-anxiety-and-depression-worldwide.
18. Dalton-Smith, S. (2017). *Sacred Rest: Recover Your Life, Renew Your Energy, Restore Your Sanity.* FaithWords.
19. Lovering, N. (2022, May 11). *ADHD Body Doubling.* Psych Central. https://psychcentral.com/adhd/adhd-body-doubling#research.
20. Cadc, C. S. M. L. (2022, December 21). Social, emotional, sensory, and more. *Psychology Today.* https://www.psychologytoday.com/us/blog/a-different-kind-of-therapy/202212/the-7-kinds-of-rest-you-need-to-actually-feel-rejuvenated.

Chapter 7

1. Slavery Law & Power in Early America and the British Empire. (2024, November 11). *Barbados Slave Code*. Slavery Law & Power in Early America and the British Empire - Documents and Images From the Seventeenth and Eighteenth Centuries. https://slaverylawpower.org/nhprc-sample-documents/barbados-slave-code/.

2. Linos, E., Mobasseri, S., and Roussille, N. *"Intersectional Peer Effects at Work: The Effect of White Coworkers on Black Women's Careers."* HKS Faculty Research Working Paper Series RWP23–031, July 2024.

3. Elakbawy, C. M. M. P. a. S., & Elakbawy, C. M. M. P. a. S. (2024, July 24). Black Women Won't Reach Pay Equity Until 2227 - IWPR. *IWPR - Institute for Women's Policy Research*. https://iwpr.org/black-womens-equal-pay-day-2024/.

4. Lean In. (n.d.). *Black women aren't paid fairly*. https://leanin.org/data-about-the-gender-pay-gap-for-black-women#the-pay-gap.

5. Lean In. (n.d.). *Black women aren't paid fairly*. https://leanin.org/data-about-the-gender-pay-gap-for-black-women#the-pay-gap.

6. Ermolenko, M. (2024, October 15). *The Glass Cliff Phenomenon and Women of Color (Explainer)*. Catalyst. https://www.catalyst.org/2024/01/31/glass-cliff-women-of-color/.

7. Thomas, K. M. (2024, January 24). The Persistence Of Pet To Threat. *Forbes*. https://www.forbes.com/sites/keciathomas/2024/01/13/the-persistence-of-pet-to-threat/?sh=b7729e963128.

8. Bryant, K., & Bryant, K. (2024b, May 7). *Claudine Gay and the Black girlboss paradox*. The Emancipator. https://theemancipator.org/2024/01/09/topics/education/claudine-gay-black-girlboss-paradox/.

9. *Maroons in the Caribbean*. (n.d.). http://www.caribbean-atlas.com/en/themes/waves-of-colonization-and-control-in-the-caribbean/waves-of-colonization/maroons-in-the-caribbean.html.

10. Morrison, C. D. (2024, November 13). *Code-switching | Linguistic Benefits & Challenges*. Encyclopedia Britannica. https://www.britannica.com/topic/code-switching.

11. https://www.youtube.com/watch?v=nopWOC4SRm4.

12. https://wzakcleveland.com/playlist/rip-paul-mooney-15-hilarious-touching-quotes-from-the-legendary-comic/item/5.

294   Notes

13. User, G. (2024, June 10). *The NEW CROWN 2023 Workplace Research Study, co-commissioned by Dove and LinkedIn—The Official CROWN Act.* The Official CROWN Act. https://www.thecrownact.com/all-press /dove-partners-with-linkedin-in-support-of-the-crown-act-to-help -end-race-based-hair-discrimination-in-the-workplaceusa.

14. Sue, D. W. (2010). *Microaggressions in Everyday Life: Race, Gender, and Sexual Orientation.* John Wiley & Sons.

15. Hurley Hall, S. (2022). *Anatomy of a Microaggression.* Sharon's Anti-Racism Newsletter. https://www.antiracismnewsletter.com/p/anatomy -of-a-microaggression.

16. Bailey, M. (2021). Introduction: What Is Misogynoir? In *Misogynoir Transformed: Black Women's Digital Resistance* (Vol. 18, pp. 1–34). NYU Press. http://www.jstor.org/stable/j.ctv27ftv0s.4.

17. Crenshaw, K. (1989). *"Demarginalizing the Intersection of Race and Sex: A Black Feminist Critique of Antidiscrimination Doctrine, Feminist Theory and Antiracist Politics,"* University of Chicago Legal Forum:Vol. 1989, Article 8. https://chicagounbound.uchicago.edu/uclf/vol1989/iss1/8.

18. Woods-Giscombé, C. L. (2010). Superwoman Schema: African American Women's Views on Stress, Strength, and Health. *Qualitative Health Research,* 20(5), 668–683. https://doi.org/10.1177/1049732310361892.

Chapter 8

1. Harts, M. (2020). *The Memo: What Women of Color Need to Know to Secure a Seat at the Table.* Seal Press.

2. https://www.insidevoices.io/.

3. *What's up with the white women doing this fake crying on TikTok* (2021). https://www.facebook.com/watch/?v=1491311547872512.

Chapter 9

1. *DSHS.* (n.d.). *Self Neglect* | https://www.dshs.wa.gov/altsa/home-and -community-services/self-neglect.

2. Webb, J., PhD. (2023, July 11). *Growing up with your emotions neglected teaches you to neglect yourself. Psychology Today.* https://www.psycholo

Notes

295

gytoday.com/us/blog/childhood-emotional-neglect/202305/self-neglect-a-telltale-sign-of-childhood-emotional-neglect.

3. NAPSA. (2022, November 9). *Neglect & Self-Neglect - NAPSA.* NAPSA - National Adult Protective Services Association. https://www.napsa-now.org/neglect-and-self-neglect/.

4. De Vries, M. F. K. (2021, September 1). *Managing a Chronic Complainer.* Harvard Business Review. https://hbr.org/2021/04/managing-a-chronic-complainer.

5. https://shkspr.mobi/blog/2024/01/no-oscar-wilde-did-not-say-imitation-is-the-sincerest-form-of-flattery-that-mediocrity-can-pay-to-greatness/.

6. Love Letters. (2023). *Love Letters.* https://loveforyall.carrd.co/.

7. Frazier, C., PhD. (2024, January 19). *Chantell Frazier, PhD on LinkedIn: Last week I asked "If I organized a love letter campaign to Black women in in academia, would y'all help? ...* https://www.linkedin.com/feed/update/urn:li:activity:7154106477232680961/.

8. Barbados Reiki Association (2024, May 22). *What Is Reiki?—Barbados Reiki Association.* Barbados Reiki Association. https://barbadosreikiassociation.com/what-is-reiki/.

Index

Page numbers followed by *f* refer to figures.

A

Abraham Hicks, 81
Abundance:
  manifesting, 61
  and quality of life, 82
Accommodating yourself, 217
"Acting as if," 95, 98
Action:
  inspired, 98
  taking, *see* Doing the work
Activism, rest as, 137–139
Affirmations:
  for aligning with your values, 46
  for connecting, 128
  for elevating your energy, 239, 242
  for knowing your strengths, 71–72
  for manifesting, 89–91, 100
  for remembering Who You Are, 26
  for rest, 163
  for soft living, 268
  for strategizing your career, 221
  for Working While Black, 200
Afropunk, 14, 17
AI (artificial intelligence), 33–34
Ali, Muhammad, 94
Aligning with your values, 29–48
  author's story of, 30–34
  community, 40–41

consistency, 36–37
directness, 37–38
exercises for, 45–48
generosity, 35
identifying your values for, 44
integrity, 34–35
joy, 40
kindness, 35–36
peace, 39–40
presence, 36
privacy, 38–39
Reiki precepts for, 41–43
in strategizing your career,
    215–216
All Things Equitable Inc., 138
Almond Beach Club, 56–58
Alone time, 235
Amadi, Liku, 250
American Foundation for Suicide
    Prevention, 1
Amplifying Black Voices campaign,
    15
Anatomy of a Microaggression (Hurley Hall),
    187–191, 190*f*
Ancestry, embracing your, 22–23
Andwele, Adisa, 20
Angelou, Maya, 34
Anger, 42
  from frenemies, 117
  toward Black women who live
    well, 248–250

297

298 Index

Appreciation:
  for aligning with your values, 46–47
  for elevating your energy, 242
  for knowing your strengths, 74
  for manifesting, 101
  for remembering Who You Are, 27
  for rest, 164
  for soft living, 268
  for strategizing your career, 222
  for Working While Black, 201
Arguments, from frenemies, 117
Artificial intelligence (AI), 33–34
Ashley-Farrand, Thomas, 89
Aura combing, 240
Authenticity, 17–19, 60. *See also*
      Remembering Who You Are
Autistic burnout, 141–142
"Avatar," 18
Avoidance, soft living *vs.*, 257

B

Background work, 60
Bailey, Halle, 178
Bailey, Moya, 191
Baker, Anita, 136
Baldwin, James, 209
Barbados, 20–21
  author's career in, 56–59
  CXC exams in, 50
  dance experience in, 52–55
  eminent people from, 20
  generosity and sharing in, 35
  hurricanes in, 266–267
  literacy rate in, 21
  National Pledge of, 21
  rest times in, 135–136
  Working While Black in, 172–176
  writing experience in, 55–56
Barbados Dance Theatre Company, 55
Barbados Landship, 53
Barbados Reiki Association, 67, 240
Barrow, Errol, 20
Bassett, Angela, 178
Beauty, in soft living, 254
Beckles, Sir Hilary, 20
Behaving things into existence, 81, 95–96
Behavioral code switching, 184–185
Being the only, 182

Being the representative, 183
Belly breathing, 267–268
Benjamin, Janelle, 138–139
Be Yourself, 69
  by curating your soft life, 245–270
  by elevating your energy, 225–244
  by learning about Working While
      Black, 169–204
  strategizing your career to, 205–224
Bhramari pranayama, 127–128
Biles, Simone, 86, 265–266
Black excellence, 139, 161, 172–175
Black girlboss paradox, 181–182
Black Girl Magic, 139, 161
Black Panthers, 137
Black women. *See also specific topics*
  in the community, 4–5
  and racism, 2–7
  soft, 264
  who live well, anger toward, 248–250
  in the workplace, *see* Working While Black
      Effect (WWBE)
Black Women Can Have It All podcast, 250
Black Women Photographers (BWP), 14
Blige, Mary J., 92
Body doubling, 159
Bolt, Usain, 86
The Book Academy (TBA), 79, 81, 98
Booker, Cory, 178
Book Proposal Power Program (BPPP), 79–81
"Born With It," 22
Boundaries:
  enforcing, 156–157
  lack of, as energy drain, 228
  negotiating your, 151
  people who break, 120–122
  in respecting privacy, 38
  setting, 219, 263
Box breathing, 241–242
BPPP (Book Proposal Power Program), 79–81
Brancker, Nicholas, 20
Brathwaite, Edward Kamau, 20
Brathwaite, Ryan, 20
Breathwork:
  for aligning with your values, 45–46
  for connecting, 127–128
  for elevating your energy, 239, 241–242
  for knowing your strengths, 69–71

Index

299

for manifesting, 96, 99–100

for remembering Who You Are, 24–26

for rest, 162–163

for soft living, 266–267

for strategizing your career, 220–221

for Working While Black, 199–200

Broken rung, 180

Brown-Jackson, Ketanji, 5

Bryant, Kimberly, 181

Burnout, 5, 138–153

  author's story of, 142–153

  autistic, 141–142

  causes of, 140–141

  defined, 140

  drivers of, 138

  as epidemic, 139–142

  handling, 149–153

  recovering from, 142. *See also* Rest

Busyness, 139–140

BWP (Black Women Photographers), 14

Byrne, Rhonda, 81

C

Calling, competence *vs.*, 62–63

Calm app, 140

Campbell, Mrs., 52

Candia-Bailey, Antoinette "Bonnie,"
  6, 149, 178

Career. *See also* Working While Black
  Effect (WWBE)

  curating your, *see* Strategizing your career

  leveraging your strengths in, 56–59

Caucacity, 2, 171–172

Cavite Chorale, 58

Celebration:

  for aligning with your values, 47

  for elevating your energy, 243

  of friends' wins, 113–114

  for knowing your strengths, 72

  for manifesting, 101

  for remembering Who You Are, 27

  for rest, 164

  for soft living, 268

  for strategizing your career, 223

  for Working While Black, 202

Cellular rest, 159–160

Chakras, 101–106

Chapman, Gary, 125

Choosing differently, 208–210, 218–219.
  See also Strategizing your career

Cilley, Marla (FlyLady), 230

Clarke, Austin, 20

Claudine Gay and the Black Girlboss Paradox
  (Bryant), 181–182

Clothing, in soft living, 254

Clutter, as energy drain, 229–230

Code switching:

  stopping, 216–217

  in Working While Black Effect, 183–186

Collective Napping Experience, 161

Collymore, Frank, 20

Comfort zone, 62

Communal rest, 160–161

Community:

  importance of, 218

  in navigating your career, 214

  organizations' prioritization of, 198

  racism in, 4–5

  seeking sanctuary in, 220

  as a value, 40–41

  as a verb, 83

Competence, calling *vs.*, 62–63

Complaining, 230–231

Connection, 107–131. *See also* Community

  author's story of, 109–111

  exercises for, 127–131

  keeping, 121–127

  qualities of good friendships, 112

  releasing, 113–121

  as self-care, 258

Consistency, 36–37, 59, 238

A Course in Miracles, 83

COVID-19 pandemic, 15, 16, 144

Creating, in manifesting, 96–97

Creative, being, 66

Creative rest, 158

Crenshaw, Kimberlé, 191–192

Cross Cultural Bridges, 139

Csikszentmihalyi, Mihalyi, 64

Culture, work, 213

Cummins-Williams, Mrs., 52

Curation. *See also* Doing the work

  two-fold nature of, 81

  of your capacity, 133–165. *See also* Rest

  of your career, 205–224. *See also*
    Strategizing your career

Index

Curation (*continued*)
of your circle, 107–131. *See also*
Connection
of your energy, 225–244. *See also* Elevating
your energy
of your soft life, 245–270. *See also*
Soft living
of your thoughts, 77–106. *See also*
Manifestation
Curious, being, 68
CXC exams, 50, 52

D

Daley, Tom, 62
Dalton-Smith, Saundra, 153
Dance, 52–55
DEI initiatives, 197
Dickenson, Samantha-Rae, 141–142
Digestive system, 159–160
Digital detox, 157
Directness, 37–38
Discipline, 59
Doing the work. *See also* Curation
for aligning with your values, 46
for connecting, 128–131
for elevating your energy, 243
for knowing your strengths, 72, 72*f*
for manifesting, 101
for remembering Who You Are, 27
for rest, 163
for soft living, 268
for strategizing your career, 221
for Working While Black, 201
Dove, 186
Dreaming big, 16–17
Dry brushing, 240
Duncan, Greg, 43

E

Ease. *See also* Soft living
boundaries for, 219
energy of, 247
experiencing, 61
facilitated by money, 256
Eat Pray Love (Gilbert), 98
Elevating your energy, 225–244
assessing energy for, 227

by choosing high vibrations, 226–227
and energy as currency, 227
exercises for, 241–244
by identifying energetic drains, 227–233
by identifying energetic increasers, 233–241
Embrace your ancestry, 22–23
Emotional intelligence, 125–127
Emotional rest, 156–157
Emotional safety, at work, 5
"Empire State of Mind," 17
Energy:
elevating your, *see* Elevating your energy
emotional, 156–157
protecting, in manifestation, 98–99
Energy drains, 227–233
clutter, 229–230
complaining, 230–231
food, 159–160, 229
lack of boundaries, 228
neglecting self-care, 228–229
noise, 231
overdrive, 228
sleeplessness, 229
socializing, 233
social media, 152–153, 231–233
Energy elevators, 233–241, 263
alone time, 235
energy practices, 238–241
ingesting the right things, 234
positive people, 235
rest, 233
routines and rituals, 233–234
saying no, 235–236
social media, 236–237
underdrive, 237–238
Energy practices, 238–241
Entitlement, 249–250
Entrepreneurship, 147–148
Evidence, examining, 215
Exhaling, 162, 264. *See also* Breathwork
Expecting good things, 16–17
Extractivists, 118–119
Extroverts, 233
Eyes, resting, 154–155

F

Failure, feeling like a, 50–52
Family, importance of, 218

Index

Farquhar, Dr., 174
The 5 Love Languages (Chapman), 125
Five-finger breath, 220–221
Flakers, 119–120
Flow, finding, 64
Floyd, George, 144
Food:
    as energy drain, 159–160, 229
    as energy elevator, 234
Frazier, Chantell, 234, 260–261
Frenemies, 112–118
Fresh, Doug E., 20
Friendships:
    author's story of, 109–111
    evaluating, 126–127
    prioritizing, 112. *See also* Connection
Fun, 263
Fundamentals, in work, 59–60

G

Gaslighting, 171, 172, 188
Gay, Claudine, 148
Gay, Maxine, 6
Generosity, 35, 124
Ghostwriting, 33
Gilbert, Elizabeth, 98
Glass cliff, 180–181
Graham, John, 58
Grandmaster Flash, 20
Gratitude:
    expressing, *see* Appreciation
    in manifesting, 99
    prayers of, 239
    as Reiki precept, 43
The Great Exhale (TGE), xviii–xx
    affirmations space in, 90–91
    The Healing Power of Laughter space in, 40
    launch of, 147
    rebrand of, 86–87
    during recovery from burnout, 152–153
    as safe space, 41
    support from, 83
    tips for rest in, 161, 162
Greenidge, Ché, 20
Gueye-James, Anta, 162

H

Hair, 185–187
Hair discrimination, 186–187
Hall, Lene, 20
Happiness, 40, 162
@HappyHappyPhoenix, 226–227
Harris, Kamala, xxi, 5, 138, 177
Harts, Minda, 208–209, 212
Hay, Louise, 81, 89
Healing Mantras (Ashley-Farrand), 89
Help, for burnout, 149–151
Henson, Taraji P., 178
Hersey, Tricia, 137, 161
High vibrations, choosing, 226–227
Hill, Elliott, 180
Hill, Lauren, 19
Hinds, Alison, 20, 22
Hindsbury Primary School, 52
Hinkson, Michelle, 54
Hiring practices, 198
Holder, Eric, 20
Honesty, 43, 150
Honoring others, 42–43
hooks, bell, 137
Humming bee breath, 127–128
Hurley Hall, Sharon, 188
Hurston, Zora Neale, 5
Hydration, 160, 260

I

"I am" affirmations, 89–90
Ideation, in manifesting, 96
Identifying your why, 97
Ikigai, 72, 72*f*
I'm Tired of Racism, 78, 93
Indeed.com, 140
Ingesting the right things, 234
Inside Voices, 213
Insomnia, 153
Inspired action, 98
Insults, 115–117, 191
Integrity, 34–35
Intentions, creating, 88
Intersectionality:
    underpinning code switching, 183
    in Working While Black Effect, 176–177, 192–193
Intersectional Peer Effects at Work, 176–177

Index

Introspection, *see* Journaling
The Introvert Sisters podcast, 78, 145
Irungu, Polly, 14–17

J

Jackson, Ketanji Brown, 178
Jay-Z, 17
Jealousy, 117–118
John 1:1, 239
Jones, Luvvie Ajayi, 24, 79, 92–94
Jones, Van, 178
Jordan, Michael, 86
Journaling:
    for aligning with your values, 46
    for connecting, 128
    for elevating your energy, 239, 243
    for knowing your strengths, 72
    for manifesting, 100
    for remembering Who You Are, 26
    for rest, 163
    for soft living, 267
    for strategizing your career, 222
    for Working While Black, 200
    to write things into existence, 88
Joy, 263
    doing work for the, 212
    elevating, 227. *See also* Energy elevators
    increasing, 62
    as a value, 40

K

Keys, Alicia, 17
Kindness, 35–36
Know Yourself:
    by aligning with your values, 29–48, 262
    by focusing on strengths, 49–74
    by remembering Who You Are, 13–28

L

Lamming, George, 20
Laughter, 40, 235, 263
Law of Attraction, 81, 82. *See also*
    Manifestation
Laziness, soft living *vs.*, 256
Leaning into your strength, 23
Life-work balance, 7
    and burnout, *see* Burnout

choosing, 209–210, 219, 220, 263. *See also*
    Strategizing your career
putting life first for, 219
rest in, 162
underdrive for, 237–238
Light, shining your, 23–24
Likeable people, 121–122
Linguistic code switching, 184
LinkedIn, 145–146, 150, 186
Lorde, Audre, 137
LoveForYall.carrd.co, 234
Love languages, 125
Love Yourself, 262–264
    by connecting, 107–131
    by manifesting, 77–106
    by resting, 133–165
Loving-kindness meditation, 202–204
Loyal friends, 123–124

M

McClurkin, Donnie, 23, 91
Male-centering, soft living *vs.*, 257
Manifestation, 77–106
    of abundance, 61
    author's story of, 78–81
    behaving it into existence, 81, 95–96
    curating thoughts for, 81–83
    exercises for, 99–106
    process for, 96–99
    speaking it into existence, 81, 88–95
    steps in, 83
    thinking it into existence,
        80–81, 83–86
    visualizing it into existence, 81, 86–87
    writing it into existence, 81, 88
Mantras, 88–89
Martinique, 253
Materialism, 247–248, 256
Matthew 7:7, 238–239
Mayo Clinic, 144
Meditation:
    for aligning with your values, 47–48
    for elevating your energy, 239, 243–244
    for knowing your strengths, 73–74
    for manifesting, 96, 101–106
    for remembering Who You Are, 27–28
    for rest, 164–165
    for soft living, 268–269

Index

303

for strategizing your career, 223–224
for Working While Black, 201–204
The Memo (Harts), 208–209, 212
Mental health:
  and cluttered spaces, 229–230
  and COVID-19 pandemic, 144
  due to burnout, 150–151
  improving, 61
  taking care of, 263
Mental rehearsal, 86. *See also* Visualizing things
  into existence
Mental rest, 155
Metta meditation, 202–204
Microaggressions, 116, 187–191, 190*f*
The Microaggressive You, 249
Microassaults, 189
Microinsults, 186
Microinvalidations, 191–192
The Mighty Gabby, 20
Mindset, of "Is this. . .IT??," 19
Minimizing others, 115–117
Miracles, making space for, 99
Misogynoir, 191–192
Misogynoir Transformed (Bailey), 191
Money:
  ease facilitated by, 256
  importance of, 218
  managing your, 258
  working for, 213
Mooney, Paul, 185
Motivation, 63–64
Mottley, Mia, 20
Movement, as physical rest, 155
Multifaceted, being, 67

N

Nadi Shodhana, 69–71
Naps, 154
The Nap Ministry, 137
Nasdaq screen, Times Square, 14–16, 18
National Adult Protective Services Association
  (NAPSA), 229
Nature bathing, 240
Negativity, 230–231
*The NEW CROWN 2023 Workplace Research
  Study,* 186–187
Noise, as energy drain, 231
Nostril breathing, 69–71
Nourishing yourself, 234

O

Obama, Barack, 178, 185
Obama, Michelle, 6, 178, 185
One-upmanship, 114
The only, being, 182
Openness to blessings, 99
Organizations:
  corporate shenanigans, 206–208
  reviews of, 212–213
  and Working While Black Effect,
    196–197
Oríkìs, 92–95
Overdrive, 228, 237
Overwork, 136–137

P

Pace, in soft living, 254
"The Path," 19
Patriarchy, 208–209
Pay inequity, 138, 178–179
Peace, 39–40
Perfectionism, 257
Performativity, de-prioritizing, 198
Permission, giving yourself, 97–98
Pet to Threat phenomenon, 180–181
Physical rest, 154–155
Pierce, Chester M., 187
Pine Hill Dairy Essay Contest, 56
Plagiarism, 30–33
Police-inflicted mortality, 174–175
Positive people, as energy elevator, 235
Positive self talk, 91–92
Practical, being, 65
Prayer, 238–239
Presence, 36, 122
Prioritizing:
  of community and safe spaces, 198
  of DEI, 197
  of good hiring practices, 198
  of psychological safety, 197–198
  of relationships, 122
  of rest, 153
  of yourself, 217, 258
  in your work, 60
Privacy, 38–39
Problems Architects, 119
Professional Troublemaker (Jones), 92
Psychological safety, 197–198
Psychology Today, 140, 159–160, 229

304 Index

Public-facing persona, 18
Puffy, DJ, 20
Purpose, doing work for the, 212–213
Putting life first, 219

Q

Quiet quitting, 217–218

R

Racial activism, 144
Racial Microaggressions in Everyday Life
(Sue), 187
Racial violence, 144
Racism, 1–7, 143
in the community, 4–5
at work, 2–6. *See also* Working While Black
Effect (WWBE)
Real Talk on Racism, 145, 147
Reframing life, 156
Reiki:
as energy elevator, 240–241
precepts of, 41–43
Touch of Light Reiki School & Healing
Centre, 67
Relationships, 262–263. *See also* Connection
Relaxation, 160–161
Reliability, 37
Remembering Who You Are, 13–28
author's story of, 14–18
by embracing your ancestry, 22–23
exercises for, 24–28
importance of, 18–19
by leaning into your strengths, 23
by respecting your roots, 20–21
by shining your light, 23–24
The representative, being, 183
Respect:
from friends, 124
for others' privacy, 38–39, 42–43
for your roots, 20–21
Rest, 133–165, 263–264
as activism, 137–139
author's story of, 135–137
and burnout, 139–153. *See also* Burnout
cellular, 159–160
communal, 160–161
creative, 158

emotional, 156–157
as energy elevator, 233
exercises for, 161–165
inadequate, effects of, 136–137
mental, 155
physical, 154–155
prioritizing, 153
sensory, 157
social, 158–159
spiritual, 159
for success, 161–162, 209
Rest Is Resistance (Hersey), 137
Reynolds, Rose, 86–87
Rihanna, 16, 17, 20
Rituals, 233–234
Roberts, Patrice, 160
Roots, respecting your, 20–21
Routines:
as energy elevator, 233–234
in soft living, 254
Rupee, 20

S

Sacred Rest (Dalton-Smith), 153
Sandiford, Sir Lloyd Erskine, 20
Sanni-Thomas, Ekow, 213
Sartorial code switching, 185
Saying no:
as energy elevator, 235–236
for life-work balance, 220
to yourself, 236
Saying yes:
for life-work balance, 220
to the wrong things, 236
Schedule, in soft living, 254
Schinn, Florence Scovell, 81
The Secret (Byrne), 81
Secrets of others, safeguarding, 39
Self-acknowledgement, 257–258
Self-care. *See also* Rest
energy practices for, 238–241
neglecting, as energy drain, 228–229
in soft living, 258–261
when recovering from burnout,
151–152
Self-compassion, 261–262
Self-confidence, of friends, 122–123

Index

Self-degradation, 92
Self-esteem, 17
  boosting, 63
  and feeling lack of worthiness, 91–92
Self-hatred, 91
Self-indulgence, 261
Self-love:
  power of, 18
  in soft living, 248, 262–264
Self-maintenance, 258–259
Self-prioritization, 258
Self talk:
  positive, 91–92. *See also* Affirmations
  taking care with, 239
Self-worth, 18–19, 116
Sensory rest, 157
7 Types of Rest Framework, 153
Shining your light, 23–24
Silks & Things, 67
Sleep, 154
Sleeplessness, 229
Smiling, 95
Smith, Stephen, 35–36
Smudging, 240
Sobers, Sir Garfield, 20
Socializing, as energy drain, 233
Social media:
  as energy drain, 152–153, 231–233
  as energy elevator, 236–237
  when recovering from burnout, 152–153
Social rest, 158–159
Soft living, 245–270
  author's introduction to, 250–253
  elements of, 247–250, 253–254
  exercises for, 267–270
  grounded in authenticity, 18–19
  moving toward, 255
  practices for, 257–264
  things that are not, 256–257
Soothing yourself, 162
Speaking things into existence, 81, 88–95
  affirmations for, 89–91
  mantras for, 88–89
  oríkìs for, 92–95
  positive self talk for, 91–92
Specificity, in manifesting, 97

Spinal breath, 45–46
Spiritual rest, 159
Starting the day, in soft living, 253
Strategizing your career, 205–224
  by accommodating yourself, 217
  advice on, 212–214
  author's story of, 210–212
  by choosing differently, 209–210, 218–219
  and corporate shenanigans, 206–208
  by examining the evidence, 215
  exercises for, 220–224
  by getting grounded in your values, 215–216
  making choices in, 208–210
  by not code switching, 216–217
  by prioritizing yourself, 217
  by putting life first, 219
  by seeking sanctuary in community, 220
  by setting boundar-ease, 219
  by working to rule, 217–218
Strengths, 49–74
  author's story of, 50–52, 56–59
  exercises for, 69–74
  focusing on your, 262
  leaning into your, 23
  lessons learned about, 59–60
  leveraging your, 56–59, 64–69
  moving from struggle to, 52–56
  reasons to focus on, 60–64
Stress, 139, 153, 219. *See also* Life-work balance
Struggles:
  author's story of, 50–52
  of Black women, 138
  moving to strength from, 52–56
Success:
  defining your idea of, 215–216
  pressuring yourself for, 261
  rest needed for, 161–162, 209–210
Sue, Derald Wing, 187, 189
Suicide risk, for Black women, 5, 6
Superwoman Schema (Woods-Giscombé), 192
Superwomen Schema, 192–195

Index

Support. *See also* Connection
  importance of, 218
  in navigating career, 213
Sutton, Paula, 248, 249
Swan Theory, 141, 142

T

Talent, 59
Tappin, Arturo, 20
TBA, see *The Book Academy*
The Tea on Tap podcast, 145, 147
Tears, white women's use of, 214
TGE, see *The Great Exhale*
Thomas, Kecia M., 180
Thompson, Obadele, 20
Thoughts:
  blissful, *see* Meditation
  curating, 81–83
  echoed in your experiences, 85
  power of, 83–85. *See also* Manifestation
  self talk, 91–92
  thinking things into existence,
    80–81, 83–86
  watching your, 98
3-6-9 method, 88
Time off, taking, 213
Touch of Light Reiki School & Healing
    Centre, 67
Transcending stress, 162
Tree breath, 24–26
Trinidad, 250–253
Trotman, Tyrone, 54
Trudeau, Justin, 20
Trustworthiness, 123, 174
Turner, Tina, 88–89
Twice as Hard series, 138–139

U

Underdrive, 145, 237–238
United States:
  literacy rate in, 21
  Working While Black in, 176–194. *See also*
    Working While Black
    Effect (WWBE)
The University of The West Indies
    (UWI), 173–174

V

Values:
  aligning with, *see* Aligning
    with your values
  getting grounded in your, 215–216
  identifying your, 44
VeryWellMind.com, 95
Vision, 84, 87
Visualizing things into existence, 81, 86–87

W

Wagner, Ellen, 139
Walcott, Sir Derek, 20
Warmth, in soft living, 254
Water, 160, 260
Way of the Winds Martial Arts System, 43
White supremacy, 208
White women, tears used by, 214
WHO (World Health Organization),
    139, 144
Why, identifying your, 97
Williams, Sada, 20
Williams, Serena, 86
Wilson, Jen, 15
Winfrey, Oprah, 142
Woods-Giscombé, Cheryl L., 191, 192
Words, power of, 239. *See also* Affirmations
Working to rule, 217–218
Working While Black Effect (WWBE),
    2–6, 169–204
  in Barbados, 172–176
  being the only in, 182
  being the representative in, 183
  Black girlboss paradox in, 181–182
  to Black readers about, 198–199
  broken rung and glass cliff in, 180
  caucacity in, 171–172
  code switching in, 183–186
  definition of, 177
  examples of, 177–179
  exercises for, 199–204
  hair discrimination in, 186–187
  impacts of, 209, 220
  intersectionality in, 192–193
  microaggressions in, 187–189, 190f
  misogynoir in, 191–192

to non-Black readers about, 195–199
to organizations about, 196–198
pay inequity in, 178–179
Pet to Threat phenomenon in, 180–181
Superwomen Schema in, 192–195
in the U.S., 176–195
World Health Organization (WHO), 140, 144
Worrell, Shelley, 54–55
Worry, 41–42

Worthiness:
feeling lack of, 91
innate, 18–19
recognizing your, 262
Writing things into existence, 81, 88
WWWBE, *see* Working While Black Effect

Y
You Can Heal Your Life (Hay), 89